# Montreal's Irish Mafia

# Montreal's Irish Mafia

## The True Story of the Infamous West End Gang

D'Arcy O'Connor
with Miranda O'Connor

John Wiley & Sons Canada, Ltd.

*Library and Archives Canada Cataloguing in Publication*

O'Connor, D'Arcy, 1941–

    Montreal's Irish mafia : the true story of the infamous West End Gang/D'Arcy O'Connor.

Includes bibliographical references and index.
Issued also in electronic format.
ISBN 978-0-470-15890-6

    1. West End Gang—History.  2. Gangs—Québec (Province)—Montréal—History.  3. Mafia—Québec (Province)—Montréal—History.  4. Organized crime—Québec (Province)—Montréal—History.  5. Irish Canadians—Québec (Province)—Montréal—History.  I. Title.

HV6453.C32Q8 2011      364.10609714'28      C2010-906142-X

ISBN 978-0-470-15890-6 (print); 978-0-470-15924-8 (ePDF); 978-0-470-67614-1 (eMobi); 978-0-470-67615-8 (ePub)

**Production Credits**
Cover Design: Mike Chan
Cover Photo Credit: *Photo Police*
Interior Design: Mike Chan
Illustrations: Ben Frisch
Typesetter: Thomson Digital
Printer: Friesens Printing Ltd.

**Editorial Credits**
Executive Editor: Don Loney
Production Editor: Pauline Ricablanca

John Wiley & Sons Canada, Ltd.
6045 Freemont Blvd.
Mississauga, Ontario
L5R 4J3

Printed in Canada

2 3 4 5 FP 15 14 13 12 11

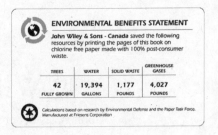

ENVIRONMENTAL BENEFITS STATEMENT

**John Wiley & Sons - Canada** saved the following resources by printing the pages of this book on chlorine free paper made with 100% post-consumer waste.

| TREES | WATER | SOLID WASTE | GREENHOUSE GASES |
|---|---|---|---|
| 42 | 19,394 | 1,177 | 4,027 |
| FULLY GROWN | GALLONS | POUNDS | POUNDS |

Calculations based on research by Environmental Defense and the Paper Task Force.
Manufactured at Friesens Corporation

*To Mouse: Whose patient suffering and assistance in my lack of computer skills was worth as much to me as her incredible research skills.*

# CONTENTS

# PREFACE

To refer to Montreal's West End hoodlums as either a "gang" or as the city's "Irish mafia" is somewhat of a misnomer, since, even if there are several familial ties, few of the subjects you'll read about here are bound to one another by a down-from-the-top hierarchy, or by any code of *omertà*.

Nevertheless, all of these characters do have one thing in common. They are a collection of petty thieves, bank and armored-truck robbers, shakedown artists, safecrackers, truck-hijackers, drug importers and distributors, money launderers, fences, loan sharks, protection racketeers, enforcers, hired killers and other assorted thugs who operate mostly in the downtown and southwestern part of the island of Montreal. And, for the most part, they are of Irish descent and are English-speaking in a city that is today 70 percent francophone.

When these Irish gangsters first began their criminal activities in the mid-1950s, they were nicknamed by the French media as *Le Gang de l'Ouest*. And the name, along with its English translation, has since stuck in newspaper, radio and TV accounts, police reports, crime commission hearings, etc. So, whether the appellation is accurate or not, Montreal does indeed have a "West End Gang," albeit consisting of a somewhat loosely knit and rather disorganized bunch of fraternal families and individuals. Their exploits, as well as their shady business relationships with the city's French, Italian, Jewish, and biker-gang fellow mobsters, is a story that has never before been fully explored.

The West End Gang's heyday was from the 1970s through the early 2000s. Nevertheless, their roots precede that, and their criminal activity is, if to a much lesser extent, ongoing today.

My introduction to some of these characters began quite serendipitously in 1979 when I moved to Montreal from New York where, as a reporter for the *Wall Street Journal*, I had written a feature article about Montreal being, during the late 1960s, "The bank robbery capital of North America." One of the first jobs I got on my return to Montreal was as an administrator and teacher in a Dawson College program at the federal Leclerc medium-security penitentiary in Laval, just north of Montreal. And because the program involved Leclerc's English-speaking inmates, I was soon meeting some of the so-called West End Gang—guys I'd never heard of before. I found some of them and their stories fascinating.

Now, three decades later, I am still intrigued by their exploits, their screw-ups, and the fact that those Irish mobsters (many of them long-since killed, and others now rather long in the tooth) can still generate headlines.

In recent years, there has been much written about Montreal's Italian mafia families, biker gangs and young ethnic street gangs. Yet relatively little attention has been paid to these "Sons of Erin" who for several decades brought crime and mayhem into the southwest corner of the city. This book is all about these men and their exploits.

## ACKNOWLEDGMENTS

This book owes much to my ability to access the files and source-support of the RCMP (especially their Quebec "Division C"), the Montreal Police Service, and the Sûreté du Québec (Quebec Provincial Police). It also relies heavily on access to and documents obtained from the Palais de justice de Montréal (the Courthouse), Cour du Québec (the Court of Quebec), Cour d'appel du Québec (Quebec Court of Appeal), Cour Supérieure du Québec (Quebec Superior Court), Bibliothéque et Archives nationales du Québec, the Canadian National Parole Board, the McGill University Law Library, and the Concordia University Library. Many individuals in those organizations were helpful in providing information, as well as guiding me through the labyrinth of voluminous files that had anything to do with the West End Gang.

More importantly, there are the cons and ex-cons, cops and ex-cops, various Irish gang hang-arounds and know-abouts, bar owners, bar tenders and barflies, hookers, pimps and drug-dealers, plus others who allowed me to interview them (either on or off the record), and helped me get a handle on the fascinating history of Montreal's so-called "Irish mafia."

But the most helpful of all were my chief researcher, Miranda O'Connor, as well as John Westlake, André Savard, John Phillips, André Potvin, William Morgan, André Bouchard and Paul Cherry, without whom I'd still be lost trying to figure out all the various connections between the "bad guys" and those who pursued them. There were also many others who granted me interviews in my quest for details about growing up in Irish neighborhoods, as well as the machinations of the West End Gang.

Finally, there are the various "munchkins," especially Julie Lewis, who did most of the tedious work of translating from French to English the hundreds of court documents, police files, crime commission and coroner reports, National Parole Board hearings, and francophone media articles. And it was mostly Miranda who transcribed dozens of audio-taped interviews onto paper. Any factual errors that may appear in the book are entirely my responsibility, and not theirs.

As for getting the book finally written and finished, I could not have done it without the enduring patience and support of my editors Don Loney and Pauline Ricablanca at John Wiley & Sons.

# CHAPTER 1

# The Irish Invasion

During the mid to late 19<sup>th</sup> century, primarily between 1846 and 1850, an estimated three million Irish immigrants fled The Hunger or, as it was also known, the Great Potato Famine, a fungal infection that ravaged their native soil. Most sailed across the Atlantic in order to take up roots in North America where, they were assured, there was arable land to be tilled, sown and harvested. In addition, they were counting on ample employment in these burgeoning urban areas. For the most part, these desperate people arrived with little more than the clothes on their back, and some with a brood of malnourished children, to establish new roots in cities like New York, Boston and Montreal.

The bulk of these émigrés chose the United States as their landfall, and most were processed through Ellis Island off the southern tip of

Irish immigrant children arriving in Canada, 1924

Manhattan. Once cleared, they either settled into Manhattan's Lower East and West Side, or else made their way north to Boston, south to New Orleans, or west to Chicago and Kansas City, all of which were growing urban centers of opportunity and blue-collar jobs.

Yet almost half a million of the Irish émigrés opted to make their landfall in the Dominion of Canada. After being crammed for five to six weeks in the holds of the so-called "coffin ships," in which they were essentially used as human ballast on lumber carriers returning from England, they were initially quarantined and processed at Grosse Île, a rocky windswept island on the St. Lawrence River, some 30 miles downstream from Quebec City. This precaution was taken because those hundreds who hadn't died at sea of cholera, typhus or malnutrition (and whose bodies had been summarily slipped over the side into the depths of the mid-Atlantic) were considered either contaminated or at risk. And indeed, many of them were. Today Grosse Île contains the unmarked graves of some 3,000 to 5,000 Irish men, women and children who came close to the "Promised Land," but who unfortunately never realized its promise. Those who did survive, later sailed up to Quebec City and Montreal, and some even as far upriver as Kingston, Ontario (then Upper Canada), where they planted their Diaspora Irish roots.[1]

1 My great-great-grandfather Charles John O'Connor arrived with his family from Limerick and was processed through Grosse Île in 1848, to later take up farming in the Gatineau area of Quebec.

Grosse Île Quarantine Shed

Many of the Irish who chose to settle in Montreal, which had been incorporated as a city in 1832, were still disease-ridden, and were confined to the "fever sheds" of Goose Village (originally known as Victoriatown) on the river's edge, where they were cared for by the Catholic order of Grey Nuns. Thousands succumbed to cholera or other diseases in those sheds, and were buried in a mass grave on the banks of the St. Lawrence River. Today there stands a monument, officially named The Irish Commemorative Stone, but colloquially known as "the Black Rock," honoring their demise. Rather ironically, the monolith bears the shape of a giant potato. It was dredged up from the river and erected in 1859 by Irish laborers who, while constructing the Victoria Bridge, had uncovered the bones of their Irish brethren who'd been interred there in the previous decade. The inscription on the 30-ton, 10-foot-high granite boulder that faces the entrance to

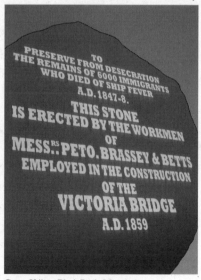

Goose Village Black Rock, Montreal

the span over the St. Lawrence River reads: "To preserve from desecration the remains of 6,000 immigrants who died of ship fever."

Those fortunate enough to survive the Atlantic crossing and the fever sheds would find housing and raise families in the impoverished working-class ghettos of Griffintown, Goose Village and Point St. Charles. There was plenty of work to be had in that southwestern part of Montreal. The eight-mile-long Lachine Canal, the Victoria Bridge and the Grand Trunk Railway yards were being built during that period, most of it with the brawn of Irish labor. Those projects in turn soon attracted breweries, brickyards, tanneries, soap factories, steel foundries and other industries. The canal, first dug in 1825 and widened twice in 1873 and 1885, provided a hydraulic power source for industries on its banks, as well as a water highway for incoming raw materials and outgoing processed goods between the St. Lawrence River and the Great Lakes. There was no shortage of jobs for those predominantly Irish settlers in Montreal during the late 19th and early 20th century, even if most of them were being paid penury wages and toiled for long hours. In 1880, for example, Grand Trunk employees were on the job 10 hours a day Monday to Friday, plus another four to five hours on Saturday. And in some of the factories along the canal, the work shift consisted of 14 hours a day, six days a week.

Life was not easy for the early émigrés from the Emerald Isle. There were many young men among them who sought an easier path in the New World. This was especially true in the United States, where Irish gangs sprang up within months of their arrival. These youths, driven from an impoverished land of British colonial oppression, had learned from experience that real wealth and power came not from hard work, but from intimidation and control of the neighborhood in which they lived.

So, not surprisingly, thousands of young males formed collectives of like-minded dissidents in the urban centers of America, particularly in New York City and Boston, where most of them had settled in the mid to late 1800s. They were at first a rag-tag leaderless bunch of thugs involved in petty thievery and fighting among themselves. But inevitably there arose individuals with the charisma and balls to become leaders of their group, creating organized Irish gangs that were named either after the leader himself or the urban district that the gang controlled.

## The First Fighting Irish

In the United States it was these gangs who, in the 1800s, first constituted what today would be labeled as members of "organized crime"—well before the arrival of the Sicilian or other Italian mafia families. As the low men on the immigrant totem pole, the "Paddies" were regarded as ignorant and impulsive rough-and-tumble yahoos by their American-born (and usually anti-Catholic) employers. For instance, at construction job sites they were often confronted with a posted sign warning that

Typical late 1800s construction sign, New York City

"Irish Need Not Apply." But many of the fighting Irish, rather than being deterred by the snub, simply chose alternative ways to make a living, albeit illegally.

These cities needed to supply the working stiffs not only with jobs, but also with entertainment, such as unlicensed after-hours saloons, brothels and gambling houses. Some of the newly arrived Irish were quick to provide those diversions, as well as loan-sharking operations that offered money to fools who were already way over their heads. Moreover, none of those enterprises could be carried out without some form of enforcement, and the Irish certainly had plenty of muscle on hand.

In Manhattan alone, particularly in the slums of Hell's Kitchen on the Lower West Side, more than a dozen Irish gangs flourished, among the earliest being the Whyos, known for their ruthlessness in dealing with opposing gang members and even with their own leaders, several of whom were purged internally during the 1880s and '90s. They were followed in the early 1900s by other Celtic mobs, often made up of members of the same family, such the Gas House Gang, the Parlor Mob, the Gophers, the Hudson Dusters, and the Westies, all of whom were equally ruthless in staking out Manhattan's territory while running their operations and keeping competing gangs at bay. Naturally, all of this provided great fodder for the many New York City daily tabloids that eagerly sought to outdo one another with up-to-the-minute salacious details on the latest gangland killing.

In Boston, which housed North America's second largest influx of Irish émigrés, the lurid tabloid headlines read much the same. In that city, the early Irish gangs were battling one another in Somerville, South Boston and Charlestown over control of the city's three B's—broads, betting and booze. And so whorehouses, gambling houses and unlicensed saloons sprang up as quickly as the city developed. The New Englanders might have had deeper puritanical roots than their New York neighbors to the south, but it certainly didn't show in their appetite for what the Irish gangs had to offer. As well, the Bostonian gangs proved to be as rapacious and dangerous as their New York City kinsmen, and as generous in their under-the-table payoffs to local cops and elected officials who were on the take.

Then, in 1918, came the Women's Christian Temperance Union—God's gift to every criminal organization. The Volstead Act, which it spawned, lasted from 1920 to 1933. Cheap jokes aside, any move to prohibit the production, sale or consumption of alcohol was about as anti-Irish as one could get. Moreover, the law was equally despised by Protestant and Jewish alike. Inevitably, the "Noble Experiment" or "Great 13-year Failure," as it later became known, would, like nothing before, contribute to the escalation of organized crime in America. Bootlegging became the crime du jour, one that attracted everyone in the American and Canadian underworld, no matter what their nationality or gang affiliation. Billions of illicit dollars were reaped during that period, by everyone from the denizens of the Ozark Mountains of Arkansas to the Gucci-shod Sam Bronfman with his mansion in Westmount.

## Booze and Corruption

As a result of Prohibition, the Irish gangs attained an even stronger foothold in American society, partly due to the fact that, unlike other European immigrants, they spoke English and had the persuasive "gift of the gab." By the early 1900s they'd already insinuated themselves into civil servant roles such as firemen and police officers in major cities like New York, Boston and Chicago. And they now had a following among fellow European émigrés, nationality notwithstanding. So it was not surprising that many Irishmen, who had already risen to become political ward bosses, were eventually able to manipulate those in elected positions, such as city aldermen and mayors, whereby, through graft and patronage, these Irish puppeteers eventually controlled many American towns and cities. The biggest example, perhaps, was New York City's Tammany Hall, which first rose to power under ward czar William "Boss" Tweed in the mid-1800s and which managed to yield influence until 1932 when its last ward-supported mayor, Jimmy Walker (dubbed Beau James), was ousted from office.

In South Boston during Prohibition, no two groups of Irishmen were more feared than the members of the Kileen and Mullin gangs. Killings over turf and the sale of illicit booze were an ongoing occurrence between the two clans. Following the end of the Second World War, other Boston Irish gangs sprang up, viciously competing with one another for control of the city's three B's.

Then along came James "Whitey" Bulger, born on September 3, 1929, one of six children in an Irish Catholic family. After serving nine years in various prisons between 1965 and 1969 for armed bank robbery, he went on to become head of the notorious Winter Hill Gang (named after a neighborhood just north of Boston proper), which he led with an iron fist from 1970 until 1994. The gang allegedly had ties to Montreal's West End Gang, and was a known money and arms supplier for the Irish Republican Army back on the Auld Sod. Police investigations revealed that Bulger controlled most of the narcotics, extortion, loan sharking and bookmaking rackets, not just in Boston, but throughout most of New England. He is known to have either personally killed, or to have ordered killed, at least 90 persons during his 25-year bloody reign, usually employing his psychopathic lieutenant Stephen "the Rifleman" Flemmi.

However, Bulger led a double life, operating as an informant about his gang's dealings with Boston's Italian mafia with John Connolly, a corrupt agent in the city's FBI organized crime squad. The FBI used this information to bust many prominent members of Boston's Cosa Nostra families during the 1980s. This reciprocal arrangement managed to keep Bulger out of jail for many years as he continued his criminal activities.

But that came to an end in April 1994 when a joint task force made up of the Drug Enforcement Administration, the Massachusetts State Police, and the Boston Police Department launched a probe into his operations. The FBI was purposely not informed, and a federal case was built against Bulger under the 1970 federal RICO (Racketeer Influenced and Corrupt Organizations) Act. The following December, Bulger was tipped off by his compromised FBI agent John Connolly that sealed indictments had been filed by the U.S. Department of Justice, and that the agency would soon be making major arrests.

None too soon, Bulger fled Boston on December 23, 1994, and he has been on the lam ever since, reportedly with his mistress Catherine Elizabeth Greig. Today he ranks second after Osama Bin Laden (who rates a $25-million bounty) on the FBI Ten Most Wanted Fugitives list, with a $2-million price on his head. The "Bulger Task Force" (consisting of seven investigators from the FBI, the Massachusetts State Police, and the Massachusetts Department of Correction) are still on his trail, running down numerous "spotting" tips in Florida, London, Ireland, Latin America and Montreal. Even though he would have turned 81 on September 3, 2010, there are many who believe that Bulger, whom the FBI say stashed millions of dollars in offshore bank accounts and in safety deposit boxes in Ireland, England, Quebec and Ontario shortly before his escape, is still alive and hiding out somewhere under various disguises and aliases.

In Canada, meanwhile, the Irish Diaspora was far smaller in number and strength, and had almost no political influence. Nevertheless, the Irish had gripes and ambitions that were similar to those of their American cousins. And they also shared their poverty and clannishness.

Perhaps the closest Canadian comparison to New York City's Hell's Kitchen or Boston's South Side would be Montreal's Griffintown and its adjacent Goose Village, which together comprised a few dozen square blocks that harbored the majority of Canada's urban Irish immigrant families at the turn of the 20th century. And immediately to the south, across the Lachine Canal, lay the sprawling ghetto and rail yards of Point St. Charles, where only slightly better-off Irish tenants could find larger flats and even a green park or two. It was these neighborhoods that would become the spawning grounds for many of the West End Gang.

CHAPTER 2

# "Most of His Children Turned Out To Be Thieves"

It was only a matter of time before many of the young Irishmen growing up in Griffintown, Goose Village and Point St. Charles began seeking out, as were their American brethren in New York and Boston, an easier way of life than working for "the man" (usually a Brit or a Scot) in his tannery, soap factory, iron foundry, printing plant, brewery, flour or sugar mill, or similar sweat shop down by the Lachine Canal. Their fathers, who toiled for the boss, received only a meager salary with which to support a large Catholic family. And on a Thursday or Friday payday, a big chunk of those wages were often quaffed down that evening by dad in one of the many neighborhood taverns.

## Griffintown

Griffintown, known as "the Griff" by its inhabitants, was anything but lace curtain Irish. It was where the poorest of Montreal's poor lived in the 19th and early 20th centuries. The shantytown was bordered by Notre Dame Street to the north, the Lachine Canal to the south, McGill Street to the east, and Guy Street to the west. It consisted of a few dozen city blocks of factories and two- or three-story brick and wood-frame, cold-water row houses that housed most of the factory employees and their families. Up the hill, particularly in enclaves like Mile End, Outremont and Westmount, the Griff was disdainfully regarded as that place to where their sewage flowed and where their non-live-in servants and coal and ice suppliers lived. In his 1942 book, *Montreal: Seaport and City*, Montreal author and McGill University economics professor Stephen Leacock snobbishly dismissed the Griff as "a wretched area whose tumbled, shabby houses mock at the wealth of Montreal."

Given its low-lying area and many wooden sheds, floods and fires were commonplace in the Griff. Perhaps its most dramatic tragedy occurred on the morning of April 25, 1944, when a Royal Air Force Ferry Command Liberator bomber taking off from Dorval airport lost power and crashed into the heart of Griffintown at the intersection of Shannon and Ottawa Streets, killing its five-man crew and 10 Griff residents.

During the 1950s and '60s, factories were shutting down and families began deserting Griffintown, moving south to Point St. Charles and Verdun where there were bigger flats to be rented and even green spaces where their children could play. By 1970, following the 1959 opening of the St. Lawrence Seaway and closure of the Lachine Canal to commercial traffic, most of the tenements and abandoned factories were razed to make way for the Bonaventure Expressway and an industrial park. Griffintown was gradually reduced to a ghost of its original self, inhabited mostly by some 2,000 working-class French Canadians, Italians and Ukrainians, which was only a tenth of its mostly Irish population a hundred years earlier. And the six streets that had once made up tiny Goose Village were wiped off the map.

Indeed, the Irish influence in Montreal has diminished greatly since the arrival of those first émigrés. According to the Statistics Canada census figures, in 1860 there were 14,179 people of Irish origin living in Montreal, making up 15.7 percent of the city's population of 90,323 inhabitants. But in the latest 2006 census, almost a century and a half later, Montreal and its on-island suburbs held only 161,000 people with claims to Irish lineage, a mere 8.5 percent of the city's 1.9 million total population. Much of this was a result of the flight of an estimated 240,000 Anglophones to Toronto and points west in the 10 years following the election of the separatist Parti Québécois in 1976 and the adoption of Bill 101 in 1977, which legislated French as the only official language of Quebec.

Perhaps the final nail in the Irish coffin was driven in 1990 when Montreal renamed Griffintown Faubourg-des-Récollets, after the order of nuns who'd first held property there in the late 18th century. This has not sat well with the city's United Irish Society and others who seek to preserve the Griff's Celtic heritage. In the past few years there have been several proposals to tear down what's left of the area, including a $1.3-billion megaproject that would create almost 4,000 low-income subsidized housing units, major box stores and other retail outlets, as well as hotels and even a concert hall. But due to the economic recession, all of those plans remain on the drawing board, are being scaled down, and continue to be hotly debated among Montreal city councilors and by several Irish associations that are desperately seeking to retain and even to revive some of Griffintown's historic past.

Those who grew up in the Griff have mixed feelings about what it was like to live there during the early to mid-1900s when it was a vibrant Irish neighborhood. There was an open friendliness among its inhabitants, who often got together to share gossip and beer on their balconies and sidewalk stoops. Yet there was also the shared poverty that often led to juvenile crime. Whether it was stealing apples off horse-drawn wagons or pick-pocketing drunks who were staggering home from the bars, petty theft was something almost every Griff kid did, or else knew that his friends did. And it would form the beginning of a criminal career for many of those young Irish lads.

John Phillips, a former West End Gang hang-around whose specialty later became passing rubber cheques and robbing jewelry stores and banks, was the product of a typical Griffintown family. He was born on September 6, 1938, the fourth of seven brothers and five sisters who were raised in a two-floor cold-water flat on Murray Street near the corner of Wellington Avenue. "With my mum and my dad there was 15 in the house in the '40s and '50s," he recalls today, "although by the time the eldest turned sixteen, they would move out. But there was always a crowd of us."

The children slept in one large dormitory upstairs, which had originally been four small bedrooms. "My father took all the walls down one cold winter because we needed to burn the wood in the kitchen's cast-iron cooking stove to heat the house," explains Phillips. And "downstairs there was one room that Dad slept in with my mother, a living room, kitchen, and bathroom with no bathtub or sink, just a toilet."

Baths were therefore scarce and far between in the Phillips household, particularly in the winter when the community's public baths were often closed. "We had a big tub in the kitchen where Mum would boil the water on the stove, and three or four of us would use the same water. We might have got two or three [baths] a winter."

These were Spartan times, notes Phillips. "My dad was kind of an alcoholic and usually out of work, so it was financially difficult for us ... and more often than not there was no food in the fucking house." But, he adds, "Whatever we were experiencing, we just accepted it as that's the way life is, since most of our neighbors lived under much the same conditions."

Inevitably, almost all of the siblings eventually turned to crime. "My father was pretty straight, but most of his children turned out to be thieves," says Phillips who quips that of the 13 kids, there was "only one white sheep in the family." Among the black sheep, John's brother David, a fraud artist, was shot to death in the early 1960s in a love triangle over a woman, and his brother Eddie was murdered in broad daylight on March 25, 1985, in retaliation for his role in the assassination of West End Gang kingpin Dunie Ryan. As for John, he would eventually become a bank robber and would end up serving a quarter of his life in various provincial and federal institutions.

Another early 20th century Griffintown kid was Charles Burke, the product of an absentee second-generation Irish father, Belfield Burke, and a Caribbean mother, Marie Terese, from the island of St. Lucia. He too dabbled in petty crime while growing up, and was a pre-teen amateur boxer in the Griffintown Block Boys Club.

John Phillips, retired West End Gang bank robber, summer 2008

He later went on to be a Canadian National Railway porter, a Montreal bar owner, and then a videographer and movie extra, which is how he now, at the age of seventy-seven, makes his living in New York City and Vancouver.

While he personally knew a lot of the West Gang types in the mid-1900s, Burke was never a member; not because he was black, but because, as he says today, "I had sense enough to stay away from them . . . Most of the Irish guys I met there grew up into the gangster world." And "almost all of them," he notes, have since been killed or are now in jail.

As an only child, Burke was raised during the 1940s by his strict Catholic mother, known as Hetty, on Lusignan Street just south of Notre Dame Street "in a little one-room house where the bathroom and everything was in the one room." He adds that by the time he was ten or eleven, "I got into shoplifting and hustling . . . And later I'm hanging out big time. I'm picking pockets, and I was one of the best in the area." But Hetty

Charles Burke, circa 2008

frowned on her son's delinquency, and she was a strict disciplinarian. "It was a regular thing with her; so [getting] a beating was part of [life], like having dinner," he says.

He recalls the time when, at the age of thirteen, he'd made a major score by picking a wallet containing "two or three hundred dollars" from the pocket of some drunken seaman on the street in the Griff. "I ran home and fell asleep on my bed with the money all around me." The next morning, "my mother sees the money and takes every cent. So I wake up and say, 'Ma, where's my money?' She said, 'I took dat money and I'll be buying some groceries and you'll get some new clothes.' I said, 'But Ma, that's *my* money!' And then, BADAM, I'm down on the floor as she hits me and says, '*That* money is going into the house.'"

Young Charles was now in a pickle because two older teenagers, Lionel Deare and his brother, were the muscle and shakedown artists who controlled that part of Griffintown, and it was understood that a percentage of any robberies in the hood was to come to them. The brothers knew about Burke's lucrative score, and approached him the next day for their cut. "I told Lionel that my mother took it, and he said he'll get it back from her. I said, 'Lionel, you don't want to do that.' But he comes to our house that evening. Now, Lionel is a tough guy; nobody would fight him. But my mother, a large woman, just grabbed the goon by the throat and said [in her West Indian accent] 'You come in dis house, mon, and I break your neck.'" Deare quickly fled with his tail between his legs. "My mother was crazy! She could kick butt like Muhammad Ali; she would beat any man, woman or child," says Burke. As for Deare, he later went on to become a strong-arm enforcer in the mid-1950s for Montreal's Italian Pretula-Greco mob, where perhaps he never had to face an opponent as fearsome as the late Hetty Burke.

## The Point

Point St. Charles, which some historians refer to as Canada's first industrialized slum, lay just to the south of Griffintown, between the Lachine Canal and the St. Lawrence River. Here the living conditions were marginally better, even if its inhabitants were just a rung or two up the social ladder. Yet they were still shanty Irish and living in an area that also spawned its fair share of potential criminals.

"The Point," as it was known, was originally inhabited by ethnic Irish, Scottish, Polish and French Canadian industrial workers in the 19th and early 20th centuries, the majority of whom were employed by local factories and the Grand Trunk Railway. As in Griffintown, most of those jobs have long since disappeared, and in the past three decades the neighborhood has been largely gentrified by yuppies buying and renovating its old houses, and its canal-facing factories have been turned into pricey condominiums.

But in the mid-1900s, the Point was the place to go in order to escape the squalor of Griffintown and Goose Village. The Irish families who relocated there had similar Celtic roots and, importantly, shared the camaraderie that existed north of the canal. Nevertheless, life there was almost as poverty-stricken as it was back in the Griff.

Brendan Deegan was a typical child growing up in the Point. He was born in 1933 on Grand Trunk Street, the fourth of ten brothers and sisters. Their father, Frank "Lefty" Deegan, worked for the railway, and was also a minor league baseball player, which meant that he was often out of town. And, like many fathers in the Point, he was not the most reliable provider. "My father was a good man, but he had the Irish curse," says Deegan today. "He drank and he gambled. So my mother, like a lot of mothers in the Point, had to wait 'til he got home on pay day."

Deegan acknowledges that times were tough growing up with a large family in a three-bedroom house with no hot running water. "But," he adds, "you never knew that you were poor, 'cause all your neighbors grew up the same way ... When we were kids, you got up to a cold [kitchen stove] fire" until Mom or Dad lit it, and "then you all hung around the

Frank "Lefty" Deegan Sr., 1931

The Deegan children in Little Burgundy, 1941

fire, put your toast on the stove and waited your turn." And often there was little or no food in the house. "If my father drank that weekend and didn't bring home the pay, we didn't know if we were going to eat the next day. So you'd steal. You'd rob a chocolate bar at the store or something like Mae Wests, Black Beauties, or whatever."

He recalls one time as a kid when he and one of his brothers were going to the store with a few coins their mother had given them to buy some groceries, and they'd dropped a quarter in the snow. "We were on our hands and knees looking for that quarter because at that time you could buy a loaf of bread, sugar and a quart of milk for about 28 cents or something. That quarter was our supper!"

Unlike some of his neighborhood friends and his older brother Frankie, Brendan eventually followed a straight-and-narrow path, becoming a (now-retired) school teacher for some 35 years. Which is not to say that his juvenile days were innocent. "My criminal career started very young . . . The trains would come in with fruit [inside boxcars] and park in the rail yards. We'd get up early in the morning, open the car doors and take the bananas and fruit and sell it . . . And we were only ten or eleven years old then."

In their early teens, the Deegan brothers were altar boys at St. Gabriel's Catholic Church on Center Street where they would occasionally steal nickels and dimes from the collection plate after mass. "But," he recalls, "the biggest heist we ever did in my church was in the bingo games." Some of the Deegan boys were the ones appointed to turn the basket tumbler with its lettered and numbered balls, and they would occasionally rig the game with a player whose card they'd copied. "We had this old man we knew who was part of the deal . . . We'd fix it so that he'd win a major jackpot, maybe five or six hundred dollars." The brothers and their bingo-player shill would then later split the winnings. "Everybody had a scam" in the Point, shrugs Deegan, "because that's the way things worked."

Unlike many Irish families in the Point, the Deegan clan managed to stay out of any serious trouble—except for the oldest brother, Frankie, who was the hustler in the bunch. Frankie had two nicknames: "Fingers" for his ability to smoothly lift wallets, and "the Machine" for his mathematical skill at figuring out the percentages in various illegal gambling games. In the mid-1960s he served almost two years in prison for embezzling funds from the CBC. But apart from being a conman, Frankie also enjoyed a sporadic career as an amateur boxer and salesman, and later as a hockey scout for the NHL. He died of cancer at the age of seventy-five on January 18, 2006.

According to Brendan, both Frankie and their father were on close terms with many of the West End Gang families, such as the MacAllisters, the Mattickses, the McSweens and the Johnstons. In fact, the youngest of Brendan's sisters still retains the memory of the time when, as a five-year-old in 1958, she and her father drove up to the family's cottage in St. Sauveur in the Laurentian Mountains. "We walked in and my father said, 'Oops, looks like the Johnston brothers have been here again.'" The evidence was bottles of liquor on the shelves, a fridge full of beer and the freezer stocked with steaks. She says, "It was only years later that I figured out that the Johnstons were using my father's place as a hideout," no doubt while on the lam from the cops between bank robberies.

Billy Johnston of the West End Gang Johnston brothers

By the time he turned twenty, Brendan Deegan decided to go straight, and had even briefly considered joining the priesthood. "I was the best Catholic ever; I always went to mass on Sunday. But still, I was a thief. It's not that I'm bragging about it; I'm ashamed of it now. But that was the way things happened in the Point in those days."

He attributes his conversion to a particular incident in the early 1950s. "What stopped me from crime was my friend Bobby Hansen . . . One day, we're all standing around and Bobby pulls out a gun and wants to shoot this gay guy. Luckily the gun didn't fire . . . And that's when I realized: 'I don't want to do this anymore.'" Shortly after that incident, Hansen used the gun to rob a store and ended up in jail.

In the 1960s the Deegan family moved a few miles west to Verdun, which was one more step up the Irish social ladder. Yet it was still an area that lay between the Lachine Canal and the St. Lawrence River. The next rung up was Notre-Dame-de-Grâce, known as NDG, which was immediately to the north. And that is where the West End Gang would establish its base in the decades to come.

# CHAPTER 3

# Calabrians and Sicilians

Well before the Irish would become a force to be reckoned with, organized crime in Montreal was in the hands of émigré Italians, notably the Cotroni and Violi families with their Calabrian roots, and the Rizzuto Family with its Sicilian roots. All had had ties to the established Bonanno and Caruana-Cuntrera Cosa Nostra mobs in New York, and they controlled most of Montreal's illegal gambling, loan-sharking, and the importation and distribution of heroin and cocaine during the early and mid-1900s.

One of the first to arrive was Nicodemo Cotroni, a thirty-three-year-old carpenter from the town of Mammola, near the southern coastal city of Calabria. He came to Montreal in 1924 with his wife Maria-Rosa and their two sons, fourteen-year-old Vincenzo, nicknamed "Vic," and four-year-old Giuseppe, nicknamed "Pep." They moved into a three-story row house on the corner of Ontario and St. Timothée streets in Montreal's southeast district. In the next seven years they would have four more children, the youngest being Francesco "Frank," who was born in 1931 and who'd eventually become head of the Cotroni criminal empire in the mid-1900s.

In the 1920s Nicodemo and his son Vincenzo legitimately worked as Montreal carpenters and cabinetmakers. But as a sideline, they became involved in the lucrative Prohibition-era liquor smuggling business. Following the repeal of the Volstead Act in 1933, they moved into illegal gambling and the drug trade, especially heroin, which proved far more profitable than selling bootleg booze. By the 1950s, the Cotroni Family had become the major conduit for high-grade "white" heroin processed in clandestine labs in Marseilles, France, and then shipped, usually by sea, to Montreal for local sale and, more importantly, for redistribution to New York and other North American cities. In 1956, RCMP and FBI authorities estimated that close to two-thirds of all heroin in North America that year had arrived through Montreal.

So important was the Montreal conduit that in 1952 Joseph Bonanno, godfather of one of New York's five major crime families, dispatched his chief lieutenant, Carmine "Lillo" Galante, north to work with the Cotronis in their gambling and heroin-import operations. After spending a busy 10 years in Montreal, Galante was extradited to the United States in July 1962, where he was sentenced by a New York court to 20 years in prison for drug trafficking.

## "Vic the Egg"

Vincenzo, known as "Vic the Egg" due to his rotund Humpty-Dumpty stature, was a professional wrestler for a brief time under the name of Vic Vincent. In the late 1940s he opened several downtown after-hours bars (locally known as "blind pigs"), brothels and gambling dens, sometimes with his kid brother Pep. Vic was arrested a few times on charges of theft, illegal sale of alcohol, and assault and battery, but usually got off with a fine or a short stint in jail. His major establishment was Vic's Café at 97 St. Catherine Street East, a club that was doing a booming business until the vice squad shut it down and revoked its liquor license in April 1955. Cotroni fought all the way to the Supreme Court of Canada to have the permit reinstated, but eventually lost his appeal.

Vic was probably the most influential and successful Montreal mafioso from the 1950s through the 1970s, aided by the fact that he had a few politicians and law enforcement officials in his pocket. He also proved to be a shrewd and respected power broker who managed to form an uneasy alliance with some of his mafia drug-importing competitors and other Montreal gangs during that period.

In 1976 he was subpoenaed to testify before the CECO (la Commission d'Enquête sur le Crime Organisé) tribunal. The Quebec government commission, headed by Judge Jean Dutil, was established in 1972 to examine the extent of organized crime in the province, specifically Montreal's Italian mafia families, the French-Canadian Dubois Clan, and the Irish West End Gang. Between September 27, 1972 and March 31, 1977, some 115 persons were subpoenaed to testify under oath. Those who failed to appear or else showed up but refused to answer questions, were cited for contempt, and automatically sentenced to anywhere from 2 to 12 months in jail.

Cotroni, whom the commission described as the "Godfather of Montreal," was one of those who refused to testify, and spent the next year in prison. He died of prostate cancer at the age of seventy-three on September 19, 1984. But he left behind an illegitimate son, Nick Cotroni, Jr., born on April 25, 1964 and named after his grandfather, Nicodemo. He was to become a small-time mafia underboss in the late 1900s.

Nick, the offspring of Vincenzo and his mistress Ghyslaine Turgeon, grew up in Miami. In July 1983 he was among dozens of people, including some 20 Canadians, such as West End Gang associate William Obront, who were arrested in a joint RCMP, FBI and DEA (Drug Enforcement Administration) operation on charges of running a $50-million-a-year drug ring in Florida. After serving a few years in a U.S. prison, Nick arrived in Montreal, where he became heavily involved in the video-poker machine racket and loan-sharking during the 1980s and '90s. On June 1, 2000, he was arrested in a north-end Montreal bar on charges of extortion, and sent back to prison. An obese man who

William Obront, 1977

weighed over 400 pounds, Nick died in prison of a heart attack in December 2001 at the age of thirty-seven.

Vic's brother Giuseppe "Pep" was also active in the family's affairs, especially as an importer and distributor of heroin and cocaine in the 1940s and '50s. He was a close associate of gangsters Frank Pretula and Louie Greco, and later a partner with them in the Décarie Boulevard Bonfire Restaurant, a popular Montreal hangout for local hoods. In August 1959, he and an associate, René Robert, were arrested in a combined FBI, RCMP, and local police sting operation on charges of importing six kilos of heroin from France to Montreal, drugs that were destined for New York. Following his trial three months later, Cotroni was found guilty and given a 10-year sentence in Manitoba's Stony Mountain Penitentiary and an $88,000 fine for trafficking in heroin. Shortly after his release, Pep died of natural causes at the age of sixty in 1979.

### "Le Gros"

Frank Cotroni, Vic's youngest brother, was probably the blackest of the family sheep during the mid-1900s. Known on the street as "le Gros" or the "Big Guy," Frank began his criminal career pulling off break and enters and shaking down local merchants in Montreal's East End. He was first busted in 1950 at the age of eighteen, and served several months in preventative detention for theft and possession of stolen goods. On July 24, 1956, he was arrested along with four of his hoodlum pals during a street melee with police in a riot that left one man shot and several cops injured. He was next picked up in September 1960 with Joseph Di Maulo and Michael Di Paolo for possession of firearms. Two months later, while still out on bail, Frank was arrested for leading 30 of his goons in the trashing of Montreal's Chez Parée Cabaret, a popular downtown nightclub once owned by

Jewish gambling czar Harry Ship. Cotroni was merely fined $200 for that crime.

During the 1960s, Frank was a key player in the so-called "French Connection," importing processed heroin from labs in Marseilles to New York via Montreal. He was also a major conduit for drugs delivered at wholesale prices in bulk to other mafia families, as well as to the West End Gang and local biker gangs. And, as will be seen in Chapter 8, he even tried his hand at breaking into a bank vault for which he was acquitted in August 1971.

Frank was back in court in 1972 on charges of trying to extort $250 a week in protection money from a Greek restaurant-owner, Dionysos Chionsis. But the case fell apart when (the apparently intimidated) Chionsis developed a sudden case of amnesia and declined to testify, so the charges were withdrawn. On November 8, 1974, Frank was again arrested, this time on charges of smuggling $3 million worth of cocaine from Mexico into the United States and Montreal, with incriminating evidence based on information from Sicilian drug-trafficker Giuseppe "Pino" Catania. Frank fought his extradition up to the Supreme Court, but lost and was shipped to the United States where he was fined $20,000 and sentenced to two concurrent terms of 15 years in prison.

He was paroled on April 25, 1979 (after having served a third of his sentence), and deported back to Montreal. However, he was picked up again on August 30, 1983, after a federal grand jury in New Haven, Connecticut, indicted him on conspiracy to distribute heroin.

While in Montreal's Parthenais Detention Centre during his fight to once again avoid extradition to the United States, Cotroni and his son Frank Jr., and associates Daniel Arena and Francesco Raso, were charged with the June 14, 1981, murder of Giuseppe Montegano, a north-end drug dealer and police informant. Frank was also charged with ordering the deaths of five rival mafia members in Montreal and Toronto between January 1980 and November 1983. Based on testimony by the Crown's main witness, Réal Simard, a professional hitman who testified to carrying out the five killings on behalf of the Cotroni mob, Frank pleaded guilty to manslaughter charges. On December 8, 1987, he was sentenced to eight years in prison, plus a concurrent six years for the Connecticut drug conspiracy.

After his release on September 28, 1995, Cotroni was arrested at his home on April 17, 1996, in a joint RCMP/Montreal and Toronto Police/Interpol drug bust. It was the culmination of a three-year investigation, code-named Operation Caviar, in which Frank and his son, plus 17 others were in the process of smuggling 180 kilos of Colombian cocaine hidden in a shipping container among sacks of Peruvian coffee into Canada via Toronto's Pearson International Airport.

Frank Sr. was handed a seven-year sentence for his role in the venture. He was conditionally paroled on October 30, 2001, but was re-arrested and briefly jailed on June 30, 2002, for violating the conditions of his parole by meeting in a Little Italy restaurant with people who had criminal records. Yet he somehow managed to obtain another conditional release two months later.

On August 17, 2004, after having spent almost half of his life behind bars, Frank Cotroni died of brain cancer at the age of seventy-two at his daughter's home in the east end of Montreal. His lavish mafia-style funeral, with a cortege of more than 20 limousines, flower-bearing cars and even a brass band following the hearse, took place the following Saturday at the Madonna della Difesa (Our Lady of Defense) church in Little Italy. It was attended by some 300 persons, including members and associates of both the Cotroni and Rizzuto families.

At that same time, a few miles to the east at the Ital Sports Bar in Rivière des Prairies, sixty-nine-year-old Vincent Melia, a known Rizzuto mobster, was enjoying his first beer of the day when a gunman entered the bar and shot him point-blank in the face. Police concluded that it was a retaliatory message from the Cotroni mob, significantly timed to coincide with Frank's funeral.

## "Frankie" Cotroni

Frank's son "Frankie," the fourth of six children, and youngest brother, born in 1960, followed his father's life of crime. He was also a pal of West End Gang kingpin Alan Ross during the 1980s. In April 1981, Frankie had a dispute over a cocaine transaction with the previously mentioned small-time dealer Giuseppe Montegano at Frankie's Agrigento Social Club in St. Léonard. The dispute was "settled" on June 14, 1981 when contract hitman Réal Simard entered the club and pumped four bullets into Montegano's head. Several years later, Simard, facing charges on other murders, turned police informant against the Cotronis, and Frankie was arrested along with his father on October 10, 1986, during

Frank Cotroni, Jr.

Operation Si-Co, and was charged as an accomplice to the Montegano killing. He pleaded guilty to manslaughter, and on January 15, 1988, received a three-year sentence.

Following his release, Frankie immediately jumped back into his family's drug business, and on April 17, 1996, was picked up during the Operation Caviar drug bust. Frankie pleaded guilty and received an 8-year sentence. He was paroled in October 2000, and appears to have stayed out of trouble ever since.

While Frankie was in jail, his forty-two-year-old brother, Paolo, a minor player in the Cotroni crime family, was killed on Sunday, August 23, 1998, by a volley of bullets in the driveway of his Repentigny home just off the northeastern tip of Montreal Island. Police suspected that the hit was ordered by Vito Rizzuto. But perhaps not, since Paolo was also a friend of Maurice Boucher, leader of the Hells Angels who were then at war with the Rock Machine motorcycle gang. Eleven years later, on March 26, 2009, Gerald Gallant, a professional freelance hitman testified that it was he, along with Frederic Faucher and Marcel Demers of the Rock Machine, who had killed Paolo. In any case, it was clear that the Cotroni Family had made some dangerous enemies.

## Paolo Violi

Another early Calabrian émigré to Canada was Paolo Violi from the town of Sinopoli. He first settled at the age of twenty in Hamilton, Ontario, in 1951, and obtained Canadian citizenship in 1956. In 1963

Paolo Violi, 1977

he moved to Montreal to open a pizzeria, and in July 1965 married the daughter of Giacomo Luppino, an influential leader of the Ontario mafia. His best man was fellow Calabrian Vic Cotroni, and the two became close business associates in control of much of the city's gambling, loan-sharking, prostitution and heroin importation rackets.

In 1970, Violi and his two younger brothers, Francesco and Rocco, opened the Violi Ice Cream Shop and adjacent Reggio Bar on Jean Talon Street in Little Italy. It was there they often conducted and discussed their "other" business, sometimes with Vic Cotroni and his associates. Unknown to them, the tenant who'd moved into the apartment above the bar in 1973 was Bob Ménard, a twenty-nine-year-old undercover cop posing as a journeyman electrician. In fact, Violi even hired Ménard to do some wiring work for him, which provided the "electrician" the opportunity to surreptitiously bug the Reggio Bar and its telephone line.

For the next two years Ménard recorded hundreds of hours of conversations, all of which were turned over to the CECO investigators. By 1975, forty-four-year-old Violi had replaced the aging Vic Cotroni as head of La Cosa Nostra in Quebec, so the wire taps, both in the bar and over the phone, provided much fodder for the commission. In 1976, Violi was subpoenaed to testify under oath about his activities. Instead, he fled to Toronto, where he was soon arrested and brought back to face the tribunal. But like Cotroni before him, Paolo stubbornly refused to answer any of their questions. He was therefore charged with contempt and sentenced to a year in jail.

Meanwhile, another Sicilian émigré to Montreal, Pietro Sciarra, who was Violi's trusted consigliere and who had testified before the CECO commission in November 1975, was gunned down on February 14, 1976. Ironically, the shooting occurred while Sciarra and his wife were leaving a Montreal North theater where they'd just watched an Italian-dubbed version of the Francis Ford Coppola film *The Godfather*.

It was left to Francesco Violi to run the family drug business while his brother Paolo was serving his time. But his tenure was short lived. On February 8, 1977, thirty-eight-year-old Francesco was found shot to death at his desk in the office of the family's importing and distributing company in Montreal's east end Rivière-des-Prairies district.

A year later, on January 22, 1978, Paolo, now thirty-eight and out of jail, was playing cards with three friends in his Reggio Bar when two masked gunmen entered the establishment and shot him dead and then stuffed his body into the trunk of his car.

Rocco Violi, 1980

The next to be whacked was the youngest Violi brother, Rocco, who'd survived an attempt on his life only three months earlier. On October 17, 1980, as he sat reading a newspaper in the kitchen of his Montreal district St. Léonard home, he was shot through the heart by a single .308-caliber rifle bullet. Police ballistics determined that his unknown assassin was a sniper who'd made a clean shot through the kitchen window from the roof of a building across the street.

Clearly, the Violi family was no longer on anyone's Christmas card list. And both the underworld and the cops realized that the uneasy truce that had existed for almost two decades between Montreal's Calabrian and Sicilian crime families over control of Montreal's drug trade had come to an end.

The Rizzutos were the obvious prime suspect in the killings, yet the murders went unsolved. Conveniently, Nick Rizzuto and his son Vito were out of the country when the shootings occurred. Later, four men connected to them—Domenico Manno, Giovanni DiMora, Agostino Cuntrera, and Paolo Renda—were charged with being implicated in Paolo Violi's murder. But the Crown was unable to prove its case, and the four were set free.

## The Ascension of the Rizzutos

Nevertheless, in the early 21$^{st}$ century, it would be the Rizzutos and their associates who would find themselves locked in the crosshairs of their gangland enemies. And they would also be targeted by an aggressive organized-crime police task force determined to take them down.

The Rizzutos had been relatively late Italian mafia émigrés to Canada. Their patriarch was Nicolo "Nick" Rizzuto Sr., who arrived in Montreal in February 1954 at the age of thirty from Palermo, Sicily, with his wife Libertina Manno (the daughter of an influential Sicilian capo) and their eight-year-old son Victor, nicknamed Vito. Back home, Nick was considered a "man of honor" within the Cosa Nostra, and he too had ties to New York City's Bonanno and Caruana-Cuntrera crime families. Like the Cotronis and Violis before them, they settled into Montreal's thriving Little Italy neighborhood.

One of Nick's first contacts was Luigi "Louis" Greco, an earlier Sicilian immigrant who'd been a petty Montreal crook and bank robber in the early 1930s. In 1944, after serving 11 years in prison for armed robbery, Greco became one of the city's top crime bosses and a major heroin importer and dealer with close ties to New York's Bonanno mob. He was also a 1940s chauffeur, bodyguard and protégé of a big-time Montreal Jewish mobster, Harry Davis, and was soon running many of Davis' Montreal gambling, prostitution and narcotics operations. When Davis was killed by a rival mobster in 1946, Greco and his associate Frank Pretula took over what remained of Davis' empire.

Greco formed a Sicilian–Calabrian working relationship with the Cotroni mob, abetted by the support of New York's Bonanno family, and soon became Vic Cotroni's second in command in Montreal's mafia underworld. He was also a partner with Cotroni, Pretula and others in the Alpha Investment Corporation, a front used to launder drug and gambling money during the 1940s and '50s, and was a co-owner with Pretula of the Bonfire Restaurant before it was taken over by Pep Cotroni.

Greco was later arrested on July 22, 1955, when a police raid uncovered a hidden arsenal of unregistered handguns and ammunition in his 4069 Dorchester Boulevard., Westmount, apartment. He was hauled off to Bordeaux prison and, despite the fact that he had $4,000 cash in his pockets, was denied bail until six days later. After several delays, his trial was held on September 30, 1955, at which time he got off with a mere $150 fine and a suspended sentence.

On December 7, 1972, Greco died at the age of fifty-seven, following an accidental explosion and fire in his family-owned Gina's Pizzeria in St. Léonard. He was perhaps the only Montreal Mafiosi of that era to meet his end not as a result of violence, sickness or old age, but simply by bad luck.

In the mid-1900s, the Rizzutos began to gradually displace the Cotronis as Montreal's major Italian crime family. Nick and his son Vito formed profitable business relationships with members of the Hells Angels and the West End Gang in the importation and distribution of cocaine. Many millions were being made on all sides. By 1982, Nick and various members of his extended family had moved from the ghetto of Little Italy to the Cartierville district of Montreal, where they had palatial million-dollar mansions built on spacious adjoining lots on Rue Antoine-Berthelet, a short tree-lined street referred to by the press and the police as "Mafia Row." Their homes, with garages and driveways full of Mercedes-Benzes, Porches, Corvettes, Cadillacs and Jaguars, were even more opulent than those of the fictional Soprano mafia clan in Somerset, New Jersey.

Nick's immediate neighbors included his son Vito and his son-in-law Paolo Renda, a Sicilian who'd emigrated to Montreal in 1958 and who had married Nick's only daughter, Maria. Renda would eventually rise to become the respected consigliere of the Rizzuto Family.

Vito, who'd arrived in Canada with his parents in 1954, became a Canadian citizen in 1966 and soon after married eighteen-year-old Giovanna Cammelleri in a classic Mob-style wedding in Toronto. In 1972, at the age of twenty-six, he and his brother-in-law Paolo were convicted of burning down the latter's barbershop for the insurance money on May 16, 1968. They each served a four-month sentence.

During the 1970s, Vito was heavily involved in loan sharking, illegal gambling, drug smuggling and money laundering, often in partnership with Montreal's Hells Angels, the West End Gang, and South American drug cartels. In 1978, after fleeing to Caracas, Venezuela, for a couple of years, he and Renda were fingered, but never arrested, for their suspected role in that year's assassination of Paolo Violi.

In May of 1981, Vito was dispatched to New York to settle a factional dispute within the Bonanno family. However, his heavy-handed method of solving the problem would come back to bite him some 23 years later.

Vito was picked up by the RCMP twice during the 1980s on charges of attempting to import large amounts of hashish and cocaine into Canada, but got off both times. In February 1988, he was arrested in Venezuela for possession of 1.5 kilograms of cocaine and served a five-year jail term there. In June 1993, he returned to Montreal, where he would succeed his father as head of the Rizzuto mob and, by managing to dodge further criminal prosecution, acquire the epithet "the Teflon Don of Canada."

The pissing and shooting match between Montreal's Calabrians and Sicilians continued off and on throughout most of the 20th century. But while the Italians were busy feuding with one another, there were two other Montreal gangs at play: the so-called Jewish mafia during the early 1900s, and the Irish mafia in the latter half of the century.

CHAPTER 4

# Montreal's Jewish Mafia

Once again, before the formation of any organized Irish mafia, it was the so-called "Jewish mafia" which, like the Italian mafia, made up Montreal's criminal underbelly in the early to mid-1900s. They too would later form sporadic allegiances with members of the West End Gang to participate in robberies and other crimes.

Beginning in the 1920s and '30s, it was East European Jewish émigrés and their offspring who were the city's major bookmakers, loan sharks, and illegal gambling house operators. And, like the Italians, some of them would inevitably be seduced by the huge profits to be made in the lucrative drug trade.

Harry Davis, born in Romania in 1898, arrived almost penniless as a young man in the early 1920s. He was a diminutive sharply dressed hustler who soon made his mark by opening an illicit betting emporium at 1244 Stanley Street in the heart of the city. There one could play blackjack, roulette, baccarat and barbotte (a popular Montreal dice game similar to craps), as well as place bets on horses running that day on tracks all over North America. The various races with their horses and odds were posted on a large blackboard, and the bookie would later that day receive the results over the phone or teletype machine. Should a gambler run short of funds, no problem. Harry and his boys would obligingly front him some cash at usurious repayment rates.

Naturally, Davis' operations and the many other gambling dens that sprang up across the city did not go unnoticed by the authorities. But this was a time when there was no shortage of municipal officials and cops who were on the take. In fact, Harry soon became the city's "edge man," who would collect the bribes from the various gambling establishments and then dutifully apportion the money among those who were turning a blind eye to what was going on.

In order to keep up appearances, the morality squad regularly carried out raids at his and other places (usually phoning ahead) and, under the province's quaint "Padlock Law," would seize a telephone or two before affixing a padlock to the offending room which, more often than not, was empty or perhaps was simply a broom closet or bathroom. Their job done (and payment assured) the vice cops could return to the station and fill out reports detailing another "successful" raid on a den of iniquity. Every gambling parlour in the city had its own such dummy room.

Things were going well for Davis until he got greedy and teamed up with another Jewish émigré, Charles "Charlie" Feigenbaum. Unlike the thin and dapper Harry, Charlie, born in 1896, was a large and somewhat slovenly man. He'd begun his criminal career as a small-time Montreal bookie and then moved on to importing one-armed bandits (slot machines) from the United States and installing the illegal equipment in dozens of Laurentian resorts north of the city. By 1925, with some 300 of his machines in place, Feigenbaum was being referred to in gambling circles as "the King of the North."

## Drugs and Death

But the lure of profits to be made in drugs was too much to resist, and in 1930 he and Davis, together with Pincus Brecher, their New York contact, began smuggling European heroin and cocaine, hidden among rolls of imported silk and other commodities shipped into the Port of Montreal. Much of the contraband was then transferred by car to Louis "Lepke" Bulchalter, head of a major New York City Jewish mob during the 1920s and 1930s. (On March 4, 1944, Bulchalter was executed in New York's Sing Sing Prison for four murders unrelated to his Montreal dealings).

It wasn't long before the RCMP got wind of Davis' scheme, and through surveillance and wire taps busted it wide open. On April 9, 1933, Davis, Feigenbaum, Brecher and six others were arrested and charged with drug smuggling. Feigenbaum, in exchange for a light sentence of only six months in jail, ratted out his associates and became the Crown's key witness during their trials.

Davis' trial, which began on October 1, 1933, lasted only five days before the jury found him guilty on all five counts of importing drugs and corrupting public officials, with most of the evidence against him supplied by Feigenbaum. Incarcerated in Montreal's St. Vincent de Paul Penitentiary, Davis received 10 strokes of the lash plus a 14-year sentence, of which he served 12.

But the thirty-eight-year-old Feigenbaum was to pay heavily for his testimony. At 5:15 p.m. on August 21, 1934, he exited his brother and sister-in-law's home at 4510 Esplanade Avenue with his eighteen-year-old son Jackie. A gunman in a parked Hudson sedan that contained two other men calmly got out and walked across the street where he pumped six .45-caliber bullets into Feigenbaum's head and chest before jumping back into the car, which sped away. Although there were plenty of witnesses to the daytime hit, Charlie's killers were never caught. Police surmised they were professional hitmen who'd been hired from out of town, perhaps New York or Chicago, and possibly by the incarcerated Harry Davis.

Even though their star witness had been eliminated, the Crown in September 1934 was able to win a guilty verdict against Pincus Brecher on charges of possession and distribution of narcotics. But a few days after his conviction, while awaiting sentencing at the St. Vincent de Paul Penitentiary, Brecher broke away from one of his guards and threw himself head first over a prison balcony and died after hitting the asphalt 35 feet below.

Davis was released from prison in 1945 and, determined to get back into the game, reopened his Stanley Street bookmaking and gambling parlor. But by then others within both the Italian and Jewish communities had taken over most of the city's rackets in his absence, and Davis' sense of entitlement was resented on the street. Within a year of his return he was shot dead at the age of forty-eight by Louis Bercovitch, a rival Jewish mobster.

Bercovitch, who sometimes used the alias Joe Miller, was born in 1909, one of nine children from the city's St. Lawrence Boulevard Jewish garment district. He became a hustler, petty thief and safecracker in his teens and twenties, and served overseas with the Canadian Army from 1940 to 1942. On his return to Montreal, he moved into the downtown bookmaking and gambling racket where, as the new kid on the block, he found himself up against some resentful and pretty heavy competition.

On the afternoon of July 25, 1946, after hearing through the grapevine that Davis had put out a contract on his life, Louis decided to meet with Harry in order to talk things out. They were alone in Davis' gambling emporium back office when (according to Louis' version of events) Harry said, "What we did to Feigenbaum, the same could happen to you." They continued to argue to the point when (as Louis would later testify) Harry reached for a gun in his belt. Bercovitch reacted by pulling out his own gun and shot Davis dead with a bullet to the chest and another to the head before fleeing the scene.

Bercovitch spent the rest of the afternoon sweating in his apartment, knowing that although there had been no witnesses to the shooting, it was only a matter of time before either Davis' mob or the police would hunt him down. He wisely chose the latter, and that evening he called Ted McCormick, a crime reporter he knew at the *Montreal Herald,* and asked to meet with him at the newspaper's office. A few hours later, McCormick was typing out the scoop of a lifetime on his

Underwood, while Louis detailed his version of what had transpired in Davis' office a few hours earlier. The reporter then called William Fitzpatrick of the Montreal homicide squad, who immediately arrived and arrested Bercovitch on a charge of murder.

Now behind bars and safe from mob retaliation, Bercovitch was sent to trial, all the while maintaining that he'd shot Davis in self-defense. On October 5, 1946, after deliberating for four hours, the jury found him guilty on a reduced charge of manslaughter, and he was sentenced to life in prison. His application to appeal the verdict was denied, and he remained a guest of the St. Vincent de Paul Penitentiary.

Ten years later, the Canadian Bar Association's criminal justice committee, after reviewing the case, determined that Bercovitch had been unfairly tried as a result of, among other things, perjured testimony by Montreal gangster Frank Pretula, and in August 1956 it recommended that he be either retried or else released from prison on a "ticket of leave" (limited supervised parole). Bercovitch, then forty-seven, declined the latter option, insisting on either an "absolute pardon" or else a new trial on the basis that he had been "framed" and "railroaded into the penitentiary" 10 years earlier. He was eventually released from prison and retired to Acapulco, Mexico, where he continued his association with some of Montreal's underworld figures such as the Cotroni Family. He died of natural causes in the early 1980s.

### The Rackets and the Payoff

Filling the vacuum left by the 1946 death of Harry Davis was thirty-one-year-old Harry Ship, a dropout from Queen's University where he'd studied business administration in the early 1930s. He would soon become one of Montreal's most prosperous bookies during the 1940s and '50s, operating out of his establishment at 906 St. Catherine Street East. Like the other Harry whom he'd succeeded, Ship was an "edge man," collecting and supplying payoffs to cops and local politicians in order to keep his businesses running smoothly. He was a conspicuous spender who lived the good life in a mansion in Montreal's upscale Outremont district, and owned several race horses and shares in legitimate nightclubs such as the popular Chez Parée night club on Stanley Street. He was also a partner with the gangster Frank Pretula and others in the Alpha Investment Corporation, which laundered drug and gambling proceeds during the 1950s.

According to a later investigation into his affairs, Ship was pulling in at least $1,500 a day from his gambling and bookmaking operations. The Quebec Provincial Police and the Montreal morality squad raided his St. Catherine Street establishment 76 times between 1940 and 1946; yet he was convicted only once on charges of "keeping a common betting house," for which he spent six months in Bordeaux prison.

Another major underworld figure was Max Shapiro, a Yiddish-speaking Polish émigré who'd arrived as a young man in the 1920s, and partnered up with Harry Davis, Fred McBurney and Harry Baris in the city's booming gambling racket. In the 1940s and '50s he was the sole proprietor of one of downtown's most successful betting emporiums on Peel Street, as well as a partner with Frank Pretula and others in the Alpha Investment Company. In 1945 he and several partners opened the huge and extremely popular Ruby Foo's Chinese restaurant on Décarie Boulevard, where he often held court before dying of a heart attack in 1958.

Shapiro and his wife Mary bore fraternal twin sons, Harold and Bernard, born on June 8, 1935. Upon the death of their father, the boys took over his stake and day-to-day operation of Ruby Foo's, but only for five years before selling out their interest. Unlike their father, the boys were serious academics, both pursuing doctorates at McGill University. Perhaps demonstrating that apples can indeed fall far from the tree, Harold later went on to become president of Princeton University from 1988 to 2001, and Bernard became president of McGill University from 1994 to 2002.

There were other Jewish hoodlums such as Harry Baris, Louis Detner, Julius Silverberg and Joe Frankel active during that period. But the only big-time Montreal Jewish gangster who was neither whacked by his enemies nor not even once busted by the cops was Harry Feldman.

Feldman, born in New York 1899, immigrated to Montreal with his parents shortly after the turn of the century, where they settled into the city's garment district on St. Lawrence Boulevard. Within a few years after the death of his father in 1911, young Harry dropped out of high school to help support his mother and younger sister and brother by delivering newspapers and running errands for people. Some of those errands included dropping off betting slips from bookies to their customers. This was to be his introduction to the Montreal gambling scene.

In 1926 he married Adele Sperling, a beautiful twenty-seven-year-old New York Vaudeville dancer and performer. The two eventually moved into a semi-detached home on Vendôme Avenue in upper Notre-Dame-de-Grâce where they raised two adopted kids, a son Irwin, born in 1930, and a daughter Roni, born in 1934.

By 1940 Feldman, reputedly a whiz at math, was heavily involved in the city's gambling rackets, and owned a three-story building at 286 St. Catherine Street West on the corner of Bleury Street in the heart of the city. The bottom floor, a tack shop selling horse-riding equipment, was a front for what went on above. On the spacious second floor were the gaming tables and the bookies who were busy taking bets on the day's horse races, displayed on a wall-to-wall blackboard. The small and dingy top floor was Feldman's "dummy room," which the vice squad, ignoring the action on the second floor, would officially raid and padlock before returning to their precinct to fill out their reports. They'd sometimes take Feldman's fall-guy Barney Shulkin to the station with them to be booked as the stand-in owner of the place. But Shulkin was long inured to the routine, and after pleading guilty and paying a small fine (reimbursed always by Feldman) he'd be back at work the next night.

Feldman's operation would later be grudgingly described by Montreal's crime-busting police chief Pacifique "Pax" Plante as "the best organized and most considerable [gambling] establishment in the city." Plante further noted that Feldman was circumspect enough that "he was never apprehended by police during the 14 years he ran his establishment." This was partly due to the fact that Feldman, although friends with the likes of Davis and his contemporaries, had absolutely no interest in getting involved with the drug trade.

Harry and Adele Feldman, Havana, early 1940s

Despite being a gangster and purveyor of illicit activities, Harry was very much a family man. His daughter Roni Shefler today recalls: "As a father he was fantastic, because he loved us kids and all our friends ... He'd take us all out in his car for ice cream or trips to Belmont Park. He was just like a kid himself when he was with us kids." She adds: "He would have dinner at home with us every night, and then he'd go to sleep between eight and nine, and then get up, put on a tuxedo and go to work. That's when he went to his club." Feldman would return home in the wee hours of the morning. "When he'd come back," remembers Roni, "he always went to my brother's room and then to my room to check on us and give us a kiss goodnight. And I always remember his smell of Old Spice and sweat and alcohol and Winchester cigarettes ... He smelled of everything; I loved that smell."

Feldman, unlike most of his business contemporaries, did not flaunt his wealth, despite the fact that by the late 1940s he was a co-owner with Louis "Puggy" Detner of several flourishing downtown night clubs such as the Tic-Toc, Chez Parée, and the Hawaiian Lounge. "My mother was always pushing him to buy a house in Westmount, but he wouldn't budge," says Roni. "My mother would drive around in a Cadillac, but my father wouldn't get into it. He drove around in an old Pontiac." Harry's only extravagance, his daughter admits, was his wardrobe. "He was very lavish with his clothing" and had a wardrobe full of tuxedos and expensive hand-made shirts and tailored suits.

In 1948 Harry Feldman decided to pack it in. He suffered a minor heart attack the year before, his friend Harry Davis had been killed with potentially further gangland violence in the offing, the Italians were putting on pressure and, the crime-busting Pax Plante was threatening to clean up the city. Harry realized it was time to get out of the game.

Roni was fourteen years old when her father's moment of deliverance occurred one evening just before dinner time. "Usually he would come in the front door and put his jacket over the stair post at the bottom. But this time we heard the door slam and he bounded up the stairs two at a time to the upstairs landing and called all of us to come out ... I remember him going into his pockets, taking out wads of money that were stuffed in his pockets, wrapped in elastic bands, and then taking the elastic bands off each bundle, and then throwing the money in the air and saying, 'I'm free! I'm free! I'm free!' And he was laughing and wheezing; he was in complete joy ... So I gathered that was a big moment in his life where he wasn't going to be involved anymore with the underworld ... It sure made quite an impression with all that money flying all over us."

Feldman died of a massive heart attack on December 10, 1951 at the relatively young age of fifty-three. Yet he died a free man—free of the shady business he'd been involved in for most of his life. And he also died a wealthy man, leaving behind an estate valued at approximately $800,000 in Montreal commercial properties that he'd acquired over the years.

Roni was never quite sure to what extent her late father was involved in the rackets. That is until one night in the early 1960s when she and her brother, Irwin, and her husband, Stan Shefler, attended a Tom Jones concert at the Copacabana club in New York. The concert had been sold out for weeks, but Stan was a friend of the comedian who was opening for Tom Jones, and he got them a front row table. "It was a long table that held maybe 12 people," recalls Roni. "Soon all these mafia-looking guys join us and ask us who we were. And when we mentioned Feldman from Montreal, this guy yells out, 'Hey, dese are Harry Feldman's kids!' And pretty soon they're pouring scotch into our glasses and saying, 'Whatever youse guys want, youse guys got!' And they're talking about what a great guy my father was ... Then I'm hearing names like Meyer Lansky and Bugsy Siegel being thrown around ... They all knew who my father was, so they must have had occasion to do business with him in Montreal ... So that kind of opened my eyes a bit wider."

## The End of an Era

Montreal's many gambling dens, bordellos and after-hours bars were magnets that attracted men and women from New York, Boston and even "Toronto The Good," all of whom were looking for a fun time. Thus, business prospered for the city's many Italian and Jewish purveyors of flesh, dice, drinking and drugs. Then along came Pacifique "Pax" Plante, head of the Montreal morality squad during the late 1940s.

Plante, a crusading vice-buster, set his horned-rimmed glasses sights not only on the Sin City operators, but also on the local politicians and cops who, through regular payoffs, had been allowing them to run their illegal enterprises for the past two decades. Plante's unannounced vice squad raids on popular Montreal establishments did not sit well with his targets. Nor did they sit well with some of his superiors in the police department or certain members of Montreal's city council. In March 1948, he was suspended from his post by Montreal police director Albert Langlois, apparently for over-zealousness on the job.

But Plante knew where the bodies were buried, and in 1949 Montreal's prestigious *Le Devoir* daily newspaper began running a series of 60 articles under his name, but actually penned by Gérard Pelletier, one of the paper's senior writers. The series, entitled "Montreal Sous le Règne de la Pègre" (Montreal Under Mob Rule), contained details of the rackets, headed up mostly by the Jewish mafia, that had been ongoing since the 1930s. The stories were replete with names, addresses and accounts about the various criminal operations and how their organizers had escaped from being busted by the authorities.

For example, in one article Plante states: "In order to gamble at [Harry] Ship's, the client must not be greatly disturbed. 906 St. Catherine is a highly accessible location . . . Upon entering you find yourself before a stairway that leads to two establishments, a hair salon and a dance room. Then on the third floor we have Mr. Ship's book [which] occupies the entire floor . . . All the way in the back is an immense classic-style blackboard that covers an entire wall on which an employee inscribes the results of the races that he receives over the phone. Towards the left is the betting counter. This is where the clients pay for their bets after having chosen their horses . . . Following this, the client can either leave and return later when the results are in, or stay there and wait for the end of the race." Plante then describes the bettors as "a varied clientele, usually dominated by working men: tram conductors, bread delivery men, milkmen, factory workers, all in general with small salaries." He goes on to say, "On Friday night the floor was covered with envelopes of paycheques, since at Mr. Ship's you could exchange a paycheque from any company, regardless of size. It was a house bonus."

Harry Ship, circa 1960

Partly as a result of Plante's whistle-blowing, a Quebec government commission was set up to look into Montreal's bookmaking, gambling, loan sharking and prostitution rackets, as well as the widespread corruption within city hall and the police department, which had been suckling for years on the underworld tit. The commission, headed by Superior Court Justice François Caron, began its hearings on September 11, 1950, and by April 1953 had interviewed 373 witnesses, including bookies, gambling-house owners, prostitutes, police officers and members of the city council. The commission's final report, issued on October 8, 1954, revealed an astounding degree of complicity that existed between Montreal's underworld and the cops and politicians who were supposed to have been upholding the law. They discovered, for instance, that many of the door-guarding "bouncers" at these illegal establishments were in fact moonlighting off-duty local cops, a sideline that was well known and ignored by their police department superiors.

As a result of the *Caron Report*, 18 high-ranking police officers were found guilty of taking bribes and were fined anywhere from $200 to $2,000. Also, the 1954 Montreal police chief Albert Langlois was fined $500, and his predecessor Fernand Dufresne was fined $7,000 on similar charges. However, the commission was unable to prove any of its charges of graft against five sitting Montreal city councilors.

But the lid had been blown off the pot. On October 28, 1954, three weeks after the publication of the *Caron Report*, a thirty-seven-year-old lawyer, Jean Drapeau, running for mayor in a reform party known as the Civic Action League, was swept into office on a platform to rid the city of its vice and corruption. Unsurprisingly, one of his first appointments was that of Pax Plante as director of the Montreal Police Service, with a mandate to erase Montreal's reputation as a city that was wide open to gambling, bookmaking, prostitution and police corruption.

Nevertheless, crime would continue to flourish in Montreal, and a new force was about to make its presence felt—The West End Gang.

CHAPTER 5

# The Emergence of
# the West End Gang

Although there was no shortage of Irish hoods on the streets of Montreal in the early 1900s, they mostly acted alone or with a couple of pals. But as a collective, the genesis of the so-called West End Gang dates to the mid-1950s, when the term was first being employed by police and the media, often in reference to crimes the Irishmen committed in concert with other individuals or groups.

The appellation *gang de l'ouest* first appears in a June 5, 1955, article in the Montreal weekly crime tabloid *Allô Police*. Entitled "La Pégre se Fusille en Pleine rue de Montréal" (The Underworld is Shooting in the Streets of Montreal), the story states that Montreal's underworld is split into "two distinct camps, the east and the west of the city." It goes on to say, "The group from the west is generally composed of English Canadians and Italians. The east is composed of French

Canadians, Italians and other European nations. The Jews are equally divided between the east and west." The article delineated St. Lawrence Boulevard as the geographical division between the east and the west, and noted, "under circumstances where they formed an alliance, the two groups unite; but this friendship never lasts long."

## Frankie

There were those who worked both sides of that dividing line. One was Frank Pretula, a notorious mobster who definitely was not Irish. He and his wife Donna occupied a waterfront mansion on Lake

St. Louis in Montreal's West Island suburb of Beaconsfield where they raised two twin boys, Frankie Jr. and Daniel, born on May 22, 1942.[1]

Frank Pretula, a tall nattily dressed man known on the street as "Frankie P," was born in Montreal of Ukrainian parents in 1917. As a young punk he began his criminal career in the 1930s, along with Louie Greco, as a bodyguard for Montreal gambling kingpin Harry Davis.

Frank Pretula, circa 1950

Following Davis' murder in July 1946, the two took over several of his operations and joined forces with the Cotroni mob, as well as becoming partners with them and Harry Ship and Max Shapiro in the money-laundering Alpha Investment Corporation. Pretula was also a part-owner with Greco in the Bonfire Restaurant at 7450 Décarie Boulevard in the late 1940s, before they were bought out by Pep Cotroni.

Frank was nothing if not a hot-tempered thug. Determined to push his competitors out of the gambling and bar business, he hired muscle from the Irish community to help harass them. His first targets

---

1 I attended elementary school on the West Island with Frankie Jr. and Danny in the early 1950s and remember them as a couple of schoolyard bullies who were always ready to pick a fight. Of course, it didn't help that some of us kids, from what we'd heard from our parents, would tease them about their dad being a gangster.

were Harry Smith, owner of the El Morocco on Clossé Street, and Ned Roberts at the Down Beat Café on Peel Street, both popular downtown nightclubs. Late Tuesday night on July 19, 1955, his goons beat up several people and trashed the two places. They then moved on in the wee hours of the morning to trash the All American Bar and the Montmarte Café, also owned by Pretula's rivals.

Two days later, Pretula's Irish soldiers were arrested for their night's activities. They included William "Carfare" Bowman, a thirty-two-year-old blind pig operator; thirty-year-old Joseph Chambers; Charles "Charlie" Chase, a twenty-four-year-old black former middleweight boxer who'd represented Canada in the 1948 Olympic Games, thirty-four-year-old Lionel Deare (who'd previously been stared down by the fearsome Hetty Burke); twenty-nine-year-old George Desmond (aka George Mathewson); twenty-seven-year-old ex-boxer Ronald "Buddy" Jones; and twenty-seven-year-old convicted armed robber Vincent McIntyre. All of them had been raised in the Griff or the Point and knew how to use their fists.

During their preliminary court hearing on September 9, 1955, the witnesses against them either declined to testify (obviously out of fear), or else retracted or changed the statements they'd earlier given to police. All seven goons were therefore acquitted. At least two of them were later arrested on unrelated charges in the years to come. George Desmond, for example, was busted by the RCMP for participating in a marijuana distribution ring, and was arraigned on November 7, 1957 in his bed at the Montreal General Hospital where he was recovering from stab wounds suffered two weeks earlier. And Charlie Chase was found guilty in March 1962 of procuring money from the avails of prostitution, for which he was sentenced to several years in the pen.

Pretula had been present during the scuffles at the El Morocco and the Down Beat and, according to witnesses, had started a fight with Harry Smith and had pulled a gun on Ned Roberts before calling in his Irish army. Roberts, a slightly built fifty-three-year-old carnival worker and gaming house operator, went to the police, and a warrant for Pretula's arrest was issued. Pretula went on the lam for several days, but at 10 a.m. on July 25, 1955, turned himself in to face charges in the affair. He and his forty-two-year-old partner Louie Greco were immediately locked up in Montreal's Bordeaux prison on charges of possessing firearms and common assault. They were both released on $1,000 bail after spending three nights in the slammer.

A preliminary hearing was set for that September 7. But when Roberts, the Crown's key witness, failed to show up in court, Pretula walked. As for Roberts, he was later tried on November 15, 1956, on charges of being a gaming-house keeper, following raids at his De Fleurimont Social Club at 1451 Metcalfe Street, but was acquitted three months later.

Although Pretula and his Irish mercenaries had gotten off scot free, the thirty-eight-year-old gangster's problems were far from over. In the fall of 1954, he and Greco had traveled to Naples, Italy, to meet with Sicilian mob boss Charlie "Lucky" Luciano (who had been deported from the United States in 1946), and they allegedly returned with a deal to ship large quantities of heroin from Europe via Montreal to the powerful Frank Costello Family in New York. Based on this information, the RCMP narcotics squad, armed with a search warrant, arrived at Pretula's Beaconsfield home on the morning of October 29, 1954.

They were not alone. Accompanying the federal agents was assistant detective-inspector William "Fitz" Fitzpatrick, a six-foot-one, 220-pound, rugged Irishman who had joined the Montreal police force in 1928 at the age of twenty-two. He became head of the homicide division in 1948 and in 1956 was made chief of detectives. Moreover, Fitz had grown up in a family of nine in Point St. Charles, and many of the people that he would eventually find himself chasing down had been his childhood neighbors in the Point. He'd also be busting their contemporaries in the Italian and Jewish criminal milieu who were involved in the rackets. It was Fitzpatrick who arrested Louis Bercovitch for the July 1946 murder of Harry Davis, and he was instrumental in the raids and closure of many of the city's blind pigs and gambling establishments during the late 1940s and early 1950s.

For some years Fitz had been keeping his eye on Frank Pretula, since he knew the gangster had ties to the mafia as well as to both the French East End and the Irish West End gangs, and was also paying off local politicians. So he was itching to bust him.

## Rotten at the Top

That chance came during the combined RCMP/Montreal police raid on Pretula's home. No drugs were found, but something much more incriminating came up. In a hidden bathroom wall safe they found $18,000 in cash, plus a handwritten list of names beside which were penciled-in amounts. Fitz and the RCMP detectives immediately recognized many of the names as members of major underworld figures, some of whom were Montreal and New York mafia capos. And they soon figured out that the list, which totaled more than $100,000, was a record of how much each gangster had contributed to the political campaign of incumbent Montreal mayor Camillien Houde who had, during his reign in the 1940s and early 1950s, tolerated Montreal's reputation as "Sin City." In 1954 he was being challenged by an upstart thirty-eight-year-old lawyer, Jean Drapeau, who headed the Civic Action League that was running on an anti-vice platform.

The mob's contributions, which included payoffs to the city's Houde-friendly journalists, proved to be money ill spent, since the Civic Action League was swept into office on October 28, 1954, the day before the discovery of Pretula's list. The bust led to no immediate charges against Pretula. However, Fitz made sure that the list of names was well publicized in the press, which proved to be rather embarrassing to many underworld figures.

As a result of Pretula's compromising record keeping, and his penchant for attention-drawing public brawls, the mafia apparently concluded that he had become a liability to their organization. In March 1956, Pretula, now being referred to in the French press as the "boss of the West End Gang," was facing charges of federal income tax evasion for defrauding the federal government of more than $220,000 in back taxes. The case dragged on for more than two years.

Then, on June 24, 1958, just before he was to meet with Crown prosecutors to discuss the tax charges against him, forty-one-year-old Frank Pretula pulled a Jimmy Hoffa, never to be seen again. The speculation on the street was that he had been whacked by either the Montreal or New York mafiosi, and that his weighted-down corpse was dumped in the St. Lawrence River or some Laurentian lake north of the city. His body has never been found.

During the 1950s and '60s Montreal was gradually being cleaned up by Jean Drapeau and his squeaky-clean police chief Pax Plante. Bordellos, gambling houses and after-hours bars were systematically raided and shut down. And those politicians and cops who'd previously had an "understanding" with local gangsters were finding it harder to supplement their civil service incomes.

Nevertheless, there still existed lots of crime and violence on the streets of Montreal, much of it involving vendettas within the emerging *gang de l'ouest* or else by or against its rivals. Much blood was shed, with most of the killings remaining unsolved to this day. Those two decades would find many Irishmen who were either on the trigger end or the muzzle end of a gun while they competed for dominance and control of their territory.

# CHAPTER 6

# The Murderous Decades

At 6 p.m. Saturday, January 10, 1948, Montreal bookie Joseph "Joey" Randolph, along with his brother Bernie and Paul Staycheff, armed with a sub-machine gun and .45-caliber revolvers, held up a barbotte gambling den on Côte de Liesse Road in the western suburb of Dorval. They escaped with $14,000 and left three of the dice players suffering from minor gunshot wounds. The three masked men were also suspected of holding up the Caisse Populaire de la Nativité de Hochelega (credit union) on Ontario Street for an estimated $1,000 ten days later.

Before the cops could solve the robberies, twenty-seven-year-old Joey "disappeared" on March 4, 1948. The gaming house was one of several operated by Frank Pretula and Louie Greco, and the word on the street was that Joey had been taken out by a member of the West End Gang.

One suspect was Johnny Goodman, who himself "disappeared" on October 5, 1948. Police speculated he'd been whacked by his own gang in order to cover up their involvement in the Randolph killing. Neither Randolph's nor Goodman's body was ever found.

On June 14, 1950, thirty-eight-year-old Aaron Marks, a small-time gambler, was involved in a brawl with two West End Gang punks, twenty-three-year-old Charles Wagner and twenty-six-year-old Keith "Rocky" Pierson, in a downtown Union Avenue after-hours bar. Marks died in hospital of knife wounds that night, and Wagner and Pierson were immediately arrested. They pleaded self-defense and were acquitted in March 1951.

Six months later, on December 6, 1950, two brothers in their twenties, Alex and Frank Balazzo, "disappeared." They were both safecrackers with ties to the West End Gang. Police presumed that they were whacked by either the Italian mafia or members of their own gang. Their bodies were never found.

Following Pierson and Wagner's acquittals in the death of Aaron Marks in January 1952, Pierson was sent to St. Vincent de Paul Penitentiary for three years on an unrelated charge of robbery with violence. But Wagner's fate was to be much more conclusive.

Charles "the Kid" Wagner was an early West End Gang hang-around and drug dealer in Point St. Charles. After having successfully beaten the Aaron Marks murder charge, he vanished at the age of twenty-six on his way home from early Sunday mass at St. Gabriel's church in the Point on March 29, 1953. His body, with a bullet to the back of the head, was found later that day tethered to a 250-pound cement block in the St. Mathieu de Laprairie creek on Montreal's South Shore. Police suspected he was whacked by the Montreal mafia or members of his own gang, either because of a drug deal gone sour, or else in retaliation for the murder of Marks. Frank Pretula was suspected of ordering the killing, and two West End Gang members, Frank "the Bat" Battaglia and James Rogers were soon after arrested and charged with Wagner's murder, but both were found not guilty on April 14, 1954.

The day after his acquittal, Battaglia was discovered strangled to death in a Montreal East alley. He was just forty years old. Police concluded that he was killed by the West End Gang to hide his connection to Wagner's death, yet nothing was ever proven. Obviously, there were people who did not like people within the Irish underworld. And inevitably, there was a lot more violence to come.

Kenneth "China Boy" Winford, a West End Gang safecracker and drug trafficker, was the target of a gunman outside his Lincoln Street apartment in July 1955. He was only slightly wounded before his would-be assassin fled. Winford was later a suspect in a May 1958 Brockville, Ontario, bank robbery, but got off. Then, at 10 p.m. on March 18, 1959, near the Laurentian village of Piedmont north of Montreal, he was found by a passing truck driver, staggering along Highway 11 with two bullets in his chest and one in his stomach. He was taken to the Hôtel-Dieu Hospital in St. Jerome and questioned by Quebec Provincial Police detectives. But he refused to say anything about the shooting and died in hospital four days later at the age of thirty-two.

On the same July evening when someone had first tried to whack Winford, two Ontario hoods, Benjamin "Baby Yak" Yakubovitch, a thirty-eight-year-old ex-boxer and drug dealer from Toronto, and John Papilla, a thirty-one-year-old mafia-connected drug dealer from Hamilton, were standing on the corner of St. Catherine and Stanley streets in midtown Montreal. They were approached by someone who fired several shots from a revolver, missing Papilla and hitting Yakubovitch in the shoulder, before running off. Once again, neither target had anything to say when the cops arrived.

On the night of November 15, 1956, a would-be assassin sprayed a fusillade of bullets from an automatic weapon through the windows of a Ville d'Anjou house in the north end of the city. It was the home of Gabby Ferland, an ex-boxer who was a West End Gang enforcer and a bouncer at the Lion d'Or Café on Ontario Street East. Ferland was fortunate enough to be out at the time, and the only fatality was his pet dog, Tiger. The shooter was never identified, but was assumed to have been a member of the rival East End Gang.

Meanwhile, on the other side of town, thirty-two-year-old Eddie Sauvageau, a 220-pound muscleman and chief enforcer for the East End Gang, was shot dead at 7 a.m. on January 7, 1957, while asleep in his Pie-IX Boulevard apartment, with two .25-caliber bullets to the head. His one-time friend and bodyguard, Bruno Marinello, turned himself in to police headquarters later that morning and confessed to killing Sauvageau over an unpaid debt related to their drug and protection rackets. Marinello, a muscular blond-haired Montreal nightclub waiter and bouncer at Vic's Restaurant on St. Catherine Street East, had connections to the West End Gang through his close friend Fernand Servant. While awaiting trial, twenty-nine-year-old Marinello committed suicide on March 5, 1957, by overdosing on barbiturates, which someone had smuggled into his cell at Montreal's Bordeaux prison's trial wing.

His buddy Servant, a twenty-six-year-old ex-boxer and West End Gang hang-around from Montreal's Rosemont district, disappeared on September 10, 1957, after he'd parked his 1956 Oldsmobile 98 convertible on Park Avenue. Six days later the abandoned car was towed to a municipal yard, where police found a loaded .38-caliber revolver under the front seat, as well as Servant's registration papers in the glove compartment. The cops contacted his wife who told them that her husband hadn't been home since September 10. Given the spate of liquidations of West End Gang members, the police kept the case open. Nine years later, in July 1966, Quebec Provincial Police frogmen fished Servant's decomposed body out of the Rivière des Prairies river in Repentigny off of Montreal's east end. His was one more gangland slaying that would remain unsolved.

On February 21, 1957, a West End Gang member, Doug Wright, the floor manager of the Main Café bar on St. Lawrence Boulevard, was shot four times and critically wounded at the age of forty-two by three East End Gang members during a 4:30 a.m. brawl in his club. Police picked up his assailants, who were later released when Wright declined to identify them.

Yet another underworld "disappearance" occurred on July 2, 1957 when Larry Petrov, a Romanian-born West End Gang member vanished at the age of thirty-six while free on bail awaiting trial for possession of narcotics. The red-haired, 225-pound Petrov was also a suspected member of a gang headed by Georges Lemay, which in January 1957 robbed an estimated $2 million in cash, jewelry and securities from safety deposit boxes at a branch of the Royal Bank of Canada. Police theorized that Lemay ordered the execution when Petrov was discovered trying to prematurely cash some of the stolen bearer bonds. On July 10, John Petrov reported his son missing and told police he feared his son had been killed. His fears were well founded. Ten days later, two women camping on the edge of Lac Ouareau in the St. Donat region 90 miles north of Montreal made the grisly discovery of a severed human leg. It was later identified as Petrov's. His murderer too was never identified or apprehended.

At 6:15 a.m. on April 23, 1959, thirty-three-year-old René Robert was exiting the infamous Café Roma blind pig on the corner of Peel Street and Burnside Avenue when he was approached by a gunman who pumped two shots into him before running away. Robert, a close associate of Louie Greco and Frank Pretula, was no stranger to violence. Despite having a .22-caliber slug in his stomach and another in his right thigh, he managed to hail a taxi that rushed him to the Montreal General Hospital. While recovering in the intensive care unit, he told police he had no idea who had shot him, even though he knew it was Gérald Turcotte, a man who'd been arrested shortly after the murder attempt.

Turcotte, a racketeer and gambling-house operator in Montreal and in Havana, Cuba, during the 1950s, was positively identified by taxi driver Guy Lafrance, who had witnessed the shooting and who was familiar with all the lowlifes that operated in that area. Turcotte refused to talk to the police and was released from custody a few weeks later when Robert, either out of fear or perhaps his intention to later settle things his own way, refused to testify against Turcotte. The cops had no alternative but to close the investigation.

Things remained relatively quiet until the night of September 17, 1965, when Leo Bougie, a 250-pound mob enforcer and bar bouncer was shot dead at the age of forty-two in the apartment of Carol Bennett, the girlfriend of James "Jimmy" Collins, a West End Gang bank robber. Bougie's body was dumped in a nearby alley behind the showroom of Chevrolet Motor Sales on St. Catherine Street West. On May 5, 1966,

Collins was acquitted on the grounds of legitimate self-defense when the jury accepted that it was Bougie who had first pulled out a gun during an argument between the two men in Bennett's apartment. Nevertheless, there was retribution to be paid.

On the evening of Tuesday, March 25, 1969, Collins, one day short of his thirtieth birthday, was shot dead with a .9-mm-caliber bullet to the back of the head by a lone gunman while he sat drinking beer in the Forum Tavern on the corner of St. Catherine Street West and Clossé Street. As was often the case, none of the 30 or so customers who were in the tavern that night was willing or able to give police a description of the shooter. The cops wrote it off as a retaliatory hit for the killing of Bougie, and the murder was never solved. It marked the fortieth "settling of scores" among Montreal gangsters in the space of 12 months. Almost all of the victims were known to police, yet none of their killers was ever prosecuted.

During that murderous decade, another internecine West End Gang dispute occurred on October 28, 1966, when Bryce Richardson pulled a gun on twenty-seven-year-old Elwood Marsman during a scuffle in the parking lot of the Hawaiian Lounge on Stanley Street. Marsman told police that Richardson had tried to shoot him. But he later recanted his testimony, and on February 9, 1967, his would-be assailant was acquitted of attempted murder.

Two months later, on April 8, 1967, thirty-year-old Richardson was paralyzed for life after being shot in the spine by Dubois gang member Yvon Belzil outside the Harlem Paradise nightclub on St. Antoine Street. The club, a popular hangout for drug dealers and prostitutes, was co-owned by Adrien Dubois and "Boxer" Di Francesco, who were aware that Richardson had ambitions to take it over. They'd made sure that it would never happen.

\*\*\*

Despite the fatality count, the West End Gang had by now grown in numbers, but its assaults from within and without were becoming more frequent and bloody by the month.

Eric McNally was one of the gang's more successful bank and jewelry store robbers and usurious money lenders during the early and mid-1960s, but had never been arrested for any major crime. In 1966, he and his girlfriend Susan Clark purchased a comfortable bungalow at 12295 Gouin Boulevard in the West Island suburb of Pierrefonds, where they had two purebred dogs, a Doberman and a dachshund, as well as an in-ground swimming pool and a collection of classic cars, rare books and paintings. They entertained often, particularly with other members of the West End Gang and their families and friends.

Eric McNally, 1968

But the thirty-year-old McNally had enemies. On the evening of April 2, 1968, he was found sprawled beside twenty-nine-year-old Clark in a pool of coagulating blood in the basement of their home. The two barking dogs were shut up in a nearby room. Crime scene investigators and a later autopsy report determined that each had been shot three times with the same .38-caliber revolver the day before. Nothing was missing from the home, so it was obvious that the killings were a deliberate assassination. But by whom?

The list of possibilities was long, since McNally had been involved with many shady characters and had stepped on a few toes during his short lifetime. Unfortunately, some of the suspects, such as Gary Snor, would soon be unable to shed any light on the murder, as they too were marked for execution.

Gary Snor, an armed-robbery specialist, had arrived in Montreal from California in the early 1960s and teamed up with McNally on a few bank jobs. Following a brief prison stint in 1964 to '66, he was extradited to the States, but came back to Montreal in late March 1968. On April 19, 1968, his decomposed body was found in a ditch beside Route 30 near the town of Lachute, 50 miles north of Montreal. An autopsy showed that Snor had been shot dead at the age of twenty-seven, with two .38-caliber bullets in his skull and two in his stomach two weeks earlier, or about the same time that McNally and Clark had been murdered. Police believed all three killings were related, but were unable to make any arrests.

Meanwhile, on the night of May 4, 1968, twenty-six-year-old Gilles Bienvenue and thirty-three-year-old Alberto Ouimet were gunned down by persons unknown in a laneway next to the Au Petit Baril Cafe, a St. Lawrence Boulevard club that was owned by the Italian mafia. Bienvenue had a lengthy criminal record, but Ouimet was unknown to police. Neither murder was ever solved.

Richard Blass, 1968

Three days later, on May 7, 1968, Richard "Le Chat" Blass and Robert Allard brazenly attempted to whack Montreal mafia godfather Frank Cotroni in an ambush outside his home. But although two mafiosi bodyguards were gunned down, Cotroni escaped unharmed.

Twenty-three-old Blass, an amateur boxer, convicted bank robber and the older brother of Hells Angels biker Michel Blass, was a West End Gang enforcer who was constantly at odds with the mafia, particularly the Cotroni Family and the Di Maulo brothers. He hated the Italians with a passion and was determined to destroy their hegemony in the Montreal drug and rackets scene. Within weeks after the attempt on Cotroni's life, Blass and his henchmen shot and killed twenty-year-old Guissepe Collizza (although he had no apparent ties to the mafia), and soon after murdered Francesco Grado, a mafia loan shark, by pumping several bullets into him as he sat in his car on Rousselot Street. Their next victim was Giuseppe Di Marco, another Italian with no mafia affiliation, whom they shot in his car and left paralyzed for life on June 9, 1968.

Blass was now marked for execution. On August 24, 1968, he survived the first of several attempts on his life by the Cotroni mob when he was shot at several times by two gunmen in an east-end bar, yet managed to escape unscathed. Two weeks later Cotroni henchmen set fire to the Le Manoir de Plaisance motel in Saint Hippolyte, 37 miles northwest of Montreal, where Blass was hiding out. Two innocent men and a woman died in the blaze, but Blass once again escaped. Then, in October 1968, he and his partner Claude Ménard were ambushed inside a parking garage by a hail of bullets in Montreal's northeast St. Michel district. Blass was grazed by a bullet to the head and had two in his back. But Ménard, driving the car, managed to flee their attackers and got Blass to the Jean-Talon Hospital, where he was treated for his wounds. It was then that Blass earned the nickname "Le Chat," based on his ability to miraculously escape death. The epithet would again apply to him in the 1970s as he eluded police before being finally hunted down after committing a series of violent bank robberies, murders and daring prison escapes.

As for Blass' original partner, Robert Allard, he was shot dead at the age of thirty-four in gangland style on the night of Sunday, May 4, 1969, by Jimmy Di Maulo, Giuseppe "Joe" Armeni and Nicolas Leo of the Cotroni mob, who pumped 12 bullets into him outside a Montreal North tavern on Jean Talon Street East. Their getaway driver was identified by witnesses as Jimmy's brother, Vincenzo Di Maulo. Although the killers were quickly arrested, they were never brought to trial, due to lack of any conclusive evidence on the part of the Crown.

On September 29, 1968, the body of thirty-two-year-old George Groom, a West End Gang member from Verdun, was found in the trunk of his car, which had been abandoned in a scrap yard near Huntington, 20 miles southeast of Montreal. He had been shot six times in the head, either on the orders of the Montreal mafia or his own mob, the likely assassin being West End Gang serial hitman John McLaughlin. But it remained yet one more unsolved murder.

Two days later, the bullet-riddled charred bodies of James Alexander Fryer and Howie Russell, both twenty-eight, were found barbequed in the trunk of a burned-out Chrysler Imperial on Chabanel Street in Montreal's garment district. Fryer, from Ville LaSalle, and Russell, from Chateauguay on the South Shore, were low-ranking members of the West End Gang. But they had obviously pissed someone off. Exactly who was never discovered.

At 10:30 on the night of Friday, November 15, 1968, Charles Gallinger, a convicted West End Gang fraud artist, was found by a passerby sprawled on the parking lot of Montreal's Dorval International Airport (since renamed Pierre Elliott Trudeau International Airport). He had been shot with a .38-caliber handgun somewhere downtown, once in the head and twice in the back, and had been stuffed into the trunk of his Ford Meteor sedan, which had been abandoned at the airport. He'd somehow managed to release the trunk latch from the inside and had crawled out to the parking lot, where he was discovered bleeding profusely. While recovering in hospital, thirty-seven-year-old Gallinger insisted to police that he had no idea where he had been shot or by whom.

Less than two months later, at 7:40 p.m. on January 9, 1969, Gallinger managed to once again dodge a bullet. He and his forty-year-old girlfriend were getting out of a car in front of their apartment building on Montclaire Avenue in NDG when two men fired at them from behind a snow bank. Gallinger pulled out his pistol and fired back. The ensuing gunfight hit no one, and the hapless assassins ran off. Gallinger (who would never win a medal for chivalry) jumped into his car and sped away in the opposite direction, abandoning his terrified girlfriend who was screaming for help on the sidewalk. Aware that he had a price on his head, Gallinger went into hiding. On February 25, 1969, a bench warrant was issued for his arrest on charges of theft. But by then he had dropped off the radar screen, never to be seen in town again.

Another minor West End Gang hoodlum, twenty-seven-year-old Gaston Roy, made the mistake of getting into a heated argument with Paul April, a notorious hot-tempered member of various gangs, in the Fort du Nord cabaret in Montreal's St. Henri district on Saturday, February 8, 1969. Later that night, as he was climbing into his van parked on Meunier Street near the bar, Roy was shot dead at close range with a single .38-caliber bullet to the back of the head.

Four nights later, Harry Livsey, a well-known West End Gang fence and safecracker who owned the Fort du Nord cabaret, met a similar fate. He was killed in his own bar on February 12 by two masked gunmen who immediately fled the scene. Police suspected he'd been rubbed out before being able to avenge the killing of his friend Gaston Roy. Although neither murder was ever solved, their probable killer was Paul April, a man who would some years later face a far more violent death.

During their investigations into the murders of Eric McNally, Susan Clark, Gary Snor, George Groom, James Fryer and Howie Russell, and the attempted hits on Charles Gallinger, one name was at the top of the Montreal homicide squad's who-might-have-done-it list: James McDonald, a muscular six-foot, 220-pound convicted armed robber and a much-feared West End Gang enforcer from Verdun. McDonald was routinely hauled in for questioning, yet the cops could never build a case against him that would stand up in court.

But on March 15, 1969, they were able to place an "Assassiné" label across his lengthy dossier. That Saturday night McDonald was in one of his favorite bars, the Cat's Den on Guy Street, just north of St. Catherine Street, having a drink with some of his pals. At 11:45, two masked men, one armed with an M-1 machine gun and the other with a revolver, entered the bar through the back door. They approached McDonald's table and opened fire, pumping 17 slugs into him, shredding his head and chest into a bloody pulp. They then calmly left the same way they'd arrived. The twenty or so customers in the bar had all scrambled for cover under their tables during the shooting spree, with three of them slightly injured by wayward bullets.[1]

Police suspected that one of McDonald's assassins was Jackie McLaughlin, later a bodyguard and enforcer for Dunie Ryan, who was destined to become the head of the West End Gang. But once again, nothing could be proven, since the bar's patrons claimed to have seen nothing.

On March 20, 1969, Leonard Wouters, a West End Gang armed robber and a former friend of Eric McNally, was found with his

---

1 Two days after McDonald's murder, I happened to be in the Cat's Den to interview the bar owner for an unrelated newspaper article I was working on. There were still blood smears on the floor and walls, and the owner described in detail the murder that had occurred there less than 48 hours earlier. My most vivid memory is his description of the "smell of shit" that, along with cordite, permeated the place immediately after the killing. He explained, "Your bowels get pretty loose when you're shot or scared to death." For some reason, my brain has retained that piece of scatological trivia ever since.

common-law wife, Gale Fetchock, machine-gunned to death in their Châteauguay home on Montreal's South Shore. Wouters happened to be a police informer, definitely not a healthy career move within any gang. Again, their murders were attributed by police as a settling of accounts, but were never solved. The gangland body count was increasing by the day.

There was a brief respite in the hits and counter-hits until 3:30 a.m. on July 8, 1969, when Martin "Marty" Rowland, a twenty-nine-year-old West End Gang associate and longshoreman, was critically wounded with a blast from a sawed-off shotgun at Danny's Villa, a St. Catherine Street club where he worked as a waiter. The shooter, who may have been a member of Marty's own mob, was never identified or apprehended. Rowland survived the attempt on his life and was wise enough to quit the rackets after that. He died of natural causes on March 15, 2009, at the age of sixty-eight. But most of his gangland contemporaries would be lucky to live so long.

The night before Rowland's shooting, Giacomo Poccetti, a twenty-eight-year-old Frank Cotroni soldier, was shot to death with seven bullets to the back, neck and head while hailing a taxi outside a Montreal North bar. He had been wounded in two assassination attempts, in December 1968 and January 1969. Police suspected that Danny Pelensky of the West End Gang had either commissioned the hit or made it himself. They were probably right.

Danny "One-a-Day" Pelensky, whose nickname came from the almost daily B&E's that he pulled off during the 1950s, became a major West End Gang figure and a close friend of Eric McNally and Dunie Ryan in the 1960s. During that decade he operated an illegal gambling casino, a loan-sharking business, and a vending machine company, while at the same time dabbling in drug trafficking.

Like Richard Blass, the Ukrainian-born Pelensky had a strong hate on for Montreal's Italian mafia, and they against him. On April 30, 1968, twenty-eight-year-old Pelensky was driving on the Laurentian Autoroute near St. Jerome when he was shot at through the window of his car, yet he managed to escape unscathed. This was only two days after his close friends Eric McNally and Susan Clark were assassinated at their Pierrefonds home. Another unsuccessful attempt was made on his life on December 30, 1969, when he was shot while driving on the Trans-Canada Highway in the West Island. He was hit by a bullet but survived his injuries.

In retaliation for the first attempt on his life, Pelensky was assumed to have been behind the murder of mafia mobster Poccetti. Now Pelensky was messing with an organization that had both a long memory and a code of vendetta. So it was only a matter of time before his number would come up. That occurred violently at 5:20 p.m. on Saturday, July 11, 1970, as he was cruising along in his 1967 Buick Wildcat on the Metropolitan Boulevard near the Decarie Expressway, and the car erupted in a massive explosion. According to the coroner's report issued two days later, Pelensky's body was recovered from the mangled wreckage "practically severed in two" with his buttocks "literally torn to shreds" and his right leg "completely detached from the torso."

An August 19, 1970 inquiry into the circumstances surrounding his death interviewed several witnesses. One was Pierre Lavigne, who happened to be two car lengths back and a lane to the left of Pelensky's vehicle, when "all of a sudden I heard a 'boom' and saw a leg fall on the road in front of my car." Lavigne screeched to a stop, but not before noticing, as he would testify, "a dark green car" that was ahead and to the right of Pelensky's Buick. That vehicle, he said, "immediately sped away" after the explosion.

The inquiry also questioned several employees of the Mama Bear restaurant on Sources Boulevard in Pierrefonds on Montreal's West Island, where Pelensky was a frequent customer. They testified that in the days immediately prior to his murder, they'd noticed several people in a car and one on a motorcycle in the restaurant's parking lot or across the street at a Shell gas station who appeared to be observing Pelensky's comings and goings. The hit was obviously in the making.

In what was left of Pelensky's car, forensic investigators pieced together debris from two electronic detonators and determined that a bomb, placed under the driver's seat, had been remotely activated by a nearby radio transmission, presumably by someone in that mysterious green car which had fled the scene. It was one more gangland murder that would remain unsolved.

Pelensky's execution had all the hallmarks and modus operandi of Yves "Apache" Trudeau, a member of the Hells Angels Laval chapter and a freelance gun-for-hire. Trudeau, born in 1944, had in the 1960s worked for Canadian Industries Limited (CIL), which was then Montreal's foremost producer of paints, chemicals and explosives, particularly dynamite and detonator caps. It was these last two products with which he was most familiar. Trudeau knew how to, with the mere flick of a switch, make someone vanish in a puff of explosive fire and smoke. His skills were much in demand by those who sought to get rid of their enemies in a way that could neither be linked nor traced back to them. Trudeau was to apply his talents even more fiercely in the decade to come.

Much of that inter-gang violence in the 1960s and '70s had to do with the fact that the members of the West End Gang were among the best and most profitable bank and armored-truck robbers and safecrackers in Montreal's underworld, a reputation they hold to this day.

CHAPTER 7

# Bank Robbery Capital
# of North America

M ontreal, like any other 20th century city, was a major center of banking institutions that held for safekeeping the hard cash of its commercial and individual depositors. So where else would one expect to find a pile of currency? When the notorious 1930s through '50s American bank robber Willie Sutton was asked by a reporter why he robbed banks, he is alleged to have shrugged and replied, "Because that's where the money is."

Indeed, that's where it was and that was where to steal it if you had a plan of attack and perhaps an accomplice or a gang at your disposal. Montreal had no shortage of either, to the point that by the late 1960s it was being dubbed in the Canadian and U.S. press "the Bank Robbery Capital of North America." During the late 1950s and 1960s more bank jobs were pulled off in Montreal than in any other North American city, some of them executed by members of the West End Gang.

In the first six months of 1969, for example, Montreal recorded 51 bank robberies, of which only a quarter were solved. During that same period, the much larger city of Los Angeles, which according to the FBI had the highest number of bank robberies in the United States, recorded only 36 similar crimes, of which some 60 percent were solved. This disparate statistic was constant throughout most of the 1960s. The anomaly was explained by two factors: Montreal bank robbers were much better organized than their American counterparts; and in Canada, particularly Quebec, a convicted bank robber would usually get off with five to seven years in prison, while an American bank robber could expect a 10- to 20-year jail term. Montreal bank robbers were often repeat offenders, continuing their trade after being released from a brief stint in jail or while out on bail or parole. There also appears to have been more easily grabbed loot available in Montreal. According to police and FBI statistics, the average take from a Montreal bank job in 1968 was $5,000, compared to $2,000 to $3,000 in other North American cities.

In addition, this was at a time when tellers kept cash in their tills; there were none of those snoopy surveillance cameras around and very few banks employed armed guards. At best there were silent alarms that could alert the nearest police station. But a speedy and disciplined gang with a wheelman outside keeping the engine warm in a car, which was usually stolen and therefore untraceable to the robbers, could be long gone before the cops arrived.

## The Red Hood Gang

Such was the legendary Red Hood Gang (Les Cagoules Rouge), which between 1956 and 1960 held up some 40 banks and Caisse Populaires (Quebec's version of credit unions) in the city and its environs, for a total of about $2 million. Their name derived from the red woolen NHL Canadiens hockey socks or tuques they pulled over their heads as they entered the bank. Their robberies usually involved four armed men, two of whom cleaned out the tills while the others held the employees and customers at bay with pointed guns. The heists, carefully planned in advance, were speedily executed as their leader, Michel Delisle, knowing that a silent alarm had most likely been activated, loudly counted down the seconds on his watch before ordering the gang to leave. Their in-and-out time was usually no more than three minutes.

Delisle was employing a tactic that would later be made famous by the notorious "Stopwatch Gang" in the 1970s; a group headed by the Ottawa Irish hood Paddy Mitchell who, with a stopwatch hanging from his neck, was extremely punctilious about the timing of their heists, some of which lasted no more than 90 seconds. The gang included Lionel Wright and Stephen Reid, a then drug addict, author and later the husband of celebrated West Coast poet Susan Musgrave. They pulled off an estimated 100 successful jobs in the United States and Canada, including a famous 1974 Ottawa airport theft of $750,000 worth of gold bars that were en route to the Royal Canadian Mint. The members of the Stopwatch Gang were eventually arrested and spent most of the 1980s in jail.

Paddy Mitchell, 1980s

Reid, who'd been given a 21-year sentence, was released on full parole in June 1987, and moved to the town of Sidney on Vancouver Island with Musgrave, whom he'd married in prison the year before. But he could not shake his addiction to cocaine and heroin. In June 1999, he was caught red-handed committing a bank robbery in Victoria, British Columbia, to support his habit, and was sentenced to 18 years in prison. He was granted day parole on January 28, 2008,

Stephen Reid, 2008

and as of October 2010, at the age of sixty, was drug-free and living in a Vancouver halfway house as a condition of his parole.

Meanwhile back in Montreal, the Red Hood Gang's clockwork efficiency had worked smoothly until Joseph "Joe" Bédard, who was head of the Montreal police armed robbery unit, threw a wrench into the cog and confronted them on March 7, 1960, while they were pulling off a bank job at a shopping center on Pie-IX Boulevard. Through an informant, Bédard knew about the planned heist, and he and his squad were waiting outside with guns drawn when the robbers emerged. A wild exchange of gunfire erupted, during which two of the robbers were wounded. Delisle managed to escape, but eleven days later Bédard tracked him down in a Côte-des-Neiges apartment, arresting him while he lay on a sofa watching TV. Three months later twenty-eight-year-old Delisle was sentenced to 10 years in prison.

Bédard was the scourge of bank robbers during the late 1950s and '60s until his retirement in 1966 when he became head of security for the Royal Bank of Canada and the Bank of Montreal. By then he was credited with having shot or captured more than 200 armed robbers. Bédard, a close friend of Harry Feldman in the 1940s, usually turned a blind eye to the city's gambling operations, which he considered victimless crime. But he abhorred the violence that accompanied most bank robberies and made it a point to nab as many of the bad guys as he could, sometimes while they were in the act of pulling off a job.[1]

* * *

In fact, Canada's lenient sentencing laws are something that sticks in the craw of every cop, Crown prosecutor and victim of crime. Until recently, the Canadian Criminal Code allowed that persons convicted of non-violent offenses were eligible for parole after serving one-sixth of their sentence. Moreover, the time they spent in custody without bail

---

1 In March 1969 I happened to meet the now-late Joe Bédard, and he showed me a gold watch that he'd received from the Canadian Bankers Association for having captured the four members of the Red Hood Gang. "And you know something," he told me with some bitterness, "they're all out of jail now, and probably back in business."

while awaiting trial counted for twice as much against their eventual sentence, due to the fact that provincial holding cells offered them none of the privileges, such as counseling, schooling and rehab programs available in a federal institution. Not surprisingly, defense lawyers who knew that their incarcerated client was guilty and would be found so in court, regularly postponed the case as long as possible in order to reduce their eventual federal prison term.

Recent changes to the Criminal Code have tightened up these loopholes, increasing parole eligibility to one-third of a sentence, and eliminating the two-for-one custody proviso. Yet it still remains true that a Canadian whose crimes are even partially committed in the United States would much rather be tried and convicted here than be extradited to the States where, for example, a 10-year sentence means spending almost all of that time in jail. It was a harsh lesson that several West End Gang members would eventually learn.

Back in the very early years, the holdup of a Canadian bank or armored truck that resulted in the death of a police officer, guard or innocent bystander was a crime that automatically merited capital punishment. Such was the case of Tony Frank, a Sardinian-born émigré to Montreal in 1907, who was a member of an early 1920s gang of robbers that included Frank Gambino (aka Mike Capuano); Giuseppe "Joe" Serafini; Giro Niegro; Louis Morel; Mike Valentino (aka Jack Foster); Salvatore Arena; Harry Stone (aka Peter Ward); and Leo Davis. It was forty-year-old Morel, a former Montreal police detective, who led the gang and who carefully cased out and planned most of their jobs.

On April 1, 1924, driving in two stolen cars, the eight bandits cut off and ambushed a Banque d'Hochelaga armored van carrying $250,000 as it was passing through a tunnel on Montreal's Ontario Street East. A shootout between the masked robbers and the four guards ensued, during which the van's driver, twenty-four-year-old Henri Cleroux, and sixty-one-year-old lifelong criminal Harry Stone were killed. The other robbers escaped with pouches containing $140,000 in cash. However, all except Arena were apprehended by police the next day.

Following a lengthy trial, during which Niegro ratted out the rest in exchange for immunity, four of the bandits on June 23, 1924, were found guilty of first-degree murder of Cleroux, and were sentenced to the gallows. Frank, Gambino, Serfani and Morel. All in their late twenties to early forties, were executed by hanging at Montreal's Bordeaux prison at dawn on October 24, 1924. Two others involved in the robbery, Valentino and Davis, managed to escape the noose and had their sentences commuted to life in prison, for which they each served 15 years before being paroled.

Another notorious Montreal bank robber was Gaston Plante, a career criminal since 1946 when he was first arrested at the age of nineteen while pulling off a job. During the 1960s he became a member of the Front de libération du Québec ("Quebec Liberation Front," commonly known as the FLQ), a left-wing separatist organization, and robbed a few more banks to finance their terrorist activities. He was captured in 1967 and given a life sentence as an habitual criminal.

On April 30, 1968, Plante, along with fellow bank robbers Yves Simard, twenty-three, and Claude Levasseur, thirty-one, escaped from the Drummondville, Quebec, jail. Plante was recaptured a month later and sent to the maximum-security Archambault Institute in Laval. Yet he managed to escape once more on August 13, 1973, before again being recaptured and sent back to prison to serve out the rest of his life sentence with no chance of parole.

Meanwhile, during a pre-dawn raid on May 9, 1968, his Drummondville jail co-escapees were tracked down by the Criminal Investigation Section at a rooming house in the Rosemont district of Montreal. A gunfight ensued, during which Simard killed thirty-five-year-old Sergeant-Detective Gilles Jean with a single shot through the heart as he kicked open the apartment door. The members of the raiding team backed away from the landing and for the next 20 minutes fired dozens of bullets and tear gas shells into the room. Simard, knowing that he was a trapped cop killer, put a revolver to his head and blew out his brains.

Levasseur, hiding in an adjacent apartment, had been taken into custody before the shootout and was later incarcerated in the St. Vincent de Paul Penitentary. But before his court sentencing, he was found on the early morning of July 21, 1968, dead in his cell, where he had apparently hung himself with a noose made from his radio headset wires.

Then there was Georges Marcotte, Montreal's notorious "Santa Claus Bandit," whose disguise was season-appropriate. In 1961 and 1962 he robbed several banks in the weeks preceding Christmas, knowing that someone dressed in a Santa Claus suit who walked into a bank with a cheery "Ho, Ho, Ho" would not only be non-conspicuous, but even welcomed by smiling employees. Behind him, however, would be one of his "elves" with a submachine gun under his coat. And waiting outside was Santa's get-away "sleigh," usually a stolen automobile with another "elf" behind the wheel. The ruse worked until December 14, 1962, when a swarm of police cars arrived while they were leaving a downtown branch of the Imperial Bank of Commerce with $140,000 of stolen loot. Marcotte sprayed one of the cars with automatic gunfire, killing officers Claude Marineau, thirty-five, and Denis Brabant, thirty-two, before he and his gang were able to speed away.

A month later police tracked down him and his two accomplices, Jean-Paul Fournel and Jules Reeves. Fournel readily became a Crown witness and named the twenty-nine-year-old Marcotte as their ring-leader. Following their separate trials, Marcotte was sentenced on May 31, 1963, to be hanged for first-degree murder of the two police officers. However, he managed to survive several stays of execution until Canada's death penalty was abolished in July 1976, and his sentence was commuted to life in prison. Reeves, meanwhile, died of a heart attack in prison in October 1974, and Fournel, who had testified against Marcotte, was later released under the witness-protection program and moved to the West Coast under a new identity.

Perhaps the most eccentric bank robber of the early sixties was twenty-three-year-old Anthony Ronald Singer who, between April 26, 1960, and November 1961, robbed 15 banks in Montreal and its adjacent municipalities of the Town of Mount Royal, Westmount and Outremont for a total of about $25,000. His usual method was to approach a teller with a note demanding cash, while showing her a gun that he had in his jacket pocket. After scooping up a few hundred dollars, he'd flee on foot and would later deposit the cash in his personal savings account at a TMR shopping center branch of the Bank of Nova Scotia, a bank that he'd twice held up.

Singer's downfall occurred on November 29, 1961, when a milkman caught him stealing two dozen eggs from his truck and collared him until the police arrived. The cops found $1,400 in his pockets, bills which were later traced back to his bank robberies. A search of his Ridgewood Avenue apartment turned up an unloaded gun that he'd used during his crime spree. During his January 1962 preliminary hearing, it was disclosed that he was something of a miser, such as insisting that his wife never throw out table scraps from leftover meals and turning off his car's ignition when coasting downhill. Nevertheless, he was found mentally fit to stand trial, and on September 11, 1962, after having pleaded guilty that August, he was sentenced to 10 years in prison for his serial bank jobs.

He was released from St. Vincent de Paul Penitentiary in 1969. But by January 1970 he was back to his old tricks and pulled off eight armed bank robberies in Montreal, Ottawa and Toronto, totaling $74,000. Singer was once again arrested on September 24, 1971, and on November 4, 1971, he pleaded guilty to eight counts of armed robbery and was given another 16 years in prison. He was paroled in 1980 and appears to have stayed out of trouble ever since.

### "Machine Gun Molly"

Hitting Montreal banks was not just a "guy thing." One of the city's most colorful and celebrated gang leaders was Monique "Monica" Proietti,

dubbed by the press "Machine Gun Molly" due to her on-the-job use of an M-1 semi-automatic rifle embellished with gold leaf. The gun was capable of firing short bursts with one pull of the trigger, hence her nickname.

Proietti, born in 1939 in the red-light district of Montreal, was an occasional prostitute from the age of thirteen to help support her mother and eight siblings. In 1956 she married Anthony Smith, a Scottish émigré gangster, with whom she had two kids. After he was deported to

Machine Gun Molly, 1960s

Scotland in 1962 for several robbery convictions, she took up with Viateur Tessier, an East End bank robber, with whom she had another child. But in 1965 Tessier was given a 15-year prison sentence for a series of armed holdups. The petite and attractive twenty-seven-year-old Proietti now found herself penniless, having to raise three young children on her own. So what was an unemployed single mom with no life skills or practical training to do?

Robbing banks was her answer. She began in 1965 as the designated getaway driver for brothers Gerard and Robert Lelièvre, but within months became their leader, given her ability to carefully plan and execute bank heists, sometimes several a month. In 1967 alone, the brothers and Proietti, with a machine gun slung across her hip, pulled off at least 20 armed robberies, netting them close to $100,000. Although heavily armed, they neither killed nor injured anyone during their frequent bank withdrawals. Monica did, however, terrify many a teller and customer when she would fire a burst from her machinegun into the ceiling while barking out orders. She was Montreal's equivalent of Bonnie Parker, sans the South Texas accent.

Her career ended violently on September 19, 1967. The trio was emerging from a Caisse Populaire on St. Vital Boulevard in Montreal North where they'd just robbed $3,000 when they heard sirens racing to the scene. Following a brief exchange of gunfire with police, the Lelièvre brothers managed to escape on foot while Monica jumped into her car with the cops on her tail. After a 20-minute high-speed chase, Proietti collided into the side of a city bus some blocks away and lay dazed behind the wheel. As the cops with drawn guns warily approached the crumpled car, Monica raised her trademark weapon one last time before being shot dead in a volley of bullets at the age of twenty-nine.

She went on to become a legend in the annals of Montreal crime, with even a feature-length docudrama film about her exploits, titled *Monica la Mitraille*, released in 2004. As one French newspaper columnist observed shortly after her death: "If Al Capone had had a daughter, he would have wanted her to be like Monique Proietti."

As for Monica's two partners, Gerard Lelièvre was picked up a few days later, while his older brother Robert managed to avoid capture until October 10, 1967, when he was found driving a stolen car in Hull, Quebec. Both were charged with the attempted murder of a police officer during the Montreal North robbery and were committed to trial.

On May 22, 1968, the brothers and four other prisoners, using a gun that Robert had somehow acquired and hid on his person, commandeered a Department of Corrections caged van that was transporting them from the St. Jerome courthouse north of Montreal to Bordeaux prison. They sped off in the van until running into a Quebec Provincial Police roadblock near the village of Ste. Monique. The four other convicts immediately surrendered, but the Lelièvre brothers, in prison-issue handcuffs and leg irons, hobbled off into the nearby woods, pursued by the cops. Shots were fired and Gerard was killed on the spot at the age of thirty-two.

His thirty-nine-year-old brother Robert was critically wounded with a bullet in his abdomen and another to his head. After recovering in hospital, he was put on trial where, on October 7, 1968, he pleaded guilty to the charges of attempted murder, and received a seven-year sentence. The Crown appealed the sentence and, considering Lelièvre's lengthy criminal record, he was ruled an habitual criminal in 1971 and wasn't released until 1980. He then fell in with the West End Gang, a career move which he would die to regret four years later.

\*\*\*

By the early 2000s, Montreal had lost its dubious distinction as the bank robbery capital of North America, to be replaced by Vancouver, where thieves, usually operating alone and in search of easy cash to support a drug habit, were pulling off far more such robberies. According to police statistics, Vancouver recorded 30 daytime bank robberies per 100,000 population in 2008, compared with only seven in Montreal and five in Toronto with respect to their much larger urban populations.

Nevertheless, Montreal thieves still held their own, since, apart from barging through the front door of a bank in broad daylight, they would often gain access to the bank's cash and safety-deposit boxes during the still of the night. The West End Gang was quite adept at this, even though it required a lot more planning, patience and physical work than simply firing a gun in the air and quickly scooping up tens and twenties and fifties from the tills of terrified bank tellers. And the potential haul from a vault robbery was always much bigger.

CHAPTER 8

# Digging for Treasure

I f you can't get through the front door, why not try the back? That's what a lot of thieves, including members of Montreal's West End Gang, did when the city had the distinction of being North America's bank robbery capital. More specifically, they dug through a wall, ceiling or floor in order to enter a vault that contained safety deposit boxes, tempting cherries just waiting to be picked.

While most Canadians were relaxing during the July 1, 1961, Dominion Day three-day weekend, Jacques Lajoie, Roland Primeau, and brothers André and Yvon Lemieux were hard at work. With cutter drills, chisels, crowbars and flashlights, they were digging their way up from a storm drain viaduct beneath the concrete floor of the Bank of Nova Scotia at 451 St. Catherine Street West on the corner of St. Alexander Street in the heart of Montreal. Their goal was the bank's subterranean vault.

Seated at a window in a building across the street, with binoculars and a walkie-talkie, was Georges Lemay, the man who had carefully planned and was now directing the job while watching out for the cops. In the wee hours of Sunday, July 2, the four diggers finally broke through the floor, and radioed their ringleader, who immediately joined them. Lemay was an experienced safecracker who easily picked open 377 safety deposit boxes in the vault. A few hours later all five were crawling back through the tunnel with $633,605 worth of cash, jewelry and negotiable bearer bonds. They drove away in their cars parked in a nearby alley, having pulled off a crime which would be undetected until the bank opened the following Tuesday. None of the loot was ever recovered.

The robbery remained unsolved until January 1962, when forty-year-old Lajoie, who had been arrested on unrelated charges, became a police informant and struck a plea-bargaining deal with the Crown to testify against Lemay and the others. During his early testimony, Lajoie, who said he had been promised $10,000 for his role in the robbery but had received only $3,500, identified Lemay as the mastermind behind the break-in. He then told the court in detail how it had been pulled off.

The case and subsequent trials dragged on for more than five years before verdicts were handed down and sentences meted out. On November 8, 1967, Lajoie, in exchange for his cooperation and the fact that he'd been incarcerated for 11 months while awaiting trial, got a token one-day prison sentence for his role in the caper. The others fared not nearly as well. Primeau, at the age of forty-one, was given a 13-year sentence, while brothers André and Yvon Lemieux were given seven and four years respectively. However, their leader, Georges Lemay, with a lengthy rap sheet for previous crimes, had gone missing shortly after the robbery and managed to evade capture for five more years.

Born on January 25, 1925, in Shawinigan, Quebec, Lemay was an accomplished safecracker during the 1950s and 1960s, and a pal of notorious bank robber, gun runner and drug importer Lucien Rivard, before linking up with the West End Gang. On July 11, 1957, he was arrested by Montreal detective-inspector William Fitzpatrick at his Laurentian chalet in Mont Rolland, 50 miles northwest of the city, and charged with possession of two unregistered .32-caliber handguns. A week later he pleaded guilty and was released with a fine of $43.75 plus time spent in jail.

Apart from the 1961 Bank of Nova Scotia tunnel job, Lemay was also pegged as the ringleader of a gang that in January 1957 had tunneled into the vault of a Van Horne Shopping Centre branch of the Royal Bank of Canada in Montreal's Outremont district and stolen an estimated $2 million in cash, jewelry and securities from safety deposit boxes.

Lemay seems to have left a few bodies in his wake. He was a prime suspect in the July 2, 1957, death of Larry Petrov, who had been part of the Outremont bank heist and had been unwisely cashing in some of the bearer bonds before the heat was off. And on January 4, 1952, twenty-one-year-old Huguette Daoust, whom Lemay had married on May 19, 1951, suddenly vanished while they were living in Miami. Exactly 12 years later, on January 4, 1964, her corpse was fished out of the water in the Florida Keys. The circumstances surrounding her death were never resolved, but were listed as suspicious by the Florida State Police.

Yet nothing was ever proven against Lemay. In the spring of 1964, the thirty-nine-year-old fugitive was living comfortably aboard his 43-foot sailing ketch *Triana* in Florida, under the aliases and fake passports of René Roy and Robert G. Palmer. He was placed on the RCMP's most wanted list on August 9, 1964, and arrested by the FBI aboard his $40,000 yacht in a Fort Lauderdale marina on May 6, 1965. He was jailed and scheduled to be extradited to Montreal. But on September 21, 1965, he managed to escape from his seventh-floor cell, reportedly by paying $35,000 in cash to guards at Miami's Dade County prison, and went on the lam again to either Mexico or Cuba. On August 19, 1966, Lemay was recaptured by FBI agents in the Golden Nugget casino in Las Vegas and was immediately transported in leg irons and handcuffs back to Montreal.

Following many procedural delays, his trial opened on October 30, 1967. Based on earlier testimony by Jacques Lajoie about the Bank of Nova Scotia robbery, Lemay was found guilty and handed a 14-year prison sentence on January 24, 1969. He was granted double time for the three years he'd spent in preventive detention while awaiting conviction, and served only eight more years.

After being released 1977, Lemay continued to get into trouble. On January 26, 1979, he and Pierre Quintal were arrested by the RCMP at a Rivière des Prairies warehouse in Montreal East where they were alleged to be operating a clandestine lab producing LSD. They were charged with possession of drugs with intent to traffic. Four months later, on May 9, 1979, the forty-one-year-old Quintal had six .45-caliber bullets pumped into his body as he was leaving the office of Frank Shoofey, a defense lawyer who represented both him and Lemay.

On October 17, 1983, Lemay, while in the Parthenais Detention Centre, was accused of having arranged Quintal's death, presumably to stop him from making a deal with prosecutors and testifying against him in the LSD bust. Also charged were Frank Laenens, thirty-five, and brothers Alain, thirty-eight, and Serge Charron, thirty-five. The Crown's key witness against them was Donald Lavoie, a self-confessed hitman with 27 kills under his belt, who was granted immunity for his testimony. He told the court that Lemay had told him about the planned hit on Quintal while the two were together at Parthenais, and that Laenens was the designated hitman. But all four were acquitted by a jury on December 13, 1984, due to "reasonable doubt," because of what was regarded as self-serving testimony from Lavoie.

Shortly before his eighty-second birthday, Lemay died of natural causes at his Montreal South Shore home in December 2006. However, his death wasn't reported until almost two years later, by his daughter Josée Lemay, on September 22, 2008.

### The Trans-Island Tunnel Affair

Georges Lemay's bank vault heists were almost trumped in March 1967 by the famous Montreal Trans-Island Tunnel Affair, an audacious plan that involved members of the Italian mafia as well as francophones and anglophones from the West End Gang, and could have garnered them $5 to $6 million in cash and securities had it succeeded.

It began on the holiday weekend of July 1, 1966, after Frank Cotroni Sr. had rented a house at 5146 Trans-Island Street, across from the City

& District Savings Bank (now the Laurentian Bank of Canada) in Montreal's Côte-des-Neiges area, and had put together a crew to pull off the job. They included Cotroni's brother-in-law Michel Désormiers and his brothers Paul and Pierre and their father Paul Sr., as well as convicted drug smuggler and expert lock-picker Joe Horvath, aka Joe Valentine, of the West End Gang.

Beset by many cave-ins and equipment failures, they spent the next nine months on and off the job, gradually burrowing their way from under the house to their objective beneath the bank, a distance of some 500 feet. Apart from spades, wheelbarrows, pneumatic cutting drills and chisels, they also had acetylene torches to cut through the steel rebar in the concrete. Their tunnel was equipped with makeshift electric lighting and pumped-in ventilation, and was shored up with wooden beams.

Finally, on March 31, 1967, just as they were about to break up through the floor of the vault, the police, who'd known of the planned robbery for a few weeks and were biding their time in order to catch them in the act, swooped down and nabbed all six of them red-handed in the tunnel. They were immediately sent to trial, where most of them either got off or received light sentences for a job not well done.

Michel Desormiers, Cotroni's brother-in-law and foreman on the Trans-Island job, spent a few years in jail for his role in the caper before going back to work for the mafia. Then, at 3 a.m. on July 15, 1983, he was shot dead at the age of thirty-nine with three bullets to the back of the head in his Lake of Two Mountains home in Montreal's West Island. His assassin, professional hitman Yves Trudeau, two years later confessed to having committed the murder on a contract from the mafia. Exactly who wanted Desormiers hit and why was never discovered. His brothers Paul and Pierre, following their short prison terms, apparently left the gangland milieu.

Joe Horvath, after spending a short stint in the can for his role in the affair, was again arrested with several others by the RCMP on May 11, 1972, and charged with conspiring to import $2 million worth of hashish from Afghanistan through Montreal's Dorval airport, and was released on $5000 bail. He was subpoenaed to appear before the CECO inquiry in February 1973, but declined to testify. While out on bail for the hashish importation charge, Horvath was again arrested in Montreal on March 1, 1974, when he was indicted by a federal grand jury in Milwaukee, Wisconsin, for trafficking in narcotics. But before he could be extradited to the United States, he died at the age of forty-five of throat cancer in Montreal's Saint-Luc Hospital on April 10, 1974.

## The Brockville Heist

Montreal's burglars also sometimes plied their trade out of town, such as in Brockville, Ontario, 135 miles west of Montreal, and the scene of Canada's largest bank vault robbery. During the pre-dawn hours of Saturday, May 4, 1958, five men laden with tools quietly jimmied open the side door of the Fullford building near the Brockville courthouse and slipped inside. Their target was the vault of the adjoining Brockville Trust & Savings Company, a subsidiary of the Montreal Trust Company. Having carefully cased the job beforehand, they knew what lay behind the Fullford's north wall and beneath the floor. With sledges, chisels, drills and an acetylene torch they hacked their way through four layers of brick and a half-inch of tempered steel plate. Three hours later they dropped from the ceiling into the bank's vault, where there were cases of negotiable bonds stacked on dollies, a bank satchel containing $20,000 in cash, and a wall lined with rows of safety deposit boxes.

The theft wasn't discovered until the bank opened Monday morning. Its value was first estimated at $3.5 million, based on the bank's missing cash and securities. But the thieves had also picked the locks and cleaned out 36 safety deposit boxes. Within days, the total haul was estimated at about $10 million, based on the additional cash, stock certificates, bonds and jewelry contained in those boxes.

Only one man, twenty-four-year-old René Martin, a Montreal safecracker and ex-convict, was ever nabbed and convicted for the theft. While fleeing the crime scene, he had accidentally dropped his bank savings account book, which showed his name and address, and he was arrested that Monday afternoon while driving in Montreal. In his pockets police found only $110, but more importantly there was a key to a locker at Montreal's Central Station. In it the cops found a duffle bag stuffed with more than $500,000 worth of negotiable bearer bonds that had come from the Brockville bank.

Martin was brought to stand trial in Brockville, where he pleaded guilty to breaking and entry and theft. He admitted that he and four others had pulled off the job, but adamantly refused to name his accomplices. At Martin's sentencing hearing on November 20, 1958, Ontario Crown Attorney Harworth Atkinson asked for the maximum sentence of 14 years, insisting, "The crime was planned and executed with skill." He added, "This was no small expedition for the Trust Company vaults and safety deposit boxes, possibly yielding the biggest haul in the history of this country and perhaps the continent."

On December 5, 1958, Martin was given a 12-year prison term. He served eight years, never once revealing the names of his four accomplices. But Montreal police were sure they included mafioso Pep Cotroni and Peter Stepanoff, Pretula associate René Robert, and West End Gang expert safecracker Kenneth Winford. In fact, three of them were at different times arrested on charges of attempting to cash bonds that were traced back to the Brockville robbery: Robert on July 28, 1958; Cotroni on November 9, 1959: and Stepanoff in 1960. But being in possession of the securities did not necessarily link them to the scene of the crime, since it was common for stolen bonds to be sold at a discount to second parties. By 1982, almost $8 million worth of the fenced Brockville securities had turned up from time to time in various parts of the world, including Switzerland, Central and South America, and the Middle East.

As for how much was really missing from the personal safety deposit boxes, there or in any other bank vault or home robbery, is anybody's guess, since both the cops and insurance companies know that a victim will often inflate the value.

André "Butch" Bouchard, a 34-year veteran of the Montreal police force, was head of its Major Crimes Division in the 1990s and chief of Homicide from 2000 until his retirement in 2004. He had previously worked on a lot of home burglary and bank robbery cases, where he became rather cynical with respect to some of the so-called victims. "They

Billy Morgan, 1950

[the victims] lied almost as much as the crooks," says the sixty-year-old Bouchard today. "I remember sometimes a guy we'd caught would say, 'Mr. Bouchard, let me tell you something. Yes, I'm a fucking crook and I'm going to plead guilty . . . The file says it was $480,000 worth of diamonds and gold and this and that. But that's bullshit! It was about $110,000. That cocksucker collected about $480,000 or something from the insurance. So I did him a favor, *ostie*. He made 300 and something in profit.'"

Bouchard also has grudging praise for the West End Gang, most of whom he says "weren't thugs selling drugs on the street like the French and the Italians . . . They had the best safecrackers and the best truck hijackers. Some of those guys were sixteen years old [and] today they're still at it."

One of those guys is William "Billy" Morgan. Born in Montreal in 1935, one of seven kids of dysfunctional Irish-Scottish parents, he grew up in various foster homes and, he says today, "I was a thief by the age of seven," stealing from local corner stores. In 1946, at the age of eleven,

Billy Morgan, 2008

he was incarcerated at the Shawbridge Boys Farm north of Montreal for auto theft and attempting to crack a safe. It was there that he met other young Irish kids who, like him, would later form the nucleus of the West End Gang.

In his teens Morgan got into shoplifting, warehouse robberies, B&E's, passing bad cheques and picking locks. "Back then I could open any lock or crack any safe, and I did a lot of that. I had a knack for it," he boasts. By the 1970s he was hanging out regularly with members of the West End Gang at the Cavalier Motel and their other drinking spots, where they plotted ways in which to make more money. Nevertheless, Morgan kept his criminal activities at a non-violent level and stayed away from the drug trade, even if some of his friends such as Jackie McLaughlin, John Slawvey, Hughie McGurnaghan, Danny Pelensky and Dunie Ryan did not. Which perhaps is why Morgan has outlived them all by many years. Today, having spent only an accumulated eight years in prison, he has shaken off his vices (except for tobacco) and lives comfortably in downtown Montreal, a seventy-five-year-old man at peace with himself.

## Easier Pickings

Apart from robbing banks by barging through the front door or tunneling into their vaults, there was one other lucrative way to hit them: get the money while it was being transferred to or from the bank in an armored truck. Here again, Montreal robbers, including the West End Gang, pulled off some successful and not-so-successful jobs.

As a Brink's armored truck pulled up in front of the Bank of Montreal in the Bell Telephone building on Beaver Hall Hill on Monday, April 30, 1971, four men with concealed weapons were casually hanging out in the crowded lobby. One of them was Raymond Lynch, a notorious bank-robbing member of the West End Gang, who had a short-barreled machine gun hidden under his coat.

Three Brink's men left the truck. One of them pushed a cart carrying canvas sacks containing $200,000 in various denominations of bills, while the other two, guns drawn and scoping out the lobby, kept pace beside him. Suddenly Lynch shouted, "Get the money!" and a burst of automatic gunfire wounded thirty-eight-year-old Brink's guard Guy Gelenais in the leg. He and the other guards began firing back at the bandits, who were rushing towards the cart. A wild shootout occurred as people in the lobby screamed and fled for cover.

When it was over minutes later, two men lay dead on the marble floor. One was sixty-five-year-old Corrado Festa, an innocent bystander hit by seven machine-gun bullets, and the other was twenty-five-year-old

Lynch, who had been shot by two of the guards. The other bandits fled and were never apprehended.

Another West End Gang armored truck robbery was attempted when a Brink's truck was ambushed on Côte de Liesse Road in Montreal's Saint Laurent district on September 12, 1973. It too resulted in a shootout, leaving a Brink's guard, Claude Vienneau, shot to death. The robbers fled with $277,000, but were captured soon after. Their leader was career criminal William "Billy" MacAllister, who on December 6, 1974, was found guilty of manslaughter for his role in Vienneau's death, and was sentenced to life in prison. He was paroled on February 2, 1981, but was destined to serve a lot more jail time in the years ahead.

Eventually the Montreal bad guys would figure how to rob an armored truck the right way; something that would happen with the March 30, 1976, "Crime of the Century."

# CHAPTER 9

# The Crime of the Century

Gilles Lachapelle, an east-end Montrealer and high-school dropout who'd served with the Canadian Army as a rifleman and machine-gunner during the Korean War in 1952 and '53, and was later posted in Japan, returned to Montreal in 1960 with his young Japanese wife, Luong. They lived modestly in a rented home on the South Shore while Gilles tried his hand at various jobs before finding a company that seemed perfect for him and his talents—Brink's Canada Ltd.

Brink's Canada is a subsidiary of Brink's Incorporated, founded in 1859 by Perry Brink in Chicago as a transporter of gold dust and nuggets from Comstock lodes, and later coins and bullion, printed currency, financial securities and other valuable goods between banks, retailers and government mints. By the 20<sup>th</sup> century, Brink's was

North America's largest and most trusted deliverer of anything that sender and receiver wanted to make sure arrived safely at its destination. With its fleet of armored trucks, the Canadian subsidiary, which opened its first branch in Montreal in 1927, was hiring dozens of new guards and drivers in the 1950s and '60s, mostly as a result of the rapidly sprawling city suburbs, all of which had chartered bank branches and retail shopping centers. Someone had to securely transport all that cash back and forth.

And that's where Lachapelle, at the age of thirty-one, found his dream job with a company that was looking for men who had military training in small arms to work as guards and drivers on their trucks. He joined Brink's as a guard in 1961, and by 1972 he was an armored-car driver—a plum job that didn't require lugging sacks of bills and coins with one hand on the dolly and the other on his holster, or else standing as point man on the sidewalk with his trigger finger on a 12-gauge shotgun. As a driver, all he had to do during a delivery or pickup was to keep the doors locked, his eyes peeled, and then let the guards, known as "hoppers," back into the truck before heading off to their next pickup or delivery. The work was boring, but it paid the rent, and Lachapelle was content. At least until his friend and co-worker Roland Brunette put a bug in his ear in 1975.

The two had vaguely formulated a scheme to rob one of the Brink's trucks, while it would be delivering $50,000 to a Cooprix market in Montreal East, but their plan was never carried out. Something far bigger was to come along.

Brunette, then a thirty-seven-year-old armed guard for Brink's in Montreal, had a few scams going on the side—nothing big, just buying and fencing stolen goods—stuff that "fell off the back of a truck." But he also had some shady and ambitious friends, particularly among the Provençal clan, the East End's most formidable family of thieves, holdup artists, pimps, extortionists and drug dealers.

The Provençal siblings, six brothers and three sisters, were raised during the 1940s through the '60s on the hardscrabble streets of Montreal's east end. The oldest brother, Roger, who was born in 1935 and ran the "family business," was always on the lookout for a major score. He was inspired

perhaps by the publicity surrounding the
famous January 17, 1950, "Crime of the
Century" involving a $2.5-million heist
of cash, cheques, money orders and negotiable securities from the Brink's Boston
company offices in the city's north end.
When that robbery was eventually solved
by the FBI in 1956 and its seven perpetrators rounded up, the story made headlines
around the world. Roger was determined
to make the same company his target and
to pull off a job in Montreal that no one
had ever before done. But he knew that

Roger Provençal, circa 1976

he'd need assistance from beyond his own clan, help that would have to
include Brink's employees as well as a few professionals from the Irish
West End Gang. The planning began in January 1976.

That's where Roger's small-time hood acquaintance, Roland
Brunette, came in. But Brunette was merely a Brink's guard, not a driver.
Provençal knew the hook would have to be sunk a bit deeper. Skillfully
using the people-who-know-people approach, Provençal had his close
associate Roch "Rocky" Carignan approach Brunette with a rough idea
of the proposed heist. Brunette, in turn, mentioned the proposition to
his Brink's co-worker Lachapelle. The bait was set, and Lachapelle was
interested. As he would later confess from his prison cell in 1983 to his
informant handler, Sergeant-Detective André Savard of the Montreal
police Bureau Enquête Criminelle (Major Crimes Division), he was
not merely an unwitting pawn, but someone who saw an opportunity
to make some big money and then move back to Japan where he could
disappear with his wife Luong. He was naïve and easily manipulated
into playing a major role in the scheme.

\* \* \*

*The following is an account of the planning and execution of the robbery, as
Lachapelle would later lay it out for Savard when he finally confessed*

*to his involvement seven years later. It therefore differs significantly from all the accounts that appeared in newspapers and magazines in the first few years following the robbery, during which Lachapelle was always portrayed as a hapless victim.*

In early January 1976, while discussing the what-if-it-could-be-done scenario, Lachapelle pointed out to Brunette that the only way a Brink's driver would open the doors to a securely locked truck was if he was given no choice. Small arms or even high-powered rifle fire could never penetrate the half-inch hardened steel body and laminated bullet-proof windshield of an armored van. But, as he knew from his army stint in Korea and Japan, a driver faced with heavy artillery would certainly be intimidated, since rounds from an anti-aircraft or anti-personnel-carrier weapon could easily punch holes into any Brink's truck. Brunette passed this information on to the Provençal gang.

On the evening of Monday, January 5, 1976, Roland called Gilles at home to say he'd pick him up shortly for a meeting about "the job." As they drove to Montreal's east end in Brunette's 1975 black Plymouth Fury, Roland explained that they were meeting somebody close to the man who would be coordinating the planned robbery. They pulled into the parking lot of the Sheraton Hotel on Ile Charron, just off the eastern tip of the island of Montreal, where a white Lincoln Continental was parked. The driver waved them over, and they left their car and climbed into the back seat of the Lincoln. The driver turned around and Roland introduced Gilles to a man he identified only as "Rocky." It was Roch Carignan, a top lieutenant in the Provençal gang. Rocky asked Gilles a few questions, digested the need for a heavy-caliber weapon and told him that the next meeting would be with someone known only as "Le Gros" (the "Fat Man"). It was he who would organize the heist and launder the money. Their brief conversation ended with a "don't call us; we'll call you" ultimatum. On the drive home, Gilles recalls wondering what had he gotten himself into.

Two weeks later, on Monday, January 19, Roland pulled Gilles aside as the two were reporting for work. He said Rocky had set up a meeting with the Fat Man for that night at an east-end motel to discuss the planned caper. They drove there and entered the designated motel room, where Rocky was waiting for them. A few minutes later there was a soft knock on the door and two men, their heads covered with brown paper bags cut with eye slits, were ushered in by Rocky and introduced to Lachapelle, although not by name. The larger of the two, whom Gilles assumed was the Fat Man since he was relatively short and appeared to weigh over 250 pounds, was Roger Provençal, leader of the infamous East End Gang. The second man was Michel Pilon, a former Quebec municipal police officer and now a key member of the Provençal mob.

Under questioning from the hooded men, Lachapelle explained that every Tuesday afternoon he and his three co-workers drove their Brink's truck into the Dollard Street laneway next to the head office of the Royal Bank of Canada at 360 St. James Street West, in the heart of Montreal's financial district. Via a triple-locked side door they routinely picked up at least $3 million in cash to be delivered to the bank's satellite branches and retail outlets. The normal procedure, he explained, was for the three armed guards to enter the bank, pick up the money and stow it in the truck. They would then go for a coffee break in the bank's cafeteria while Gilles waited in the locked truck for their return 15 minutes later. It was during that 15-minute window of opportunity that the robbery should occur.

But Lachapelle emphasized that he could only be believably forced to open the door to the truck if he was faced with something powerful and frightening enough to intimidate him, such as an armor-piercing weapon. The Fat Man assured him that that would be no problem. And he promised that half of whatever the job netted would be handed over to him, Roland and Rocky, to split up as they chose. He also ominously warned Gilles that at this point there was no backing out. The two hooded men left the motel room, saying they'd be in touch via Rocky to set up the actual day of the robbery. Lachapelle, as he would later admit, was left wondering if he'd gotten himself in over his head. But it was too late to turn back.

## "Is This What You Wanted?"

More than a week went by before the next meeting on the evening of Wednesday, January 28, when Roland picked up Gilles at his home and the two drove to the Sheraton Hotel parking lot on Ile Charron and pulled up alongside Rocky's white Lincoln Continental. Rocky handed Gilles a blindfold, ordered him to put it on and to get into the rear seat of the car. He then told Roland that his part of the job was finished and that he should now drive home.

A man seated next to Lachapelle in the back of the Continental muttered that he was about to see what he was looking for. Gilles instantly recognized the hoarse voice of the Fat Man. After a long drive, Rocky wheeled the car into an underground garage and came to a stop. Gilles was told to take off his blindfold and get out of the car. The Fat Man, once again with a paper bag over his head, got out on the other side and brought Gilles over to a white Ford Econoline van that was parked nearby. He flung open the van's back doors and asked, "Is this what you wanted?"

An astonished Lachapelle was staring into the muzzle of an air-cooled Browning M2 .50-caliber machine gun with a 54-inch barrel mounted on a tripod and a bandolier of 300 rounds of armor-piercing cartridges running from its magazine to a green metal ammunition case on the floor of the van. He immediately recognized the U.S. Army–issue weapon, even though he'd not been this close to one since the Korean War.

"We'll be in touch," grunted the Fat Man as he slammed the van doors shut and abruptly walked away towards another parked vehicle. Gilles got back into Rocky's car and was driven home.

Browning M2 machine gun like the one used in the Brink's robbery

Three weeks passed, with Gilles becoming increasingly more nervous each day. Then on Thursday, February 19, he got a call at home from Roland to tell him that Rocky would pick him up the following day after work outside a restaurant near the Brink's depot on Shannon Street. Gilles spotted the Lincoln parked at the curb and got in, this time in the passenger seat. Rocky, noticing Gilles' agitation, assured him that everything was going fine. They drove west to the International Motel near Dorval Airport, got out and walked down the motel corridor to room 36, where Roger Provençal and Pilon, both with paper bags cut with eye slits over their heads, let them in. The Fat Man came to the point, informing Gilles that the Brink's job was set for next Tuesday, February 24. He then explained that as soon as the three guards entered the bank for their coffee break, the white van containing the machine gun would back into the alley and stop about 50 feet away. Its rear doors would open to reveal the machine gun aimed squarely at the Brink's truck. Rocky would then exit the van's passenger door and approach the armored truck. If everything seemed okay, Gilles was to flash the truck's head-lights and then unlock the side door to let Rocky in. They would then follow the van to wherever Rocky directed him. The money would be quickly transferred into another vehicle, the bandits would flee and Gilles would be left handcuffed to the truck's steering wheel. When the police arrived they would find him there, as well as the white van and machine gun. He then simply had to tell the cops the story that they'd rehearsed many times.

On the following Tuesday, shortly before 2 p.m., Gilles pulled into the Dollard Street laneway and let out the three armed guards, two of them with shotguns and the third with a .357 Magnum revolver. They returned several minutes later with two dollies laden with sacks of cash and coins, which they loaded into the back of the truck before heading back inside for their afternoon coffee break. Gilles then saw the familiar white van slowly back into the alley in front of him. But before flashing the all-clear, he glanced into his rear-view mirror, where he saw three men in overcoats entering the alley from St. Paul Street. Were they local businessmen? Were they cops who'd been tipped off?

Who could know? So he panicked and took his finger off the headlight switch. Meanwhile, Rocky had gotten out of the van and was casually walking towards the Brink's truck, waiting for the signal. When all he saw was Gilles with his hands on the steering wheel and shaking his head, he returned to the van and immediately sped off. Mission aborted!

Two days later, as Lachapelle was leaving the Brink's garage, Brunette pulled him aside and asked him what had happened, and told him that the Fat Man was in a foul mood. Gilles explained that he was willing to do his part, but that last Tuesday things didn't look right. On Friday, Brunette grabbed him again to inform him that Rocky would be picking him up after work near the same restaurant as last time.

The Lincoln Continental was parked by the curb in the same place. Gilles got in. Neither he nor Rocky said a word as they drove west to the International Hotel in Dorval and entered room 36 where the Fat Man and Michel Pilon, both of them again masked, awaited them. The Fat Man, clearly pissed off by the aborted run, told Gilles that the robbery would be happening the following Tuesday and that this time there would be no turning back. The Fat Man also informed him that it had become too risky to drive the van around the city with its mounted gun in the rear; so that particular van would not be in the alley that day but would be left where the Brink's truck and Lachapelle would eventually be found. All Gilles had to do, he said, was to stick to the prepared script when he was questioned by police.

At 2:40 p.m. on Tuesday, March 30, 1976, Lachapelle stopped the truck next to the Royal Bank's side door. It was their seventh drop-off and pick-up stop of the day. The three Brink's guards got out and returned ten minutes later with two dollies containing 92 zippered and tagged leather bags full of cash and coins, which they loaded into the back of the truck. Gilles pushed a dashboard panel button to lock the rear doors as his companions returned to the bank for their routine afternoon coffee break. A white van, although not the same one that he'd seen before, slowly backed into the alley in front of his truck, stopping about 50 feet away as if preparing to unload something. Seconds later he saw Rocky sauntering down the laneway in front of him. This time there was no one in his rear-view mirror. Gilles flashed the truck's headlights as Rocky approached the truck's passenger door to let him know that the coast was clear. He then punched the console button to unlock the passenger door. Rocky climbed in and said, "Let's go!"

Following the van and Rocky's directions, Gilles turned left on St. James Street and then left again on University Street a few blocks away, and onto the Bonaventure Expressway heading towards the Champlain Bridge. Just before the tollbooths, Rocky told him to take the Nun's Island exit and guided him to a deserted area between a tennis club and a railroad yard where he parked the truck. The van that had held the machine gun was already ominously parked in front of him. The other white van and another vehicle, containing Jean-Louis Ouimette of the East End Gang and Claude Meredith of the West End Gang, pulled up on either side of him. As Rocky jumped out, a hooded Michel Pilon approached the driver's side of the Brink's truck where he pushed Gilles down to the truck floor and handcuffed him to the steering wheel before punching a dashboard button that electronically opened the rear doors. From his position on the floor, Gilles heard the bags of money being quickly transferred to the van, which then immediately sped away with the other car behind it. The entire operation, from start to finish, had lasted a mere 24 minutes and not a single shot had been fired.

Lachapelle, noticing that the handcuffs were not properly locked, managed to free himself. He then smashed his eyeglasses, to make it look as if he'd been assaulted and ran to the tennis club where he told the receptionist to call the police and report a robbery.

Meanwhile, back in the Dollard Street laneway, the three Brink's guards had returned to their truck, horrified to find it gone. They ran back into the bank to sound the alarm. Within minutes, the area was surrounded by cop cars, and the guards were being questioned on the spot by holdup detectives. A headquarters dispatch call at 3:04 p.m. soon had the cops racing towards Nun's Island where they found the empty Brink's truck and a highly agitated Lachapelle standing beside it, blabbering on about the robbery and pointing to the white van with its ominous .50-caliber machine gun parked in front of him.

The city's (and North America's) biggest ever armed robbery, amounting to $2,775,884 in 61 bags of cash (consisting of 10-, 20-, 50-, and 100-dollar bills) and 29 boxes containing $5,000 worth of Olympic gold coins, had gone down with hardly a hitch. It was to become the "New Crime of the Century," surpassing even the 1950 Boston Brink's robbery. And it would soon prove to be the Montreal police department's most frustrating and dangerous case to solve.

CHAPTER 10

# The Rubber Duck Squad

*Ah, breaker one-nine, this here's the Rubber Duck. You got a copy on me,*
*Pigpen? C'mon. Ah, yeah, ten-four, Pigpen, for sure, for sure . . . Mercy*
*sake's alive, looks like we got us a convoy.*
                    —from the 1975 song "Convoy" by C.W. McCall

Montreal's armed-robbery detectives were both stymied and under a lot of public pressure to solve the March 30, 1976, Brink's robbery, which the French-language press was now calling the "Crime of the Century." No one had ever before robbed the Brink's company of that much cash, nor had a bigger heist ever occurred in Montreal. The company was offering a $25,000 award for the arrest and conviction of the culprits, and its insurer, Commercial Union Assurance Company, posted an unheard-of $100,000 reward for the recovery of the stolen money.

Within the next two days, investigators established that the Ford Econoline van had been stolen in Montreal's North End the previous February 18, and its phony license plate had been stolen on March 11. The machine gun, which was examined and taken apart by the department's ballistics experts, was still coated with packing grease and probably would not have fired in any case. Using serial numbers, they traced the weapon and its metal ammunition box and cartridges to an army-surplus dealer in Kentucky who had legally sold it the year before to a certain John Fuller. That turned out to be the alias of John Sheppard, a Montreal hoodlum who was well known to police and who was a confederate of both Dunie Ryan, then head of the West End Gang, and Roger Provençal, head of the East End Gang.

Considering the robbery's intricate planning and smooth execution, police were certain that either or both of these organized groups were behind it. And given the fact that members of the West End Gang had close ties to some of those who had pulled off the infamous 1950 Boston Brink's robbery, the heat was focused on them.

In the following days, the Montreal cops pulled in and questioned more than a dozen suspects. They included the truck's driver, Gilles Lachapelle, who steadfastly stuck to his prepared script and even passed a lie-detector test; John Sheppard, who denied any involvement; and Dunie Ryan and Roger Provençal, neither of whom had anything to say and both of whom had ironclad alibis for the day of the robbery.

The case was going nowhere, yet the pressure was on from both the media and the public to solve it. And that's when sergeant-detective André Savard entered the picture.

Savard started out as a Montreal rookie cop in 1961 at the age of twenty-one. He chuckles today, recalling that his first assignment was at the Montreal Botanical Gardens. "I've got a gun, and my job was to make sure people didn't step on the flowers. What was I supposed to do? Shoot them?" He was soon after transferred as a beat cop in the city's Ville Émard district just north of Verdun, and then to nearby St. Henri, NDG, and Côte-des-Neiges, all of them tough bilingual neighborhoods. By 1972, he'd been promoted to sergeant-detective and assigned to the night patrol. He was given the task of cleaning up Montreal's popular downtown Crescent Street, where two motorcycle gangs, Satan's Choice and the Popeyes (absorbed into the Hells Angels in 1977), were intimidating the street's bar owners for protection money, as well as selling marijuana and hashish to the mostly anglophone habitués of those bars.

"Those bikers were nuts; they had everybody scared, even the big doormen. So what we did was take control of the street. I had about 10 guys working with me on night patrol, and every time we'd see one of those guys, we'd pick him up, frisk him, seize his motorcycle and tell him we didn't want to see him here again." Within a year, says Savard, his squad had rid the street of the biker thugs.

However, in the late 1960s and early 1970s a less intimidating but

André Savard, 1976

equally rapacious group was also prominent in the bars of Crescent Street and other downtown watering holes. This was Savard's first encounter with the West End Gang. He recalls the Johnston brothers, the McGuire brothers, Peter White and John Slawvey all hanging out on Crescent Street, as well as on nearby Bishop and Stanley streets, during that time. "The Irish liked to drink in those places and even controlled some of them," says Savard, going on to explain they did this by strong-arming their owners into paying protection money.

He recalls one incident when Johnny Vago, owner of the popular Crescent Street Sir Winston Churchill Pub and Winnie's, opened the Don Juan bar on Stanley Street. Soon after its launch, the West End Gang shake-down boys arrived and informed Vago they'd be back the next night for their first payment. Vago put in a call to his cop friend André Savard. "So the next night," says Savard, "me and another [plainclothes] officer are sitting there when these guys come in and ask to talk

Peter White, 1975

to the owner. I say I'm the manager and ask them what they want. They say they've come to collect. Hah! We busted their asses on the spot ... One of them was Peter White [Dunie Ryan's Bostonian cousin] who was a real mean son of a bitch."

By April 1976 Savard, a burly thirty-six-year-old detective, was assigned to the armed-robbery squad, where he was nicknamed "Dirty Harry." His specialty was tracking down and eliciting information (using both on- and off-the-book methods) from suspects in cases he was working on. He was itching to try his hand at breaking the Brink's robbery case that appeared to be going nowhere. He finally got his chance, and was given command by his division inspector to set up a seven-man squad created specifically to solve that crime. Because Savard suspected that the West End Gang was a major player in the robbery, he chose his team from Montreal's downtown Station 10, where the cops were either bilingual francophones or anglophones.

Apart from Savard, the unit consisted of sergeant-detective Jean-Pierre Gilbert, plus five constables who were all in their mid to late twenties: Yves Arpin, Eddie Gravely, Jean-Claude Malette, Kevin McGarr and Ross Trudel.

In order to keep their mission a secret (since it was known that there were some cops on the force who were friends of, and maybe even on the take from, the West End Gang), the group of seven gathered not in police headquarters but in a room at a nearby private club on St. James Street West, only a block or two away from where the Brink's robbery had occurred. They dubbed it Room 4.07, in reference to the Montreal courthouse room number where preliminary cases were heard. They called themselves "the Rubber Duck Squad," a name borrowed from the 1975 song "Convoy," a popular country-and-western tune at the time. They each had a code name (Savard's was "Big Ben") that they would use over the radio as they traveled in convoy in unmarked cars during their raids; the reason for this was to conceal their transmissions from cops in other units, including their backup mobile squad, whom they suspected might relay information to the West End Gang.

It was that particular gang that they intended to hit, and hit hard. "I knew that the Irish gang was the most likely to pull off the [Brink's] job," says Savard today, acknowledging that they may have been abetted by others. "So that's who we were going after ... Instead of just waiting around for tips from informants, we were going to hit the clubs and bars where the Irish hung out."

Which is precisely what the Rubber Duck Squad did night after night for the next few weeks. They were basically turning over rocks in order to see what crawled out. And in the process they managed to intimidate and turn a few informants. The raids, which were conducted mostly in clubs and motel bars in Montreal's downtown and NDG west end, achieved some limited success, but they also resulted in a few close calls for the squad.

**BIG BEN**                    **CONVOY**

**RUBBER DUCK CREW**

André Savard's Rubber Duck Squad ID badge

Their first target was Peg's Motel, on the corner of Westmore Avenue and St. Jacques Street in NDG. Its bar was a regular hangout for members of the West End Gang, at that time headed by Peter "Dunie" Ryan. Then in quick succession, the squad raided the nearby Raphael Motel, Nittolo's Garden Motel, and the Cavalier Motel on Upper Lachine Road. They also hit similar hangouts, such as Smitty's and the Country Palace on Sherbrooke Street West in NDG, as well as the downtown Sahara Club, Shack Club, Lorelli, The Little Club, The Irish Lancer, Molly McGuire's, Cat's Den Lounge, and Chez Giustini.

They also managed to surreptitiously place wiretaps on the pay phones of some of the clubs, occasionally done "off the book" without the legal hassle of having to first obtain a judge's warrant. "We knew guys who could climb telephone poles and clip into a couple of wires," grins one former member of the squad. All of these places had one thing in common: they were patronized by West End Gang members and hangers-on during the 1970s.

Most of the raids turned up nothing. But during some of them Savard and his boys found illegal handguns, small caches of drugs, or else individuals who either had outstanding warrants against them or, by virtue of simply being on the premises, were in violation of their parole conditions. The latter were hustled back to headquarters where some, to avoid being sent back to the can, begrudgingly supplied Savard and his team with bits and pieces of what they knew or had heard about the Brink's robbery, even if they themselves hadn't been directly involved in it. Thus, towards the end of April 1976, the evidence was slowly falling into place and a case was being built.

"We were raiding all those clubs and motels, putting on a lot of pressure, finding guns and drugs hidden in some of them," recalls Savard today, adding that it was "especially the Irish places, because that's where we were directing our investigation." And as in any police investigation, unearthing and flipping informants was a major part of their operation.

One of their first important informants was Fred Kadafi (an alias for a West End Gang errand-runner and drug-deliverer), whom they picked up on April 22, 1976, and brought in for questioning. It was he who supplied the name of John Sheppard, the provider of the .50-mm machine gun. But no strong evidence could be found against Sheppard at that time, and he was released after several hours of grilling.

The following night the Rubber Duckers, backed up by members of Montreal's mobile squad, again swarmed Peg's Motel at 1:45 a.m., taking its 10 bar patrons by surprise. Nothing of any significance was found in the bar itself, but when the cops used the motel's master keys to check the empty units, they found an arsenal of revolvers, sawed-off shotguns, boxes of ammunition, empty Royal Bank and Canadian

Imperial Bank of Commerce canvas money bags, stolen American Express travelers cheques, blank Quebec driver's permits, and a pound of hashish—all in Room 14.

Since the room wasn't registered to anyone, no arrests could be made. The motel's owner, Peg O'Neill, expressed complete shock and surprise about the cache. Yet Savard, who'd long suspected O'Neill of being a member of the West End Gang, was certain that the Rubber Duck Squad had stumbled into a bunker used by the gang for previous crimes—and perhaps for the Brink's robbery itself.

Understandably, the West End Gang did not take kindly to all of this heat. Also, some of the clubs that were raided were owned by people with municipal or Quebec political connections, and it wasn't long before calls were being made to the chief of police. As a consequence, Savard was called onto the carpet many times.

"Oh shit yeah, we were disturbing their business so we could get someone to talk . . . But what we were doing was out of the ordinary, not standard procedure that would be tolerated by the department," admits Savard, going on to say, "certain places we were hitting at the time belonged to a few politicians in the government, so a lot of complaints were made." Each morning following a raid Savard had to report to his headquarters captain, who was getting the heat from higher up. "He'd say, 'André, you gotta be careful. We're not supposed to be cowboys, and people are complaining.' So when I'd leave his office I didn't know if we were gonna be on the [Brink's] case the next day or not."

But the Rubber Duck Squad was left intact, primarily as a result of the favorable publicity it was getting from the media (particularly the weekly crime tabloid *Allô Police*, and Montreal's premier French daily newspaper *La Presse*) every time a bar was busted and guns or drugs were seized. Savard and his squad had the press and the public on their side, and the police department knew it.

Savard's informant, Fred Kadafi, next gave his handler the name of Julius Alter, a compulsive gambler and petty thief during the 1950s and '60s, and who later formed ties with the West End Gang in the 1970s. Kadafi told Savard that the word on the street was that it was the sixty-one-year-old Alter who'd laundered most of the Brink's job money through his contacts in Las Vegas.

On Monday, April 26, 1976, Savard and two of his men, armed with a search warrant, confronted a surprised and nervous Julius Alter in his apartment at 2400 Van Horn Avenue. The search of the apartment turned up nothing, but Savard left with a strong hunch that he had just met someone who was closely involved in the crime.

Eventually, the investigation started becoming a bit hairy and scary for the Rubber Duck Squad cops. The West End Gang, pissed off by the constant harassment, decided to fight back.

## Warning Shots

The first retaliatory shot came late Saturday night, May 1, 1976. Savard and his partner Jean-Pierre Gilbert were sitting in their unmarked car in the parking lot of Peg's Motel, preparing for yet another raid. Suddenly two high-powered .303 rifle bullets smashed through the car's rear window, narrowly missing both of them. According to a later informant, the sniper was John Slawvey, a West End Gang hitman who had been perched on a nearby rooftop.

Four nights later, on Wednesday, May 5, Constable Kevin McGarr was walking across the parking lot of the nearby Nittolo's Garden Motel when a late-model car, its lights off, roared towards him. McGarr leapt out of the way, narrowly escaping being hit. The driver was twenty-year-old Raymond Ricciardi, another West End Gang punk, who was arrested the next day on charges of attempting to murder a peace officer.

The following night, McGarr and his Rubber Duck partner Ross Trudel, acting on an anonymous tip, went to search The Little Club, a popular West End Gang hangout on Bishop Street. It was a trap. Trudel noticed a shotgun leaning in plain view against a backroom wall. He leaned over and started to pick it when it suddenly went off, its 12-gauge pellets fortunately missing both cops. Upon examination, they discovered that the trigger was wired to fire as soon as the gun was moved. But there was no way they could prove that the booby trap was meant for them.

Then, at 10 p.m. on Saturday, May 8, McGarr and Trudel, in search of someone they wanted to bring in for questioning, entered the upstairs Molly McGuire bar, another West End Gang watering hole, across from the Montreal Forum. Although the place was crowded, their suspect wasn't there. But while the cops were leaving the bar, two men and a woman at a table began cursing them and warning them to "drop the (Brink's robbery) investigation." As he was about to call for backup, McGarr was jumped by all three, and two other goons hurled Trudel down the club's stairs and barricaded the door.

McGarr was savagely beaten by his attackers, who punched and kicked him, broke a beer bottle over his head, and slashed open his cheek with the broken shards. He was unconscious with a fractured skull and bleeding profusely when the backup cops stormed the bar. By then the attackers had fled. McGarr was rushed by ambulance to Montreal General Hospital where he was stitched up and spent two weeks recovering from lacerations, broken bones and a mild concussion.

Now retired after 26 years on the force, where he went on to serve as a detective in its drug and anti-gang units, McGarr is currently based in Ottawa as president and CEO of the Canadian Air Transport Security Authority (CATSA). He still bears a facial scar from the Molly McGuire incident.

His fellow Rubber Duck squad members, enraged by such an audacious attack on one of their own, managed to track down and arrest the assailants within a matter of days, since the three had been identified by McGarr and Trudel as well known West End Gang associates. They were thirty-five-year-old Edward O'Neill, his thirty-three-year-old brother Thomas, and thirty-year-old Sheila Dalpe. All were taken to Station 10 for questioning.

One officer who participated in the interrogation of Edward O'Neill, an avowed cop-hating bully, admits that, given the circumstances, the procedure was "maybe a bit off the books ... one of those lock-the-front-door-and-turn-up-the-radio interrogations." Their prisoner appeared to have accidentally fallen down a flight of stairs and broken a few teeth by the time he appeared in court.

Eventually, McGarr's attackers were found guilty in Quebec court on reduced charges of "grievous and common assault on two police officers." On October 27, 1976, the O'Neill brothers were each sentenced to six weeks, and Dalpe to 10 days in a provincial jail.

Still, it would take another eight years before the Brink's robbery case could be closed once and for all. And during that time more blood would be shed between the Rubber Duck Squad and the perpetrators of the Crime of the Century.

CHAPTER 11

# Follow the Money

The Rubber Duck Squad was ruffling a lot of feathers among the West End Gang. One man, John Slawvey, aka Johnny Wilson, a suspected participant in the Brink's robbery, had a real hate on for André Savard, and had previously tried to assassinate him and his partner Jean-Pierre Gilbert while they were on surveillance in their car. The six-foot-four, 242-pound gorilla known as "Big John" was an armed robber, truck hijacker and occasional hitman for the West End Gang.

He was also a known cop killer, having slain a Montreal motorcycle cop, Jean-Guy Sabourin, during a $50,000 East End Gang payroll robbery from the downtown Simpson's department store by three men, including Donald Lavoie of the Dubois Gang, on December 17, 1971. Sabourin, thirty-eight, happened to be ticketing a car outside of the store's Metcalf Street entrance when the robbers burst out.

Slawvey mowed him down with a burst of machine-gun fire before he could even draw his revolver. Although there'd never been enough evidence to try him for the killing, both the good guys and the bad guys knew Slawvey had done it. Hell, he'd even boasted about it among his cronies.

On the afternoon of May 14, 1976, Savard was relaxing with his squad at their Room 4.07 Club meeting place when he was called to the phone. On the other end of the line was his trusty paid informant, Fred Kadafi, to tell him that it was John Slawvey who had fired at him and Gilbert in their car outside of Peg's Motel two weeks earlier. Savard asked him how he knew, and Kadafi said, "I got it straight from the horse's mouth." Slawvey had been bragging about it to him and others in a bar a few nights before.

Savard rounded up some of his squad and they decided to arrest Slawvey that night when he arrived home at his St. Regis Apartments building on 2555 Benny Street in NDG. They intended to bring him in to police headquarters, where they would question him about his suspected involvement in the Brink's case and the attempted murder of two police officers.

On that same night, Billy Morgan and a few of the West End Gang boys were sitting at a table in the bar of Peg's Motel, drinking and shooting the shit till the wee hours of the morning. As Morgan remembers it today, "There was Porky [Carl McGurnaghan], myself and Big John and a cluster of other thieves and gangsters . . . At about 3 a.m., Slawvey says, 'I'm going home,' and he got up to leave." He was going to his apartment, where his girlfriend, Heather Irving, was waiting for him. Morgan said later that McGurnaghan had convinced Slawvey to leave his gun with them, since he might be stopped for a traffic violation on the way home and be found in possession of an illegal firearm. So, to the best of Morgan's knowledge, Slawvey was unarmed when he left the bar. Of course, it's always possible he had another gun in his car.

Meanwhile, in the underground garage of the St. Regis Apartments, Savard and four heavily armed cops had been lying in wait since midnight to arrest Slawvey. Some of them were stationed behind concrete pillars, waiting for a walkie-talkie transmission from Eddie Gravely, who was slouched behind the wheel of an unmarked van parked across the street from the entrance to the garage, watching for Slawvey's arrival.

At 3:30 a.m. Gravely radioed the others that their target, driving a blue 1974 Chrysler Imperial, had just entered the garage and was alone in the car. The minutes ticked by as Slawvey parked, got out and headed for the elevators. Savard, armed with an M1 semi-automatic rifle, stepped out from behind a pillar to confront him about 20 feet away. He shouted: "Police! Don't move!" Then things became chaotic as bullets erupted from different directions.

According to Savard, "Slawvey said he wasn't armed, put his hands up and started to walk towards me. But then he makes a quick move towards his waist, and so I fired a shot." Savard's M1 jammed before he could get off another round. Immediately the cavernous underground garage was a cacophony of noise as three other cops, Jean-Pierre Gilbert, Lucien Lefebvre and Ross Trudel, emerged from behind concrete columns and fired 20 rounds of various-caliber bullets into Slawvey, leaving him a pulpy mess of punctured flesh at the age of thirty-eight. His ex-wife, Nancy Carter Slawvey, identified his body at the Montreal morgue two days later.

His killing was regarded by some as an ambush against an unarmed man. When the homicide detectives arrived on the scene, they found a fully loaded Hopkins & Allen .38-caliber revolver lying beside Slawvey's body, the gun that Savard said Big John had pulled out when confronted in the garage. "Well, of course there'd be [a] gun beside the body!" cynically observes one seasoned former police detective who was not part of the shootout.

On June 9, 1976, a coroner's inquest into the shooting cleared the police of any criminal wrongdoing. After hearing from several witnesses, Coroner Roch Heroux stated, "There is only one verdict to render: The police continue to protect themselves in the way they know best." He went on to say, "The day when we don't have people like Slawvey is the day when police won't be in danger and won't be under the obligation to protect themselves, [because] when police

John Slawvey, circa 1976

protect themselves they are protecting the public." Nevertheless, some remained suspicious about the circumstances surrounding Slawvey's death.

In 1995, Jean Belval, a disgruntled former Montreal police officer, testified before the Quebec Police Ethics Commission and to the Quebec Public Security minister about what he alleged were crimes committed by provincial and Montreal police officers during the 1970s, including perjured court testimony, as well as what he claimed was the "premeditated execution" of John Slawvey by André Savard and four other cops, as well as police "executions" of bank robbers Richard Blass in January 1975, and later Jean-Paul Mercier.

Belval was on medical leave, due to burnout, from the Montreal police department from 1984 until June 27, 1995, during which time he was involved in various real estate transactions, including a 1994–1996 Marché Central financial scandal. He was also being investigated for fraud and forgery in connection with loans obtained from his police credit union and other institutions. He declared bankruptcy in 1994, leaving creditors on the hook for between $6 and $9 million in unpaid loans. He was also accused of hacking into confidential Quebec Provincial Police database files on June 16, 1995, and was shortly after fired from the force. On November 3, 1998, he was found guilty of that charge and received a suspended sentence. On October 19, 2002, he was acquitted of the real estate fraud charges, in exchange for his dropping his obstruction-of-justice complaint before the Quebec Police Ethics Commission against provincial police officers Guy Tremblay and Roger Primeau, whom he'd accused of planting evidence in the form of incriminating documents against him.

Today, the fifty-eight-year-old Belval is written off as a "lunatic" and "shit-disturber" by cops who had once been his fellow officers.

One who harbors total contempt for him is former Montreal detective André Bouchard. "Belval was a prick; a piece of shit," Bouchard exclaims, adding, "I knew him when he was an undercover cop, and he actually thought he was a bad guy . . . We had to get him out of so much shit that he got into . . . And then he played the game, complaining that he couldn't work in uniform . . . They suspended him and did everything, and the fucking city had to pay him [severance pay] money. [Belval] was a real piece of crap, *ostie!*"

Around 10 p.m., the night after Slawvey's death, Savard was again called to the phone at the Rubber Duck Squad 4.07 Club. On the line was Sidney Leithman, Montreal's top defense lawyer for members of the West End Gang, the Dubois brothers and the Italian mafia, and a man whom Savard respected even though the two had often clashed verbally during court hearings. After a bit of chitchat, Leithman came to the point, saying, "There's a lot of talk going on and I think you should be careful, André. There's a lot of people not happy [about the death of Slawvey], and you can push only so much . . . Call this a warning if you want, but be careful and take care." Leithman then hung up the phone.

Savard was still mulling over Leithman's message when he was called to the phone an hour later. This time it was his district captain calling to say that they'd heard from a reliable source that the West End Gang had put out a $50,000 contract on Savard's life. This was the first time anyone had heard of someone openly gunning for a Montreal cop. That night two members of the Rubber Duck Squad accompanied Savard to his duplex bachelor apartment in Montreal North, where they slept on sofas with their guns within easy reach. The next morning Savard was booked under another name into the downtown Richelieu Hotel with two cops stationed outside his door. He lived there for two weeks, until the threat on his life seemed to have subsided. And everywhere he went there was always an armed plainclothes cop close beside or behind him.

Savard remembers those days as a time when "I'd pick up my car at the police station only after it had been checked out by the technical squad to see if there was a bomb under it." For months he also kept his gun handy, even sleeping with it within easy reach under his bed. "I was living at home with a big .44 Magnum I always carried around," he says. "I had had a chair blocking the front door; that's how I slept at night." Savard admits, "No matter how tough you are, it doesn't make a bit of difference if you think somebody's after your ass and wants to kill you."

The contract on Savard's life, which he still maintains was ordered by West End Gang leader Dunie Ryan, was never carried out, and he continued his pursuit of those who had committed the so-called Crime of the Century.

After taking down Slawvey, the Rubber Duck Squad continued investigating others involved in the robbery. Their first lead had come from Fred Kadafi, the informant who supplied them with Julius Alter's name in late April 1976. They now had the man whom they could prove had washed most of the Brink's loot in Las Vegas; consequently, they had a strong case against him. But it would take almost eight more years before Savard could gain Alter's confidence.

Meanwhile, on June 1, 1976, based on other names that Kadafi had supplied, the Rubber Duckers, backed up by flying squads from the Montreal and Quebec Provincial Police force, tracked down and arrested Réjean Duff, a twenty-year-old hood who had stolen the van used in the robbery, as well as Michel Pilon, thirty-eight, and East End Gang leader Roger Provençal, forty-two. They were arraigned in court the next day and charged with conspiracy in the heist. Provençal's brothers Bernard and Jacques, and sisters Françine and Murielle and their mother Grace, were also arrested but released without charges, even though about $75,000 in cash was found in their homes.

Réjean Duff, circa 1976

Pilon and Provençal were each released on $25,000 bail four days later. Duff, however, was kept in custody when one of the Montreal armed-robbery unit detectives told the court that releasing Duff would pose "a danger for him." How right he was.

When Duff had been picked up, he was happily tooling around in a brand-new Chevrolet Camaro SS that he'd recently purchased for $7,000 cash. After being grilled by police (during which time he claimed to have been beaten), Duff admitted to stealing the van that was used in the heist, but insisted that he'd not taken part in the actual robbery. He said he'd been paid $70,000 from the proceeds, some of which was seized during his arrest, and another $35,463 found hidden in the home of his uncle, Laurent Duff. He eagerly gave up the names of Roger Provençal and Michel Pilon as active participants in the crime.

That August, Duff, represented by defense attorney Frank Shoofey, was set free, since there was no evidence connecting him to the scene of the crime. But in January 1980, his lime-covered remains were found buried in a farmer's field in Ile d'Orléans near Quebec City.

Gilles Bourré, aka "the Priest," was a freelance hitman who, after being busted by the Quebec Provincial Police in a 1981 drug deal, became one of André Savard's informants and told him that he'd been paid $25,000 by Roger Provençal to whack Duff, which he did in June 1979 in order to keep him from testifying at Provençal's trial. Bourré, who got his nickname from wearing a priest's black Roman collar while calmly transacting assassination jobs and payment fees with interested clients in the pew of a dimly lit Quebec City church, "disappeared" sometime in the mid-1990s.

### A Break in the Case

The Rubber Duck Squad was disbanded in June 1976 and its members transferred back to their original stations and duties. But that did not stop Savard, now assigned to the Major Crimes Division, from behaving like a dog gnawing at a bone that still had some meat on it. Clearly, the $2.7-million robbery was an open case, despite the fact that Montreal police director René Daignault had boasted to the press immediately after the 1976 arrests, "We have solved the Brink's robbery." That would not be true for many more years, and even then it would remain unsolved with respect to recovering most of the loot or convicting its architects and principal participants. A lot more inside information was needed.

"Any cop will tell you," says Staff-Sergeant André Potvin, the current head of the RCMP's Montreal Drug Section, "informants are among our most important tools in solving a case." He speaks from many years of experience. It's a truism echoed by other cops, including Savard, who says, "I think you'll find that the best cop is the one with more informants. But there's a talent to getting the informant; it's not easy. And I think I had that talent, because when I worked in homicide and armed robbery, I had control of a lot of them."

Former bank robber and West End Gang member John Phillips admits, "One of the reasons I decided to go straight was because [fellow] thieves were becoming informants. People whom you knew for 30 years or more were suddenly ratting on you ... And then a lot of guys who weren't informants would be suspected of being informants, and their life would be on the line."

A hood becomes a "rat" for various reasons: money (all police departments have informant slush funds), a way in which to get a reduced sentence, moral guilt, revenge and the need to disappear under a new identity in a witness-protection program where the rat-hunters can't find them.

The latter two motives applied to Julius Alter, a grade-seven school dropout who was a compulsive gambler and petty thief in the 1940s through the 1960s, and a later associate of the West End Gang. He was arrested on November 25, 1980, for possession of $700,000 in stolen bonds and a stolen Renoir painting worth $300,000. He was found guilty on August 4, 1981, and due to his age of sixty-six and ill health received only 36 months probation and 120 hours of community service at Montreal's Jewish General Hospital. In January 1984, after he'd been fingered by the cops as someone who had laundered approximately $500,000 from the Brink's job, he was wounded by shards of flying glass when two bullets were fired through the window of his car, probably by John Sheppard. He realized that the West End Gang had put out a contract on him, and he was scared.

"So when he ends up in the hospital," recalls Savard, "he calls me and then became my informer. But he was not an open book; he was giving me some information, but not enough, so I kept leaning on him for more." Alter, quite understandably, was very paranoid. "So I used to meet him at the Côte-des-Neiges cemetery, *ostie*, he was so scared." There the two could talk with no one (who was alive, anyway) around to observe their meetings. Savard kept doling out small amounts from his informants' budget, and gradually elicited names of those connected in one way or another with the job: John Sheppard, John Slawvey and Dunie Ryan of the West End Gang, plus the brothers Roger and Bernard Provençal, Réjean Duff and Michel Pilon of the East End Gang. Alter, knowing there was a gangland contract hit on his head, moved from Montreal at the age of seventy in 1985, and has probably since died a natural death.

Prior to that, Philippe Vanier, a small-time hood, had approached the holdup squad in 1979 to say he had information about the robbery. He claimed that he had been cut out of the planned heist by Brink's employees Gilles Lachapelle and Roland Brunette. He was pissed off to the point where he agreed to wear a wire to meet with them and incriminate them in the crime. His recorded conversation with the two several days later proved to police that Lachapelle and Brunette had at least been accessories to the crime. A search warrant turned up $12,000 in cash and Olympic gold coins at Brunette's St. Hubert home, but nothing on Lachapelle's property. Based on their incriminating taped conversation with Vanier, the two were arrested and charged with collusion in the robbery. Their trial by jury began on December 3, 1979, and on December 21 both were found guilty and sentenced to four years in prison.

Another break in the case came in August 1981 when Bernard Provençal, Roger's younger brother, was sentenced to nine years in prison after having been found guilty of drug trafficking. His conviction stemmed from a bust the previous October when he'd been arrested at his St. Bruno home, across the St. Lawrence River from Montreal, by the RCMP for conspiring to import 10 kilos of cocaine into Canada. Desperate to get a reduced sentence, he said he could supply information about the Brink's robbery as well as other crimes, even if it meant testifying against his own brother. The RCMP alerted the Montreal robbery squad detectives, who questioned him at length. Bernard hadn't taken part in the heist but knew of its details from what his older brother had told him. He gave up the names of his brother Roger, Gilles Lachapelle, Roch Carignan, John Sheppard and Julius Alter. As an added bonus, Bernard also gave them names of those who'd been involved in an unsolved $2.2-million robbery from an Alliance (now known as Securicor) armored truck at 51 St. James Street West in Montreal that previous March 26.

In exchange for his cooperation, Bernard's sentence was reduced to two and a half years. He was released in 1984 and, under the name of Paul Bernard Robinson, settled in Granby, Quebec, dealing in used cars. But in March 1985 he was again arrested, this time in connection with stolen cars. He served a couple of years, but was nabbed again in early 1990 on robbery and murder charges. After serving more time, he was re-arrested in July 1999 and charged, along with two others, with participating in five bank robberies in Drummondville, Quebec. In 2001, after two years behind bars, he pleaded guilty and was sentenced to six more years in prison.

Paul Gill, a racetrack driver and Roger Provençal's brother-in-law, had been busted by the RCMP with Bernard in October 1980 on the same drug-importation charge. Gill, known as "the Chemist" for his ability to produce high-grade hashish from bulk marijuana in a Laval laboratory just north of Montreal, was also turned in August 1983 in exchange for a reduced sentence, and agreed to testify against Roger about both the Brink's and Alliance robberies.

Soon after, another unexpected informant popped up. Claude Grenier, a member of the Dubois brothers, had had his left arm blown off by a shotgun blast in July 1981, and was found bleeding to death on a downtown Montreal street by paramedics. He suspected that his unidentified assailant was a member of the West End Gang, and he knew they'd try again. So while recovering in hospital, he asked to speak with Savard, hoping to get police protection. Savard made it clear that in exchange Grenier would have to reveal everything he knew. Grenier then told him about a Brink's truck holdup that he and two others had carefully cased and were planning to pull off soon at a Quebec City shopping mall. He said their plan was to ambush the two armed guards with automatic weapons while they were transferring money from their truck to a bank, and then make a fast getaway. He named Bruce Phillips (no relation to John Phillips) as the leader of their crew and the one who'd set up the prospective robbery.

Warrants were immediately issued for Phillips and the other suspect, who were quickly arrested in Quebec City by the provincial police and brought back to face trial in Montreal on charges of conspiracy to commit armed robbery. They were found guilty in 1982 and given a four-year sentence. While being led out of court at his sentencing hearing, Phillips, a 230-pound brute with a legendary nasty temper, turned to Savard and shouted, "I know where you live with your family, and I'll get you!"

Savard shrugged it off, knowing that Phillips would be locked away for most of the next four years. But within a few months Phillips was set free, following a successful appeal for a new trial. Savard was once again sleeping with a .44 Magnum within easy reach under his bed, especially since he was now a married man with a two-year-old son. But three days after Phillips' release, Paul Galliano, an SQ detective, called Savard from Quebec City with the news that Phillips and his girlfriend had just been found dead, lying side by side in bed in their apartment. Phillips had been shot through the mouth with the gun lying next to him. A coroner's report later ruled it a murder-suicide.

## "It's the Big Fish We Want"

In early 1983 the Brink's robbery, now in the hands of two other detectives, was still unsolved, even though informants had led the cops to some pieces of the puzzle. They had a file full of sworn affidavits from people like Bernard Provençal, Rejean Duff, Paul Gill, Fred Kadafi, Julius Alter and Claude Grenier. But none of those men had been at the scene of the crime. The investigators knew they needed to put more pieces together before having a strong enough case that would stand up in court.

Savard, worried that the case would end up cold, asked his captain to be reassigned to it. He was given permission, although with the warning to refrain from any of those "cowboy style" raids on bars. Two constables were assigned to work with him, one being Eddie Gravely of the former Rubber Duck Squad.

At this time, Gilles Lachapelle was nearing the end of his four-year prison term at the La Macaza minimum-security institution, 100 miles north of Montreal. Savard decided to pay him a visit. So far Lachapelle had only admitted to his own involvement in the robbery, refusing to incriminate anyone else. Savard filled him in on the confessions of Bernard Provençal and Réjean Duff, and the fact that Roger Provençal had arranged for Duff's execution. He also pointed out that once out of jail, Lachapelle and even his wife Luong could be Roger's next targets in order to keep him from testifying. "It's the big fish we want," said Savard, "and you can help us." In return for Lachapelle testifying against Roger, Savard promised him complete police protection and the opportunity to relocate with his wife under a new identity. He left the prisoner, telling him to think it over. A few days later Lachapelle called the detective and said he was ready to testify. Savard drove back up to La Macaza where he finally got a full first-hand account of how the robbery was planned and executed, as well as the names of others who were involved back in January through March of 1976.

Savard next visited Paul Gill in prison to urge him to testify against his brother-in-law, with the guarantee of police protection while they moved his family to a nearby safe location. Gill took the bait and gave up the name of Bernie Colangelo, Roger Provençal's chauffeur and "homme à tout faire," a man not part of the Brink's robbery, but who was involved with Roger in the March 26, 1981, $2.2 million Alliance armored truck robbery. In exchange for their freedom, Gill and Colangelo later testified against Provençal and others.

The next target was Jean Charbonneau, Roger Provençal's accountant, who laundered money from his various drug deals and the Brink's robbery. He was picked up in late 1983 by Eddie Gravely while driving his Cadillac to work one morning, and taken to an empty classroom in an abandoned east-end Montreal school, where

Savard was waiting to grill him. While Charbonneau had not been a direct participant, the detectives had found approximately $200,000 from the Brink's robbery stashed in cereal boxes at his Laval home. Savard, employing the same tactic that he'd used on the others, told Charbonneau about the information they'd already received, and that it was clear that Provençal intended to get rid of anyone who might have evidence against him. After being offered police protection and the chance to relocate with his wife and two children in Florida, Charbonneau signed a statement admitting his role of hiding and washing some of the Brink's robbery loot. He also told Savard that he'd attended a meeting in January 1976 with Roger and John Sheppard where they had discussed how best to procure a .50-caliber machine gun to be used in the robbery.

The Major Crimes Division now had four reliable witnesses ready to testify on behalf of the Crown against Roger Provençal and others who were actually present at the Brink's robbery. The trials took place in early 1984, resulting in different outcomes.

In January 1984, fifty-four-year-old Gilles Lachapelle and forty-three-year-old Roland Brunette pleaded guilty to their involvement and later testified against Provençal. They had two more years added to their previous sentences, and both appear to have stayed clean after serving their time.

Roch Carignan also pleaded guilty on January 25, 1984, and was sentenced to eight years in prison. He was paroled on April 20, 1989 and began working as a volunteer for the Old Brewery Mission, a downtown homeless shelter. On the evening of Tuesday, November 19, 1991, an armed stranger rang the bell at his home in Lavaltrie, 20 miles east-southeast of Montreal, and fired four bullets from a .9-mm machine pistol into him, wounding him seriously before fleeing. Carignon survived, but his assailant was never apprehended.

Later that month, Michel Pilon, forty-six, pleaded guilty to the robbery, and was sentenced to two years on top of a four-year drug charge conviction he was already serving.

John Sheppard was set free due to insufficient evidence against him. Jerry Wadsworth, one of the jurors in Sheppard's February 1984 trial, today recalls that the Crown had "only circumstantial evidence" against him, so according to the judge's instructions, "we had to find him not guilty." Wadsworth remembers that the names of Roger Provençal and Paul Gill "repeatedly came up" during Sheppard's trial, and "we heard a lot of [police] wiretapped conversations between them." But, he adds, "none of it was conclusive enough." He and his fellow jurors were therefore unable to render a guilty verdict against Sheppard.

The trial of "the big fish," Roger Provençal, began on March 12, 1984, with 44 witnesses testifying against him. The Crown wound up its case two weeks later. Provençal's defense lawyer, apart from sarcastically pointing out that all of the Crown's witnesses were convicted felons of one sort or another, offered no witnesses in support of his client who himself declined to take the stand. It was now up to the sequestered jury to deliberate and deliver a verdict. One of the Crown's main witnesses, Roger's accountant Jean Charbonneau, died of a heart attack in Florida soon after delivering his testimony.

At 10 a.m. on March 30, 1984, exactly eight years after the Brink's robbery, the jurors filed into the courtroom where they declared Roger Provençal not guilty. The assembled cops, journalists and trial witnesses were aghast. One seasoned court reporter turned to Savard and said, "This is the worst miscarriage of justice I have ever seen!" Savard today shakes his head and says, "It reminds me of the [1995] outcome of the O.J. Simpson trial."

Thus ended Montreal's "Crime of the Century," with less than $500,000 of its $2.8 million in stolen loot ever recovered. Most of that, amounting to $290,000, was found in June 1980, hidden in the basement of a Greene Avenue home in lower Westmount owned by indigent eighty-four-year-old Fred Meilleur, a former friend of John Slawvey, who had probably stashed it there without Meilleur's knowledge. In fact, Meilleur was as astounded by the discovery as were the cops, and later commented, "Had I known I was rich, I wouldn't have bothered being on welfare."

But what irritated Savard and his Rubber Duck partners the most was the fact that after eight long years, it was only the minor players from the East End or West End Gang who were eventually convicted.

Members of the Rubber Duck Squad and other Montreal detectives being feted by the Brink's company, 1986

Roger "the Fat Man" Provençal, whom Savard figures "probably got about a million from that robbery," went on to be heavily involved in the drug business in Montreal's East End, and was often seen meeting with various members of the mafia, the West End Gang and the Hells Angels. He later served time on assorted robbery and drug charges before being released from prison in 1989.

On September 2, 1991, the corpse of his right-hand man, Robert Décarie, was found with a bullet through the head in the trunk of his Mercedez Benz in Laval. Then it was the Fat Man's turn. On November 9, 1992, Roger Provençal at the age of fifty-seven was assassinated by two rival East End Gang members in a hail of machine-gun bullets as he was leaving a store on Beaubien Street. His murder was never solved, and there were few mourners at his funeral. His brother Bernard, interviewed in prison, simply said "[He] died like he lived; with violence."

Savard, bitter over the not-guilty verdict at Roger's trial, retired from the police force in 1992 at the age of fifty-two and moved with his wife Nicole and son Patrick to Roanoke, Virginia. But they later returned to Montreal, where today Savard is a partner with retired Montreal police drug squad sergeant-detective John Westlake in a successful private investigation business.

CHAPTER 12

# An Uncommon Thief

If ever there was an achievement award for a Montreal thief with the most imagination and a flair for dramatic escapes, it would have to go to Rory Shayne. Despite his Irish-sounding name, Shayne was actually of German descent, having been born Berkhard Bateman on March 23, 1951, in Hamburg, Germany. At the age of two, he was abandoned by his German mother and Canadian father and placed in a Hamburg orphanage and then in a foster home, where he was severely maltreated. At the age of four, his foster mother slashed him in a fit of rage with a kitchen knife, and then tried to cover up her crime by scalding his cheek and neck with boiling water, claiming that he'd pulled a pot off the stove himself. He still carries an ear-to-ear scar and the horrific memories to this day.

In 1960 he was adopted by a Bellville, Ontario, couple and he moved to Canada where he acquired the name of Rory Shayne. But he was a troubled youth with a long life of crime ahead of him. His first conviction was at the age of twelve when he was sent to juvenile court in Mount Forest, Ontario, for petty theft. In 1967, he was found guilty of auto theft and several break and enters in Ontario, and received a six-month sentence. In February 1970, he was arrested for shoplifting at a Toronto Eaton's department store and served another month in jail.

After his release, Shayne, nineteen and sporting shaggy blond hair, headed west to British Columbia, where he upped the ante on his criminal career, first by robbing several Vancouver hotel check-in clerks of a few hundred dollars of cash in their tills. Then, on September 24, 1970, with a rifle in hand, he brazenly strode into a branch of the Canadian Imperial Bank of Commerce in Victoria, British Columbia, and robbed it of $8,050. He escaped in a hijacked taxi, meanwhile shooting at and wounding two policemen who were pursuing him. His cab ride ended up at a nearby marina in Saanich, where he commandeered a 22-foot sailboat at gunpoint and ordered its owners, Peter Wells and his wife El Rae of Portland, Oregon, and their friend Roger Smith of Vancouver, to cast off the lines and head south.

Twelve hours later, as the sloop was sailing down the Pacific coast of Washington, it was intercepted by the U.S. Coast Guard cutter *Richmond Beach* near the San Juan Islands. Realizing he was hopelessly outgunned, Shayne gave up, much to the relief of his three terrified onboard hostages. He was jailed in Seattle and later deported to Victoria, where he faced charges of armed robbery, attempted murder and kidnapping.

On October 20, 1970, after pleading guilty, Shayne was given a 12-year cumulative sentence which he began serving in British Columbia. In 1975 he was transferred first to the Archambault maximum-security and then to the Leclerc medium-security penitentiaries in Laval, just north of Montreal, to serve the rest of his sentence.[1]

---

1 I first met Rory in the fall of 1978 while I was teaching English literature and creative writing in a Dawson College program at the Leclerc prison. He was one of the brightest and most imaginative of the 15 or so students in the class, and during our twice-weekly sessions would show me short stories and film treatments that he had written in his cell. When on one mid-December day I arrived at the prison and Rory was not in class, the other students gleefully informed me that Rory had "gone over the wall."

On December 14, 1978, the twenty-eight-year-old Shayne was granted an escorted day pass (known as a Code 26) to go shopping in Montreal. This is a standard pre-release perk given by the National Parole Board to convicts who are nearing the end of their incarceration, in order to help introduce them back into society.

Shayne's escort was Audette LeCorre, a prison psychologist who also happened to be the wife of Michel LeCorre, director of Quebec's regional federal penitentiaries. At the Alexis Nihon Plaza in Westmount, Shayne excused himself to use the men's room, from which he never emerged, at least not through the door where LeCorre was patiently waiting for him. He had given her the slip through another exit and became a fugitive on the run for the next three months, during which time he busied himself by robbing banks, trust companies and jewelry stores, either alone or with various accomplices.

One of those was John Phillips, who'd been Shayne's fellow inmate at both Archambault and Leclerc in the mid-1970s, and John pulled off some jobs with him after his escape. Today, the seventy-two-year-old Phillips, who has long since abandoned his life of crime, describes Shayne as "a really smart guy" but also "fucking crazy." In fact, says Phillips, Shayne was technically not a member of the West End Gang, since Dunie Ryan, its leader at the time, considered him a loose cannon and wanted nothing to do with him. "Dunie once said to me, 'John, if you don't get away from him, you're both gonna get shot to death [by the cops] on the street . . . I'm telling you, it's crazy what you guys are doing,' because me and Rory were holding up a lot of banks together." This was during the time that Shayne was on the run in the winter of 1978-79.

In January 1979 they robbed an estimated $50,000 in cash and travelers cheques from the Provincial Bank of Canada on St. Catherine Street across from Eaton's department store, hitting it three times in the space of a month. During two of those robberies, Rod Sutherland, a former Archambault fellow convict, was also on the job. His role was to assist their escape while they fled across the street to Eaton's and down the stairs that led to an underground Metro station, should any bank guards or cops be on their tail. "We both ran down the staircase and passed Rod who [one time] had a shopping bag full of marbles" and [another time] had "a five-gallon can of oil" that he would pour onto the stairs behind the fleeing bandits. "If anyone was chasing us and runs down those stairs, they're gonna kill themselves for sure," chuckles Phillips. The two thus managed to make a clean escape during all three robberies.

But Phillips was becoming uncomfortable with Shayne and his wild bank-robbery methods. "I told him, I says, 'Look, we gotta break up. I talked to the boys [of the West End Gang] and they say that it's too fucking dangerous and we're gonna get blown away together.'"

Phillips' other concern was that Shayne was a serious gun nut. "Every time we made any money, he spent [his share] on buying more guns. He had a bullet-proof vest, a bazooka and anything that was for sale. So if he grabbed 10 or 15 thousand bucks in a fucking score with me, he'd spend it on guns." Phillips adds, "I said to him 'the only thing you want to do is to arm yourself, and you got more fucking guns than Heinz has got pickles already. So we're gonna break up; I'm packing it in.'"

Rory Shayne, 1979

## Helicopter Heist

And pack it in he did. But Shayne now had a new accomplice, his thirty-six-year-old girlfriend Micheline Rachel Dubiel from Montreal's West Island suburb of Pierrefonds. She was a 1970s version of Montreal's 1960s Machine Gun Molly, or perhaps Rory's modern-day partner of Bonnie and Clyde. Together the two pulled off several bank heists, including one of the most audacious getaways the local cops had ever encountered.

At 10 a.m. on Friday, February 23, 1979, Rory and Micheline arrived at Cartierville Airport in Montreal's Saint Laurent district and climbed into the back seat of an Olympic Helicopters Ltd. Hughes

396HS helicopter that they had previously chartered and paid $636 for, ostensibly, a two-hour round trip to Quebec City. Both were stylishly dressed in leather pants and jackets; Rory all in black and Micheline all in red. And both took canvas tote bags on board.

Their pilot was thirty-two-year-old Nguyen Huu Lee, who had immigrated to Montreal from Saigon in 1976. He was a seasoned pilot, having spent five years in the South Vietnamese Air Force, flying Chinook and Huey helicopters in the early 1970s during the Vietnam War, where he had accumulated some 4,000 hours in combat missions against the Viet Cong. He had begun working for Olympic only three weeks prior to this flight.

According to Lee's later court testimony, minutes after takeoff Shayne pulled a Colt .45 out of his bag and showed it to him. Micheline also put a gun to his head. Shayne reached over and ripped off Lee's radio headset and ordered him to fly east and land on a municipal golf course near the Olympic Stadium. Once on the ground, Shayne got out and climbed into the right front seat beside the pilot and, taking a chrome-plated machine gun out of his bag, said, "Today you have to take me to rob some banks." Lee flung open his door and tried to make a run for it through the snow-covered field. But a warning burst from Shayne's weapon brought him up short, and he trudged back to the aircraft where Shayne handcuffed one of his wrists to the steering column yoke of the helicopter. Micheline meanwhile was busy pasting blue and white Montreal police decals on the fuselage of the helicopter.

They then ordered Lee to fly to the Place Côte Vertu shopping mall in Saint Laurent and set down in the parking lot facing a branch of the Royal Bank of Canada. With Micheline holding a gun behind Lee's head, Shayne hopped out with his machine gun and a gym bag, and within minutes scooped up $11,752 from the startled bank cashiers. The many shoppers at the mall thought they were witnessing either a police operation or an action movie in the making. Shayne dashed back to the helicopter with the bag of loot and ordered Lee to take off. He instructed him to fly a few miles east to the Sauvé metro station and to land on the street behind it. The two desperados then made a clean getaway via the subway. It was a cleverly planned and executed bank robbery and escape—unlike any that the Montreal police armed-robbery squad had dealt with before.

But within 10 days, based on fingerprints they'd taken from the helicopter, the Montreal cops knew who the fugitives were and arrested them on Friday, March 2, in their St. Léonard apartment. During a search of the premises, police found a Sten MK2 .9mm submachine gun, a .12-caliber sawed-off rifle, four different-caliber revolvers and enough ammunition to start a war. The two were arraigned the next day without bail.

On April 9, 1979, after having pleaded guilty to robbery, hijacking and kidnapping, Micheline Dubiel was sentenced to five years in prison. The feisty Dubiel escaped from the Tanguay women's prison on July 2, 1979. She was captured soon after on Gouin Boulevard by the Quebec Provincial Police, but two weeks later escaped once more, only again to be recaptured. In 1983 she was tried and found guilty of escaping custody and forced to serve out the rest of her sentence. According to John Phillips she later became the girlfriend of Talbot "Toby" Murphy and eventually the wife of Ronald "Ronny" McCann, both of whom were prominent West End Gang members in the late 1980s.

As for Shayne, he had many more years to serve. But he had no intention of doing the time if he could help it. Following his arrest with Dubiel, he too was charged with armed robbery, hijacking and kidnapping. At Shayne's trial on April 4, the helicopter pilot Nguyen Huu Lee described the "two terrifying hours" he'd experienced that February morning, saying that it was scarier than anything he'd faced as a pilot during the Vietnam War. Today, his widow, who still lives in Montreal, says that her husband, who died in 1986 in a helicopter crash while working for an oil-exploration company in Sudan, "always talked about that robbery as something very frightening."

On April 15, Shayne was sentenced to 12 years for the helicopter job. But, to the Crown's dismay, the judge made it concurrent with the 20 years he was already serving for the Victoria, British Columbia, crimes, which meant there was no extra prison time added. Nevertheless, Shayne still had a future trial date ahead of him to answer charges in the six other robberies he'd pulled off during his ten weeks of freedom from Leclerc.

Meanwhile, he was locked up in the maximum-security St. Vincent de Paul Penitentiary in Laval where, on August 25, 1980, he once again made a bid for freedom. This time he was accompanied by eight other convicts, most of whom were serving life for murder. Armed with smuggled-in guns, they managed to take four unarmed guards and six instructors hostage in the prison's welding and sewing workshops. They then bolted out to the prison courtyard, where they commandeered a service truck, seizing its two occupants and intending to crash the truck through the prison gate. But they were met by a hail of rifle fire from the prison towers, which killed one of the inmates, John Connearney. The others retreated against a wall, holding their hostages in front of them as human shields.

It became a Mexican standoff, with the convicts demanding drugs and a van in which to drive out of the prison. The authorities replied with a definite no, and decided to starve them out by refusing them food and water. Eventually, at 10:30 a.m. on August 28, the would-be escapees, who could see dozens of high-powered rifles pointed at them from every angle by guards and Quebec Provincial Police officers on the prison towers and roofs, gave up after a 74-hour siege. All of them were then confined to six months in solitary confinement.

In December 1980, Shayne was back in a Montreal court, this time facing charges on the other robberies he'd committed in January and February 1979, which had netted him some $260,000. Following a two-week trial, during which tellers from various banks pointed him out as the one who'd shoved a gun in their face, he was found guilty and given 18 years, to run concurrently with his other sentences. Before pronouncing sentence, the judge asked Shayne if he wished to make a statement. The prisoner rose and morosely said: "I never had a chance. From the age of nineteen I've been locked up in penitentiaries . . . I don't know anything but the inside of a prison cell." There were no tears shed in court by the bank-teller and customer witnesses whom he'd terrified with his gun.[2]

On December 15, 1981, Shayne's arraignment began in Room 4.05 of Montreal's Palais de Justice, on charges of complicity in his role in the attempted break-out and hostage-taking at the St. Vincent de Paul Penitentiary. Shayne, seated in the prisoner's box and shackled in leg irons, suddenly made an audacious attempt to gain freedom. Seated near him was Gary Martin, a twenty-seven-year-old wet-behind-the-ears defense lawyer who'd recently been assigned to the case.

As Quebec Superior Court Justice Paul Martineau entered the courtroom, Shayne jumped to his feet and aimed a gun at him, clicking it twice. A clerk pushed the judge back into his chambers and Shayne then waved the weapon at two court constables, Michel Miron and Claude Manseau, and the court stenographer, Colette Lapointe, who had dived under her desk. He then screamed to the guards to unshackle his legs. But everyone was frozen on the spot.

Martin, who still vividly remembers the bizarre scene, immediately went over and tried to calm down his client. "And then he points the gun at me," recalls Martin. "I figured it was a phony gun carved out of wood or soap; I was sure he wasn't packing a real piece . . . I was more concerned about the guards who had big Colt .38s, and I was between them and Rory . . . So I asked him, 'What are you going to do now, shoot your lawyer?' Because he was pointing [the gun] at me at the time, he was so frustrated. I thought it was all part of the act, you know . . . So I wasn't scared of Shayne at all; I was sure it wasn't a real gun. But I was worried about the guards." The standoff lasted for about five minutes until, according to Martin, "Shayne sort of turned around and the two

---

2 On January 15, 1979, I was about to enter my branch of the Bank of Montreal at Place du Canada when I saw the outside lobby roped off with police tape. I asked a cop what was happening and he told me there'd been a robbery and that the bank was closed. The next morning I read in the newspaper that the suspected culprits were my former student Rory Shayne and Micheline Dubiel, both armed and holding about 20 employees and customers at gunpoint lying on the floor while they scooped up about $28,000 in cash and travelers cheques. Almost two years later I ran into Shayne in jail again, not having seen him since his December 1978 escape. I wryly noted that he'd been pretty busy since I last saw him in class, and told him that one of the banks he'd robbed was one in which I would have been one of those customers on the floor had I been there half an hour earlier. I pointed out that I would have recognized him, and asked him what would he have done. Rory then gave me one of his lop-sided grins and answered, "I guess I would've had to fuckin' shoot you." To this day I still don't know whether he was serious or just pulling my chain.

guards jumped him at that point . . . And his gun went off . . . It went click-click, but misfired, and the bullets just fell to the ground." It was, in fact, a real gun: a four-inch-long Italian-made .22-caliber starter's pistol, modified to shoot real bullets.

Sergeant-Detective André Savard happened to be in the hallway outside of Room 4.05 that day, waiting to testify at another trial. He recalls, "A Crown attorney came rushing out, shouting, 'There's a guy in there and he wants to shoot the judge!' So I went in there with my gun, but the guards had [already] disarmed him . . . This guy was really nuts."

Perhaps not nuts, but definitely desperate. How Shayne, who had been carefully searched before entering the courtroom, managed to procure and hide a gun remains a mystery. One theory was that it had been previously taped by someone under the seat of the prisoner's box. The other possibility, which Martin accepts, is that Shayne had hidden it in his rectum while either in the Parthenais Detention Centre or the courthouse holding cell. "Knowing Rory," says Martin today, "I always believed he had it there . . . and it misfired because the bullets were damp from being up his ass." Martin adds that Shayne's intention "was obviously to escape from the courthouse. The hostages were only a means to the end."

Shayne was immediately sent to the CDC (Correctional Development Centre) a super-maximum penitentiary in Laval. Nine days later Martin visited him there. "I went to square it out with him. I told him, 'You son of a bitch; you tried to shoot me, you fuck! I didn't know it was a real gun.' He laughed it off . . . But then I felt bad for the guy, because it was Christmas Eve and he didn't even know it. He was in solitary, no windows, no nothing in there. He was wearing a one-piece orange suit and sneakers with no laces." Martin adds, "That's the last time I remember seeing Rory Shayne, except when I testified at his trial."

Shayne's final trial took place in April 1982 to face charges of attempted murder and using a firearm to hold hostages while trying to flee the Palais de Justice courthouse. Ironically, the hearing was in the same Room 4.05 from which he'd tried to escape. On April 21, 1982, after several days of testimony from Justice Paul Martineau who said the accused had tried to fire at him, plus testimony from other witnesses, Shayne was found guilty and sentenced to life in prison. Following several appeals, his final one was rejected by the Supreme Court of Canada on June 18, 1984.

He spent the next few years in various federal institutions, and was last recorded in the SHU (Special Handling Unit) of the Prince Albert, Saskatchewan, Federal Penitentiary in 1986. There are several versions from former inmates of what later became of him, including that he was killed during a prison escape, although there is no record of that. According to Billy MacAllister, who was his friend at the Archambault, Leclerc and Millhaven penitentiaries, Shayne was deported to Germany sometime in the late 1980s. Since it doesn't appear that Shayne ever legally became a Canadian citizen, his former lawyer, Gary Martin, tends to agree. "Back in those days," he says, "if you had a life sentence you would be eligible for parole after seven years." He adds, "Right after the seven [the Canadian authorities] would have thrown him on a plane and sent him back to where he came from."

So today Rory Berkhard Bateman Shayne might be languishing in a German jail finishing up the rest of his life sentence. Or, perhaps more likely, he's up to his old tricks, this time planning a major score against the Deutsche Bundesbank.

CHAPTER 13

# The King of Coke

I f anyone can be dubbed the Godfather of Montreal's so-called Irish mafia during its heyday of the 1970s and '80s, that person is Frank Peter Ryan, a charismatic and affable Irishman who commanded the allegiance and respect of dozens of his cohorts, most of whom were anglophone Irish who, like Ryan, grew up in working-class neighborhoods in the city's downtown and southwestern enclaves.

Ryan, an only child, was born on June 10, 1942, and raised by his devout Catholic mother, May, on Milton Street in Montreal's "McGill Ghetto" after his alcoholic father, Frank Sr., abandoned them in 1945. His mother referred to him as (Frank) "Junior," which as a toddler he mispronounced "Dunie." It stuck and would become his nickname for life.

Intelligent, yet bored with school, Dunie dropped out at the age of sixteen, and formed a local street gang which engaged in relatively

Dunie Ryan, circa 1980

minor crimes such as break and enters, shoplifting, and thefts from transport trucks, often on the bustling St. Lawrence Boulevard (aka "the Main"), just around the corner from his home. He was arrested several times, usually for being in possession of stolen goods, and by the age of twenty-one had accumulated two years off-and-on in juvenile detention centers and the St. Vincent de Paul Penitentiary.

Once out of jail, Ryan had higher ambitions than merely stealing and fencing appliances or fur coats from delivery trucks and local warehouses. He wanted to make a real score. So on August 23, 1966, at the age of twenty-four, he and three companions, twenty-three-year-old William "Billy" MacAllister, twenty-six-year-old René Lachapelle, and twenty-five-year-old Clifford Piva, drove down to Lynn, Massachusetts, to hold up the Essex County Bank and Trust Company, which Dunie's Bostonian cousin, Peter White, had assured him was ripe for the picking. Their point man and local accomplice was William Breen, a former police officer from the nearby town of Somerville.

They pulled off the job the next day, and scooped up $49,953 from the bank's tills. But it turned out that Ryan and his fellow bandits were themselves ripe for the picking, as they were arrested by Lynn police within hours of the armed robbery. Ryan was soon after put on trial, found guilty and sentenced to 15 years in prison for his role in the heist. His accomplices received similar sentences.

After serving a third of his time in an Indiana federal penitentiary, Ryan was paroled and deported back to Canada in the fall of 1972. That December 2 he married Evelyn Lemieux, an attractive redheaded French-Canadian girl from Quebec's Gaspésie region, and the two moved into a Ville LaSalle duplex in Montreal's southwest corner. However, Ryan had no intention of settling down to family life or seeking legal employment. In fact, he never held an honest job during his entire short lifetime.

Determined to make a living by doing what he knew best, Ryan quickly financed himself by pulling off several downtown jewelry store robberies, for which he was never caught. He also renewed acquaintances with some of his former colleagues, as well as other Irish and French-Canadian thieves, most of whom regularly met to drink, play pool, shoot the shit and plan future scores at Smitty's, a dingy Sherbrooke Street Country and Western bar in Notre-Dame-de-Grâce in the city's west end. By dint of his charm and easy-going personality, Ryan soon became the ex officio leader of what some referred to as the "Irish mafia," which actually was more of a cooperative than a mafia-style oligarchy. He was an astute businessman, and he invested the take from his jewelry store scores by fronting money for other crooks planning various jobs, as well as lending money at usurious rates, laundering stolen cash and negotiable securities for a 10-percent commission, and buying stolen merchandise which he would sell for a hefty profit.

By the mid-1970s Dunie was accumulating some serious coin. Naturally, given his record, the Montreal police were watching him like a hawk, and had even wiretapped the pay phone in Smitty's bar, where he conducted much of his business. Yet they managed to nail him only once, for a 1977 break and enter, which netted him a mere 61-day jail term. It would be the last time Ryan would see the inside of a Canadian prison as an adult.

In the fall of 1979, Ryan was subpoenaed to testify before the CECO (la Commission d'Enquête sur le Crime Organisé) tribunal to explain the source of his wealth, since he hadn't held a legitimate job since being deported back to Canada. The tribunal had been mandated to examine the extent of organized crime in the province. During his appearance, Ryan simply told the commissioners that he'd left the United States after his prison stint with some $100,000 stashed away from bank robberies and other thefts there, and that he'd parlayed that into the money-lending business in Montreal. The panel members, their eyes undoubtedly rolled back in sarcastic disbelief, could come up with no incriminating evidence to disprove his claim.

### "Mother" Ryan

By 1980, Ryan, at the age of thirty-eight, was in the catbird seat. He had now set up shop in the bar of the Cavalier Motel on St. Jacques Street West, where an assortment of Anglo-Irish and francophone petty crooks, smash-and-grab artists, truck hijackers, safecrackers, bank robbers, pimps and protection racketeers arrived daily to pay homage and do business with him in a place they dubbed "the Zoo." For it was Dunie who could launder their money and fence the pilfered goods from their various robberies, always, of course, with a healthy commission to himself. Nevertheless, more than his business acumen, it was his easy-going manner and charm that had the local hoods gravitating towards him. He was low-key and non-threatening, but above all, he was extremely loyal and generous to his entourage of thieves, many of whom referred to him as "Mother."

John Phillips, a former bank robber and friend of Ryan's, today describes him as being "an honorable thief" who would "help anybody that came out of the can, anytime! He'd say, 'Well, I'll see what I can do for you. Here's five hundred bucks; get yourself some clothes or whatever the fuck you need.' Dunie was like that. He was generous to a fault."

Another acquaintance, a one-time major drug dealer and pimp who hung out with Ryan at the Cavalier Motel, says, "Dunie took care of everybody. He had guys on the payroll, and half of them didn't even do fuck-all. They used to go by [the Cavalier] to get their rent money, and whatever they needed, he would give it to them. I got to know him well. He always wore a mink coat and fur hat [in the winter], and he was always on the move, always checking out the action."

Billy Morgan back in the 1960s and 1970s was one of the city's top safecrackers, and did much of his fencing through Ryan. "I was in the Cavalier every day. I lived there from 10 o'clock in the morning until 8 o'clock at night." Morgan remembers one particular evening in the late 1970s when he entered the bar and "there was Dunie sitting alone at a table in the corner with a bottle, and he usually didn't drink. We got to talking about growing up and the things we did to make money." Morgan noticed that Ryan was sporting an expensive fur coat and diamond rings. "I was flabbergasted. He told me that he'd moved into importing hash through his connections in the States. Those guys had set him up in the drug business in Montreal." As for Ryan's generosity, Morgan confirms, "At Christmas time he would give a mink coat to anybody that worked for him." And if you were a loyal henchman who'd just been released from a stint in prison, Morgan explained, "He'd say, 'Here's a couple of Gs; here's a pile of coke.'" Ryan, as Morgan describes him today, was "a very generous man" who was "very articulate" and who "never got mad. He was a perfect gentleman."

## Cocaine Cooperative

It wasn't long before Ryan realized that the really big money was not to be made by brokering stolen merchandise like fur coats, liquor, cartons of cigarettes and TV sets hijacked from trucks or boosted from warehouses. Nor was it to be made by fencing jewelry and negotiable securities looted by safecrackers from bank safety-deposit boxes and private homes. The big bucks lay in the importation and distribution of illicit drugs, especially large quantities of hashish and cocaine. And in Montreal during the 1980s there was an insatiable market for the product, to the point where supply could hardly keep up with demand. So, although he personally eschewed the use of recreational drugs, Ryan had no compunction about hopping onto this lucrative gravy train—a rail line that since the beginning of the 20th century had been controlled almost exclusively by Montreal's two dominant Italian mafia families—the Sicilian-connected Rizzutos and the Calabrian-connected Cotronis.

Through his various contacts in the United States, particularly his cousin Peter White, Ryan soon established business relationships with hashish suppliers in Pakistan and Afghanistan, as well as with several Colombian cartel suppliers of cocaine. Deals and shipment schedules were set up, money paid up front, and drugs delivered, usually in large quantities, which Dunie's henchmen would cut up, repackage and distribute. More often than not, the middlemen that he sold to were motorcycle gangs, such as the Rock Machine and its archrival, the Montreal chapter of the Hells Angels. Ryan cared not to whom he sold, as long as their money was green. He was, after all, a businessman. And the cash was rolling in like never before.

It didn't take long for the local Italian mafia to begrudge the fact that an upstart Irishman was competing in what they considered to be both their business and their long-held territory. The message was sent out to him, along with veiled threats. But Ryan shrugged it off. As he once commented to a colleague, "mafia, shmafia. If there's gonna be a war, we've got the IRA." Indeed, although it was never proven, Ryan was known to be a financial supporter of the Irish Republican Army via its American Irish affiliates in Boston. And that support was sometimes repaid with arms smuggled into Montreal from Northern Ireland. Dunie did, after all, proudly wear a gold Claddagh ring on the third finger of his right hand, as did many other members of Montreal's West End Gang.

The Italians never carried out their implied threats against Ryan. Instead they began using him and his organization, such as the Irish Matticks family who controlled the Port of Montreal, to provide them with imported hashish and cocaine, which they in turn could distribute on the street at a profit through their own network. Ryan also set up similar cooperative deals with the Hells Angels and other local biker gangs. But he stubbornly made it clear that he was not interested in forming any sort of importation partnership with them. He was simply the conduit through which they could obtain drugs for resale, take it or leave it. By 1982, he was being hailed as Montreal's "King of Coke" by fellow mobsters, the media and the police. "If you wanted blow back then," today says one of his former major buyers and distributors, "Dunie was the man to see."

But as apparently laid-back as he may have appeared to be to his fawning acolytes, Ryan was certainly not averse to employing violence whenever he felt it necessary to keep the troops in line and, above all, honest.

Patrick "Hughie" McGurnaghan, whose criminal record dated back to 1956, mostly on fraud and bookmaking charges, was an habitué of the Cavalier Motel bar, and was a wholesale purchaser of cocaine from Dunie Ryan. He was part of an Irish family gang from Point St. Charles, and his younger brother Richard "Ricky" McGurnaghan was later shot in the head at the age of forty-two by rival gang members on

March 18, 1991, in his Olympic Tavern at the corner of St. Madeleine and Wellington Street in the Point.

Hughie, a short and stocky five-foot-six, 180-pound drug distributor for the West End Gang, had a major flaw. He seemed to be snorting more product than he was selling on behalf of Ryan. He was carrying a massive debt of about $100,000, and had apparently stiffed Ryan on a recent drug deal. After McGurnaghan ignored several warnings from Ryan, the boss had had enough, so he brought in Montreal's most prolific

Patrick "Hughie" McGurnaghan

contract killer, Yves "Apache" Trudeau from the Laval chapter of the Hells Angels, to take care of things. Hughie would be taught a lesson, one that, more importantly, was directed to others in Ryan's entourage who owed him money or who dared to cross him.

On the night of October 26, 1981, Billy Morgan and a few friends were hanging out in a bar with McGurnaghan. "We were sitting around playing cards and fuckin' around. Hughie came in all dressed up in this white shirt . . . and buying me booze. We had a very good night . . . But he left in a very serious mood . . . And the next day, Boom!" That was the last Billy would see of his friend.

A little after noon the next day, Tuesday, October 27, McGurnaghan left the Château Maisonneuve apartment complex in Westmount, where he was sharing an apartment with his brother-in-law, Kevin Moore. He was met outside the main entrance by his long-time pal Joe Frankel, a major bookie and money-launderer from Côte St. Luc.

Yves "Apache" Trudeau

They climbed into McGurnaghan's 1977 Mercedes 280SE beige sedan, which had been left overnight in the building's outdoor parking area. Their ultimate destination is not known, but they drove east on York Street, then up Victoria Avenue and east again on Sherbrooke Street before turning south a few blocks later on Melville Avenue, adjacent to Westmount Park.

Yves Trudeau, a diminutive five-foot-six, 135-pound psychopath who had spent a busy night beneath the Mercedes in the Château Maisonneuve parking lot, was in a car not far behind them. And on his lap was a radio-controlled activator. It would require one flip of a toggle switch to accomplish his mission.

A few hundred yards down Melville Avenue the car exploded with a blast that blew out windows in the triplex apartments across the street from the park. A satisfied Yves Trudeau continued driving east on Sherbrooke Street. Mission accomplished.

Dawson College philosophy professor Sholom Glouberman was sitting in his living room when the blast shook his windows. He ran outside and saw the smoking Mercedes that had been flipped over into the park. As Glouberman recalls it almost 30 years later, "I opened the car door and the guy had no feet. There was a smoking hole in the bottom of the car. The guy was conscious but bleeding to death, and screaming, 'Get me out of here!'" Hughie McGurnaghan was in shock and in the throes of dying at the age of forty-four. Another neighbor, a doctor, fastened tourniquets on his upper legs. Minutes later the police and an ambulance arrived.

It was too late for McGurnaghan. But his fifty-six-year-old passenger, Joe Frankel, managed to survive with only lacerations and perforated eardrums. He would live to commit several more crimes before dying of cancer some years later.[1]

"Mother" had made his point, a fact that did not go unnoticed by Dunie's entourage. The message was: "You don't fuck with Dunie," as one of his former colleagues puts it today. Other Ryan associates who

---

[1] My companion Ann Elsdon and I were seated at the kitchen table of our apartment on York Street that day when we heard the explosion five blocks away. We shrugged it off as perhaps some construction activity. We only learned of its source in the next morning's newspaper.

were out of favor with the boss would also wind up dead under mysterious circumstances.

John "Jake the Snake" Jackie McLaughlin was a 1960s bank robber and freelance killer from Verdun, suspected in at least a dozen underworld hits, including that of George Groom in 1968, James McDonald in 1969, Gary Dow in 1970 and Michael French in 1982. In 1974 he became Dunie's bodyguard and much feared strong-arm man, and occupied a room at the Cavalier Motel, paid for, along with a generous salary, by Ryan. But McLaughlin was exhibiting serious psychopathic tendencies. He just loved to kill, even on hits not commissioned by the West End Gang. And that was beginning to bring some heat down on the Cavalier Motel, Ryan's base of operations.

In early 1983 Ryan sent McLaughlin and his twenty-four-year-old girlfriend, Maria Kraus-Hillebrand, east to New Brunswick to stay on a farm owned by a mutual gangland friend, Noel Winters, where he was to lie low until the heat died down in Montreal. But McLaughlin's bloodlust traveled with him, and over the next few months he committed several murders in New Brunswick, none of which were gangland related. Then came a falling out with his host, and McLaughlin was shot dead at the age of forty-five by Winters sometime in late 1983. On April 23, 1984, the decomposed bodies of McLaughlin and Kraus-Hillebrand and their pet bull terrier, Buster, were found by the RCMP buried in a shallow grave near Winters' home outside of Saint John, New Brunswick. Police speculate Winters had killed the couple out of fear that McLaughlin had been sent to whack him for failure to pay for a shipment of drugs he'd received from Dunie Ryan.

Winters hanged himself at the age of thirty-four in his Dorchester Penitentiary cell in New Brunswick on April 24, 1984, the day after police announced that they'd found the bodies, presumably because he knew he was a dead-man-walking if he was ever incarcerated with any of McLaughlin's friends. At the time of his suicide, Winters was serving two life sentences for the murder of a sixty-four-year-old Saint John, New Brunswick, man and his thirty-two-year-old son that past February.

By 1983, Ryan and his wife Evelyn had moved from their Ville LaSalle duplex into a large home at 541 Montrose Drive in the upscale suburb of Beaconsfield on Montreal's West Island. They now had two young children, nine-year-old Tricia, and five-year-old Troy. Ryan entertained many of his cronies at the house, as well as at a nearby Lake St. Louis yacht club, where he kept his 36-foot cabin cruiser. Things were looking good for Dunie Ryan. He was wealthy, he was respected, and he was at the top of his game.

Nevertheless, there were seeds of envy and discontent growing within his organization. He had buffaloed the cops, the Quebec Organized Crime Inquiry, the Italian mafia and the biker gangs. But as Julius Caesar once observed, *"Yon Cassius has a lean and hungry look."*

# CHAPTER 14

# The Death of Dunie Ryan and Its Fallout

B y early 1984 there were two senior West End Gang members, Alan "the Weasel" Ross and William "Billy" MacAllister, who envied the power being wielded and the money being made by the man at the top and, according to police and inside gang sources, both were hungry to wrest control of the gang from Dunie Ryan. Another mob member, Paul April, hungered for the millions of dollars that the drug lord reportedly had stashed away in the form of cash, gold ingots or diamonds somewhere in the Laurentian Mountains. And there were yet others who, for their own reasons, simply had it in for Ryan. Thus, a palace revolt was slowly simmering, and it was only a matter of time before the pot would come to a boil and the blood of the King of Coke and others would be shed.

Paul April, early 1980s

At about 4 p.m. on Monday, November 12, 1984, a woman in her mid-thirties showed up at the front desk of Nittolo's Garden Motel, which was attached to an Italian restaurant of the same name with a back-room bar that was then the West End Gang's regular hangout on St. Jacques Street in NDG. She paid $60 in cash to rent Room 40 for two nights on the ground floor. But the woman, who registered under the name Sylvie Gagnon, never occupied it that night or the next.

The next evening Dunie Ryan had an early dinner with two Ottawa business associates at Rube's restaurant in Hudson, west of Montreal near the Ontario border. He left them and drove to Nittolo's, arriving there at about 8 p.m. to meet up with some of his crew, including Paul April, in order to take care of business in the rear bar.

April, a convicted bank robber and the former brother-in-law of Billy MacAllister, had joined Ryan's West End Gang earlier that year after having served nine years for robbery and attempted murder of a police officer. On February 16, 1970, he and three others were arrested following a wild gunfight with police while stealing $52,000 from the Canadian National Bank in Drummondville, Quebec. A police officer, Douglas Lyons, was shot and paralyzed for life during the shootout. The four were convicted on September 30, 1971, and sentenced to 10 years in jail for armed robbery and attempted murder. After his release from prison, April became the West End Gang's principal distributer in the city's east end, and he was now in hock to Ryan for an estimated $200,000 worth of cocaine from a previous shipment.

There are two versions of what was said between them: April either told him that a hot-to-trot woman was waiting for him in Room 40, or that he wanted to privately settle the outstanding cocaine debt with him in that room. In either case, Ryan was last seen leaving Nittolo's bar by a side door as he followed April to the adjacent motel. It was a setup.

Hiding in the bathroom with a sawed-off shotgun was Robert "Bob" Lelièvre, a career criminal and a former member of Monica "Machine Gun Molly" Proietti's holdup gang. Also in the room was Alan Rose, Larry Schlaer and Edward "Eddie" Phillips, a petty thief and errand boy for Ryan. According to his brother John, it was Eddie's wife, Sharon, who had booked the motel room under the pseudonym Sylvie Gagnon.

As soon as the two entered and closed the door, April pulled out a pistol and Lelièvre emerged from the bathroom with his shotgun pointed at Ryan, who instinctively picked up a chair and flung it at his assailants. But the chair harmlessly smashed through a bay window, and Lelièvre pulled the trigger, bringing Ryan down. April then ordered Phillips to put a coup de grâce bullet through Ryan's head, which he did with his revolver. They immediately fled, leaving Montreal's forty-two-year-old King of Coke very much dead. Police believe that both Billy MacAllister and Larry Schlaer were involved in Dunie's assassination, though neither was present at the time of the shooting.

A chambermaid working on the second floor heard the shotgun blast and called the motel manager, who called police. The cops arrived at 8:53 p.m. and found Room 40 in total disarray, with Ryan's bloodied body sprawled on the floor. According to the coroner's report, Ryan had taken a direct hit to the chest from a .12-caliber Browning shotgun loaded with SSG slugs, and a .45-caliber bullet through his left cheek. The police assumed that the murder was a settling of accounts rather than a robbery, since the victim had a diamond-encrusted Rolex watch on his wrist, a gold chain around his neck and $6,350 in cash, mostly in one-hundred and fifty-dollar bills, in his wallet and pockets.

Nittolo's restaurant, 1960s

Nittolo's restaurant and motel exist no more: the place closed in the early 1990s and was later razed to make way for a Loblaw's supermarket. But after it was shuttered up, 39 feral cats who'd previously hung around outside its back door waiting for restaurant kitchen scraps, kept coming back to find shelter in the motel's dilapidated ground-floor rooms. For several years, Jean Smith, an octogenarian from NDG, known locally as "the Cat Lady," would arrive each day to bring them food. Smith, aware of the violent murder that had taken place in Room 40, today recalls, "It was always spooky in there. Very eerie."

Ryan's funeral was held four days later at St. Augustine of Canterbury Church in NDG. It was attended by his elderly mother May, his wife Evelyn and their two teenaged kids Tricia and Troy. Another 200 or so other people, many of whom, police surveillance photographers noted, were known members of the West End Gang and the Hells Angels, also showed up to pay their last respects. Among them were Alan Ross, Michel Blass, Yves "Apache" Trudeau and Laurent "L'anglais" Viau, president of the Hells Angels Laval chapter, a major distributor of cocaine supplied by Ryan during the early 1980s. At the time of Ryan's killing, Viau owed him $185,000 for previous drug deliveries.

The four men were observed by police huddled together in conversation on the steps of the church immediately following the funeral, and the cops surmised that they were discussing what would come next. For it was clear that Dunie's death would have to be avenged. And indeed it was.

## Special Delivery

Neither Paul April nor Robert Lelièvre, the cops duly noted, attended the funeral. Nor did Billy MacAllister, who happened to be in jail for breaking bail conditions at the time of Ryan's murder and funeral. April and Lelièvre were now living at 1645 de Maisonneuve Street West, a high-rise building directly across from downtown police Station 25. The two-bedroom ninth-floor apartment had been leased by Lelièvre only two months earlier, and was a place where they and their friends would often gather to relax over a few beers or lines of coke and discuss future jobs.

On Monday, November 19, Yves Trudeau, who had previously committed several murders with April, dropped by their apartment. Noticing that they did not own a working television, he promised to get them one. Trudeau, a Hells Angels Laval chapter contract killer, had been commissioned by Alan Ross to whack Paul April for $200,000, and he now had a plan. As he would later testify at a coroner's inquest on August 28, 1985, "I accepted the job [from Ross]. He gave me a $25,000 advance, along with debts erased for the Hells Angels" who owed Ryan several hundred thousand dollars for drugs delivered prior to his death.

A few days later he called April to say that their mutual friend Michel "Mike" Blass, a Hells Angels member, would be delivering the TV and a VCR player the next night. Michel was the younger brother of the notorious Richard Blass who, on January 24, 1975, was killed at the age of twenty-nine during a wild 4:30 a.m. shootout with Quebec police at his Val David hideout in the Laurentian Mountains just north of the city. April knew the Blass brothers well, and told Trudeau that Michel could drop by anytime.

Shortly after 3 a.m. on November 25, Blass and Trudeau parked in an alley behind the apartment building. While Trudeau waited in the car, Blass lugged the TV set and VCR up to Apartment 917 where forty-two-year-old April, fifty-five-year-old Lelièvre and two friends, Gilles Paquette, a seventy-two-year old petty crook, and Louis Charles, a fifty-three-year-old armed robber who had been Lelièvre's cellmate at the St. Vincent de Paul Penitentiary, were snorting coke and eagerly waiting for what was in effect a Trojan horse. Blass set up the equipment, even giving them a documentary video cassette entitled *Hells Angels Forever*. He then raced down the building's fire stairwell to join Trudeau in the car, which immediately sped away.

Packed inside the television console were 15 kilos of C-4 plastique explosive and a timing mechanism set to detonate 30 minutes after the VCR was turned on. At 4:15 a.m. a powerful explosion reduced all four occupants of the room to dismembered body parts and shredded tissue, blew out all the windows and damaged several other apartments on the eighth and ninth floors. "The Mad Bomber" had successfully accomplished another mission. As he would later boast in court, "I showed them the power of the Hells Angels."

Police officers across the street in Station 25 raced to the scene. They first assumed that a bomb had accidentally gone off while the dead men were putting it together, which was the story initially reported in the press. But this assumption was discarded the following August when Trudeau admitted to his involvement in the bombing, named his co-conspirators, and described how it was done.

Trudeau had been the founder of the 1960s Popeyes motorcycle gang, which in 1977 was absorbed into the Montreal Hells Angels. He broke away in September 1979 to form the Laval-based North Chapter, a group known for its violent behavior and excessive drug use. He was also a freelance killer who did "jobs" for anyone, no matter what their gang affiliation. In August 1985, hearing that he was on the Hells Angels hit list with a $50,000 price on his head, he sought protection by turning police informant, the first full-patch Hells Angels member ever to do so. In exchange, he admitted to participating in 43 murders; 29 with a gun, 10 with bombs, three with a baseball bat, and one by strangulation during his 15-year professional career as a gun-for-hire thug between 1970 and July 1985. He also testified against Michel Blass and many others with whom he had committed murder.

On February 28, 1986, Trudeau was sentenced to life imprisonment on multiple charges of manslaughter. He was granted parole in 1994 and lived under the identity of Denis Côté until March 2004 when he was arrested and pleaded guilty to sexually assaulting a thirteen-year-old boy, for which he received a four-year prison term. On July 15, 2008, at the age of sixty-four and suffering from incurable bone-marrow cancer, he was paroled from the Archambault Penitentiary in Ste. Anne des Plaines north of Montreal, and confined to a palliative care facility where he was expected to die within two to three years.

As for Michel Blass, he was arrested in September 1985 and became a police informant against others, including his own defense lawyer, Réal Charbonneau, at his trial in February 1986, in exchange for copping a plea on a reduced charge of manslaughter in 12 contract killings, including the four men who were killed in the apartment bombing. On July 2, 1986, he was handed a life sentence and was paroled in 1995 after serving nine years, and then given a new identity under the name of Michel Simon in the government's witness-protection program.

Two years later Blass was being sought by the Quebec Provincial Police as a "person of interest" in the case of a forty-five-year-old Prevost, Quebec, antiques dealer Étienne Therrien, who disappeared on March 21, 1997, while on an antique-buying trip with a lot of cash to the Trois-Rivières area, where he was supposed to meet with Blass. On July 3, 1997, two detectives in an unmarked car spotted Blass and began tailing him near Joliette, Quebec. Shots were fired at their car, and Blass was arrested and booked on various charges, including the attempted murder of peace officers. The next day police discovered the remains of Therrien buried in a shallow grave nearby in Saint-Michele-des-Saints. They pinned his murder on Blass who, on October 5, 1998, was found guilty and sentenced to 20 years in prison.

## A Dead Man Tells No Tales

Following the apartment bombing, there remained some more internal housecleaning to be done in the wake of Ryan's murder. Even though two of his killers, April and Lelièvre, were no longer alive, there was also the matter of Eddie Phillips who'd taken part in the assassination.

"I shot a dead man!" Eddie Phillips told his brother John shortly after Ryan's death, realizing that the only reason April had ordered him to fire a bullet into Ryan's head was to make him complicit in the murder. Following the deaths of April and Lelièvre, Phillips was afraid that he might be next on the "dead men tell no tales" hit list. His fears were well founded.

On March 25, 1985, the diminutive five-foot-three, forty-one-year-old Phillips was invited to have lunch and drinks with Billy MacAllister at the Victoria Station chain restaurant and bar in the Town of Mount Royal on Jean Talon Street. He arrived there at 12:45 p.m. Shortly after, as he was walking from the restaurant to his car in the rear parking lot, a black Honda motorcycle pulled up beside him and the passenger on the back seat got off and fired five bullets into his back, chest and face, before hopping on the bike, which immediately sped away.

From left to right, John and Eddie Phillips, 1967

The motorcycle was being driven by an unidentified man wearing a white helmet and visor.

Eddie's brother John, as well as former Montreal police Sergeant-Detective John Westlake, are certain that Billy MacAllister had set up the hit. Moreover, André Savard, the homicide detective who investigated the slaying, today maintains that MacAllister was the one driving the motorcycle. But no proof was ever established.

It was later ascertained that the shooter on the back of the bike was David Singer, a small-time mobster and drug dealer from the Montreal suburb of Beaconsfield who worked as a gopher for West End Gang member Larry Schlaer in the latter's automotive garage. He too was a marked man.

Singer had first been busted by the RCMP on February 24, 1976, along with Schlaer, Larry Morrison and others following the delivery of two tons of hashish, with an estimated street value of $9 million, on a twin-engine turboprop Lockheed airplane that landed the night before on an isolated airstrip near Drummondville, Quebec. The RCMP, who'd been previously tipped off, observed from a distance the landing and the unloading of the plane's cargo into two cars. The suspects were then tailed and arrested en route to Montreal. Singer spent two years in prison for his role in that caper.

Following the murders of Ryan and Phillips, Singer, now living in Pompano Beach, Florida, was the next witness targeted for elimination. On May 12, 1985, he was found shot dead at the age of thirty-one with three .38-caliber bullets to his head and chest, his body sprawled across the back seat of a stolen car that had been abandoned in Tigertail Lake Park in Dania, Florida, just south of Fort Lauderdale.

But in this case, a dead man *could* tell tales. Apart from his wallet with ID and the gun that had killed him, one of the items investigators discovered in Singer's pockets was a piece of paper with Alan Ross' wife's Montreal telephone number on it. This helped the Florida police, the FBI and the DEA to connect some dots that led to Singer's murder and, indirectly, to a later major drug conviction against Ross. Eventually they were able to put together the circumstances surrounding the killing.

Two days before his body was found, Singer had been "taken for a ride" in the stolen car by two West End Gang hoods, Allan Strong and Raymond Desfossés. Their mission, which allegedly was ordered by Alan Ross, was to get rid of the first-hand witness to the murder of Eddie Phillips.

Strong, who also went under the aliases of Jean-Guy Trépanier and Yvan-Jacques Rousseau, was originally from Cantley, Quebec. He'd been serving a 10-year sentence for armed robbery at the Cowansville penitentiary until his escape on May 9, 1973. He was next arrested, at the age of twenty-seven, during a gun battle with police following an aborted Montreal bank robbery on March 15, 1974, during which an innocent bystander was shot and killed by a stray bullet. His accomplices were William Lydon, twenty-nine, and William White, twenty-three, both of whom were prison escapees from the Massachusetts Correctional Institute. After his release in 1984, Strong became an international drug trafficker with ties to Colombia's Cali cartel, and was second in command to Alan Ross, who had taken over as leader of the West End Gang following Ryan's assassination. Shortly after that, Strong fled to Florida.

Raymond "Trifluvien" Desfossés, was a Trois-Rivières, Quebec, garage owner and drug dealer, and a West End Gang henchman during the 1980s. On August 8, 1984, he was arrested on charges connected to a June 29, 1984, armed robbery of $134,000 from a Brink's guard outside the Knob Hill Farms food terminal in Pickering, Ontario. His trial began in September 1988 in nearby Whitby, but ended in a mistrial a month later due to procedural errors. While out on bail, he was traveling back and forth between Quebec and Florida.

Both men were staying at Strong's Fort Lauderdale apartment at the time of Singer's death. As he would testify in June 1992 in a Florida federal court, John Robert Quitoni, a former New Jersey police officer who had served time in a Texas prison for drug convictions, met with Strong and Desfossés at the apartment on May 10, 1985, and at their request supplied them with a loaded .38-caliber revolver. That night, the two men picked up Singer at a nearby hotel under the pretext of taking him to where he could purchase cocaine. With Desfossés driving and Strong in the back seat beside Singer, they drove a short distance south before Strong pulled out the gun and pumped three bullets into their victim.

They now had to dump the body and the stolen car. Near the town of Dania they were pulled over by a Florida State Trooper, Michael Foti, for running a red light. As the cop approached their car, Strong handed the gun to Desfossés who leaned out the window and shot Foti in the leg. They sped off, ditching the car and its dead occupant in nearby Tigertail Lake Park.

According to Quitoni's 1992 testimony, he met with Strong and Desfossés at the apartment a week later where the two related the details of Singer's murder. The two killers, who had long since fled Florida, were now internationally wanted men.

At 3 p.m. on March 24, 1992, Desfossés was intercepted by the RCMP while driving his Mercedes-Benz at 105 miles an hour on Autoroute 40 in Louiseville, Quebec. The following month he was ordered to be extradited to the United States for the attempted murder of Highway Patrol officer Foti. He fought his extradition all the way to the Supreme Court of Canada, by arguing that the key witness, Quitoni, had perjured himself. But the Supreme Court refused to hear his appeal, and he was extradited to Florida in September 1997, where he could have gotten the electric chair for Singer's murder. On May 29, 1998, he pleaded guilty to a reduced charge of non-premeditated murder, and received a 12-year sentence.

While in jail that November, he and Roger Forgues, Pierre Tremblay, and Jean-Denis Grégoire were accused by the RCMP of plotting to smuggle 210 kilos of cocaine into Canada back in 1989. After serving six years in the United States, Desfossés was sent back to Canada. He was again arrested on September 8, 2004, in Trois-Riviéres by the RCMP for conspiring with 24 others, linked to the Italian mafia, the Hells Angels and the West End Gang, to import huge quantities of cocaine by boat into Quebec in August 2003. In 2005, he pleaded guilty and was sentenced to 13 years in prison. Then, on the basis of testimony from police informant Gérald Gallant, he was re-arrested in a Laval federal prison by the Quebec Provincial Police on March 26, 2009, on charges of killing Richard McGurnaghan, who had been shot dead at the age of forty-two in his Point St. Charles tavern back in 1991, and for the July 7, 2000, shooting death of Robert Savard in a North End restaurant, as well as four other murders. The sixty-year-old Désfosses, dubbed by police as "the Trois-Rivières King of Drugs," was still locked up in late 2010.

As for Strong, he too left Florida shortly after Singer's murder, moving first to Portugal, and then to the French Riviera, where he lived the good life while trafficking in amphetamines and other drugs. But both the RCMP and Kevin McGarr, a former member of the Rubber Duck Squad and later a Montreal police narcotics detective, doggedly remained on Strong's trail for the next 10 years.

He was eventually arrested in Amsterdam on February 6, 1994. Following a failed penitentiary escape there, Strong was extradited to Canada, and then to the United States, where he went on trial in Tallahassee, Florida, on March 6, 1996. Three weeks later, based on testimony from a former henchman, Jean-François Leboeuf, and by detective McGarr, and RCMP anti-drug agent Jean Corbeil, he was found guilty of drug trafficking and possession, as well as the murder of David Singer. Strong, then fifty years old, was sentenced to 25 years in a U.S. federal prison, where he still languishes today.

Nevertheless, the killing of Dunie Ryan and its subsequent bloodletting still had to be answered to by Alan Ross. As the heir apparent to the King of Coke, he would become one of North America's biggest drug dealers.

CHAPTER 15

# The Emperor of Coke

As soon as Dunie Ryan was knocked out of the West End Gang driver's seat, his number-two man, forty-year-old Alan "the Weasel" Ross, took over the wheel. If Ryan had been the King of Coke in the late 1970s and early '80s, his successor would become the Emperor of Coke, dealing in quantities that Ryan could only have dreamed of.

But first there was that messy business of avenging Ryan's death and permanently sealing the lips of tell-tale witnesses in Montreal and Florida, murders for which Ross was never initially charged. He'd managed to remain in the background by giving out orders and doling out money, yet never getting blood on his hands. Once that housecleaning chore had been taken care of, he could move on to much more important business.

Alan Ross, 1988

Ross started out as a petty thief and small-time pusher in the 1960s, but his criminal career didn't get seriously kick-started until 1976 when he, perhaps more than his mentor, realized the enormous profits to be made in the importation and distribution of hashish and cocaine—and not just in Montreal, but throughout all of North America. He became, in effect, the low-price, high-volume emperor of the drug trade, dealing with suppliers from South America and the Southeast Asian Golden Triangle of Burma, Thailand, Afghanistan, Turkey and Pakistan. Like any savvy business man, Ross understood the basic principle of buying cheap in bulk at wholesale prices from the Third World and then selling the goods at retail prices for a hefty profit in Canada and the United States.

Ross, who lacked Ryan's charisma and generosity, was nicknamed "the Weasel" by his colleagues ("le Belette" by his francophone friends), both because of his ferret-like features and his ability to weasel out of being busted for many years. The RCMP and the Montreal drug and homicide squads had been trying to get hard evidence on him since 1976, as did the FBI and the U.S. Drug Enforcement Administration in later years. He proved to be frustratingly elusive, despite the fact that in August 1985 Yves Trudeau had fingered him in a coroner's inquest as the one who'd set up the four apartment bombing murders the year before. But an accusation from a hired killer testifying in order to get police protection and a reduced sentence was one thing, proof was another.

Ross was always ready to pay big bucks to those who could keep him informed on what the various police agencies were up to. One such person was his attorney Sidney "Sid" Leithman, Montreal's top criminal defense lawyer. From the 1960s through 1980s, Leithman represented members of the West End Gang, the east-end Provençal gang, the Dubois brothers, the Cotroni and Rizzuto mafia families, the Hell's Angels and Rock Machine, and even several members of Colombia's Medellin and Cali drug cartels who happened to get arrested in Montreal.

Sidney "Sid" Leithman

Leithman, the son of a de Bullion Street Jewish tailor and schmatta merchant, obtained a law degree from McGill University in 1960, passed the bar exams a year later, and for the next 30 years took on most of the city's high-profile gang-related gambling, extortion, armed robbery, murder and drug cases. His reputation as an aggressive defense attorney who could get a client acquitted, or at least off on a much-reduced charge and sentence, was such that whenever a gangster was arrested, his immediate request often was: "Get me Leithman!" The workaholic, cigar-chomping lawyer and reportedly frequent cocaine user soon became a millionaire by successfully defending his well-heeled clients who paid in cash up front. He'd even gotten Dunie Ryan off several times, in exchange for which (apart from cash, of course) Ryan had given him a traditional Irish Claddagh ring, which he wore on the third finger of his right hand. The lawyer would often proudly show it off to clients and fellow attorneys in the hallways of the Montreal courthouse.

Ross had given his attorney a retainer of $300,000 in the late 1980s to keep him abreast of any evidence that Canadian and American authorities were accumulating and what charges they were trying to pin on him. Leithman had many sources in Canada and the United States whom he could tap in order to keep his client up to date and free from the long arm of the law.

But Ross' consigliere would eventually be of no more help. At 6:30 a.m. on Monday, May 13, 1991, Leithman climbed into his black Saab 900/Turbo sports convertible at his Simcoe Avenue home in the Town of Mount Royal and headed for his downtown office on Phillips Square. Thirteen minutes later he was shot dead at the age of fifty-four, with four .45-calibre bullets pumped into his neck and head when he pulled up to a red light at the corner of Rockland Avenue and Graham Boulevard, a few blocks from his house. According to witnesses, a Jeep backed up in front of the Saab, preventing it from proceeding through the intersection. A man raced out from behind a bakery across the street, shot out the passenger side window and then stuck his arm inside, firing four more times at the driver before escaping on foot. It was all over in less than a minute. The investigating homicide detectives recognized it as an obviously pre-planned professional hit.

Leithman's murder came as a shock to Montreal's legal community. Yet it was not the first time it had happened to one of their own. Six years earlier, at 11 p.m. on October 15, 1985, forty-four-year-old Franklin "Frank" Shoofey who, after Leithman, was regarded as the city's second-most successful defense lawyer representing prominent

gang members, was emerging from his downtown fifth-floor Cherrier Street office when someone stepped out of the elevator and fired five bullets into his head and escaped down the stairs. The assassination was thought to have been ordered by the Italian mafia and possibly carried out by Michael "Crazy Mike" Fidanoglou, a 1980s bank robber and freelance hitman who is still serving a life sentence for subsequent bank robberies and attempted murder.

Franklin "Frank" Shoofey

Many suspect that the motive for Shoofey's killing was that he was a big supporter of Montreal's ne'er-do-well Hilton boxing family, and that he'd annoyed certain Mafiosi who had bet heavily and lost on some of the Hilton brothers' fights that were thought to be rigged.

A lawyer who worked for Shoofey at the time of his murder today says, "We all thought that it was because of his involvement with the Hiltons," who were "a really bad family ..." and, "I think their involvement with [notorious U.S. boxing promoter] Don King led to Frank's killing." But she insists that Shoofey's death, unlike that of

Leithman's, had nothing to do with the drug trade, adding that Shoofey "can be reproached for a lot of things," such as vainly wearing a "terrible toupee," but he was "a health nut who ate grapes and other health food" and had no interest in either the personal trafficking or use of cocaine or any other drugs.

However, retired Montreal police homicide detective André Bouchard today sees the murder differently. "When the Hiltons went to fight for Don King, that pissed off the Italians for sure ... But Cotroni and his gang had nothing to do with [Shoofey's] killing . . . It was something else completely different." Bouchard adds, "We know who killed him . . . I can't tell you the whole story because we can't charge him. But he's in jail right now and he'll be in jail for 25 years, because we got him on something else." He maintains that Shoofey's murder was for "the craziest reason in the world. Everybody thinks it's because of the boxing, but that's bullshit."

## Colombian Cocaine

The murders of Montreal's two most prominent criminal defense lawyers in the space of six years remain unsolved. But in Leithman's case it almost certainly was connected to his association with Colombian drug cartels. He knew and previously defended cartel members who were nabbed in Montreal. For example, Jairo "el mocho" Garcia, a Colombian national and Montreal resident in the 1980s, was allegedly a major distributor for the Cali cartel and a good friend of Alan Ross, Allan Strong and Leithman. In October 1983 he was arrested by the RCMP on charges of importing 16 kilos of cocaine into Montreal. But in 1985, with Leithman as his attorney, he was acquitted and returned to his native country.

Garcia's cohort in Montreal was Inès Cecilia Barbosa, a Colombian national who was known in drug circles as "La Madrina" (the Godmother). She first showed up in Montreal in the late 1970s, and throughout the 1980s ran a wholesale drug ring with ties to the Cali cartel. Her job was primarily to funnel laundered money back to the cartel. According to the RCMP, Barbosa transferred at least $75 million in cash from Montreal to Colombia between 1989 and 1992. She was eventually arrested in December 1996 for importing 17 kilos of cocaine into Montreal. She served two-thirds of her six-year sentence in the Joliette Women's Institution, 50 miles northeast of Montreal (where she became a close friend of the notorious Karla Homolka). On June 2, 2006, at the age of fifty-nine, Barbosa, under pressure and death threats from the Cali cartel, to whom she owed millions of dollars for cocaine deliveries, committed suicide with an overdose of barbiturates in her downtown MacKay Street apartment.

On the morning of his death, Leithman was scheduled to appear in court on behalf of Diego José Ganuza, a Colombian pilot who had been arrested with others by the RCMP in March 1989 and charged with importing 2,628 kilos of cocaine on his private twin-engine plane into St. Norbert, Quebec, about 60 miles north of Montreal. The feds had been tipped off and were expecting the plane's arrival. The Medellin cartel bosses immediately hired Leithman to defend Ganuza. But Leithman, who had assured them that he had a direct pipeline into the federal force, was unaware that Douglas Jaworski, a middleman in the smuggling operation, had become an RCMP informant. The following year, a second Colombian private plane laden with cocaine was likewise pounced upon by the RCMP the moment it landed in Fredericton, New Brunswick.

Back in Colombia, the cartel was enraged about losing tens of millions of dollars worth of product in those two seized aerial deliveries, and they placed the blame on Leithman. So it was time to waste him, if for no other reason than for legal incompetence. A contract on his life was put out, one that most likely was executed by a local gun-for-hire thug connected to either the Montreal mafia or the Hells Angels.

Three months after Leithman's death, his client Ganuza was given a 25-year prison term and fined $500,000, mostly on the basis of Jaworski's testimony. Others who were swept up in the two airplane cocaine seizures were also handed lengthy sentences.

Meanwhile, investigators, particularly Kevin McGarr of the Montreal police drug squad, were attempting to connect the dots to figure out the connection between Alan Ross and whomever might have murdered his lawyer. Most of the dots led to Colombia, where Leithman had traveled several times in the years prior to his death to meet and party with cocaine drug lords. Colombia was also where the cops were certain Ross was obtaining most of his imported cocaine.

One dot that indirectly led to Ross was a scribbled telephone number on a piece of paper that detectives had found in Leithman's pocket the day he was murdered. It was the unlisted home number of RCMP Inspector Claude Savoie.

Leithman, as he'd assured his Colombian friends, did indeed have a pipeline into the federal agency. And to whom better should that pipeline lead than to Savoie, head of the Montreal RCMP anti-drug squad from 1989 to 1991. It would later come out that the two met regularly on a casual basis, trading information to the point where Leithman was sometimes informing on his own clients. But the quid pro quo was that the lawyer learned details about ongoing drug cases and planned RCMP raids, important intelligence that he would then pass on to his clients. Exchanging such information was obviously a breach of trust and ethics on both of their parts, yet it served each of them well. It was similar to the "you show me yours and I'll show you mine" questionable relationship that Boston Irish gangster Whitey Bulger had formed with the compromised FBI agent John Connolly during the 1980s.

But Savoie took it much further than that when he became a direct conduit for one of Leithman's principal clients, Alan Ross. This time Savoie's compensation was money rather than information. It began in late 1989 at a meeting in Leithman's office when the lawyer introduced his client to Savoie, and suggested that the two might be of assistance to one another. A deal was tacitly struck, and over the next 18 months Ross delivered about $200,000 in cash to Savoie in exchange for inside RCMP information regarding its investigation into him and other members of the West End Gang.

His fellow RCMP officers soon smelled something fishy and, in April 1992, Savoie was quietly transferred to the force's Ottawa intelligence department, where he was assigned to administrative duties while an internal investigation got underway.

Dan Burke, then an investigative reporter and freelance researcher for the CBC's current-affairs program *the fifth estate*, began looking into the story, even interviewing Lavoie off-camera for three hours in his Ottawa office. Burke also had the advantage of knowing Ross and several other West End Gang members when, as a teenager, he'd played pool with them at their Smitty's bar hangout, and also knew them when he'd worked as a busboy at Nittolo's Restaurant back in the 1970s. Today Burke says his impressions of those places and its habitués were "like a scene out of [the Martin Scorsese film] *GoodFellas*. That's what it was like."

The program eventually compiled strong evidence against Savoie and his connection to Leithman and Ross, and so had the RCMP's internal investigation division.

At 9:15 a.m. on Monday, December 21, 1992, Savoie, alone in his Ottawa office, picked up his service revolver and blew out his brains. This was just hours before he was slated to be questioned downstairs by RCMP internal investigators, and a day before *the fifth estate* was to run its incriminating documentary concerning his connection to Alan Ross.

As retired Montreal drug squad sergeant-detective John Westlake, who knew Savoie, today bluntly states, "He had no choice but to kill himself because of the circumstances of his family and the disgrace of going to jail. Have you ever heard of an inspector in the RCMP going to jail? Very rare. They'd kill themselves before that."

Westlake and others knew that the corruption within the Montreal RCMP drug squad was even more complex, given that one of their undercover agents, Jorge Manuel Leite, was in fact a double agent. He was a Portuguese native who'd immigrated to Canada in 1979 at the age of twenty-eight and settled in Cambridge, Ontario. In 1987 he applied and was accepted for admission into the RCMP, mostly because he was fluent in five languages. He spent the next four years as a constable in the Montreal RCMP drug section where, due to his command of Spanish, he handled cases involving the Colombian Cali cartel.

And then Leite switched sides. In 1991, he was suspected of working as a mole for the cartel, feeding them, via Inès Barbosa, information about Canadian police operations, and receiving over $500,000 in payoffs from Barbosa between March and May of 1991. He had also met with a Cali cartel underboss, Diego Ortiz, in Colombia during that time, while ostensibly working as an undercover RCMP agent for Claude Savoie.

On May 22, 1991, a week after Leithman's murder, Leite abruptly resigned from the force and flew with his two young daughters to Portugal, where he held dual Canadian-Portuguese citizenship. A few days later, his wife Maria quit her part-time nursing job at Montreal's Reddy Memorial Hospital to join him and their children. They moved into a luxurious villa in the village of Calhandriz, 25 miles northeast of Lisbon. The next year Leite was charged in absentia by the RCMP with bribery, fraud and breach of trust. But he managed to remain on the lam for another seven years.

On November 26, 1998, Leite was picked up by Portuguese police, held in a Lisbon jail under an Interpol warrant and charged with corruption and fraud between March and May 1991 while serving with the RCMP. During his trial at the Vila Franca de Xira judicial tribunal in Lisbon, he admitted to receiving $45,000 cash and a $30,000 Toyota Previa van from Colombian drug traffickers via Luis Lopes and Barbosa in exchange for inside information. But he insisted that he'd handed all the money over to his RCMP supervisor Claude Savoie for whom he'd been working as an RCMP undercover agent, and denied being a corrupt cop in league with either Savoie or the Cali cartel.

On January 19, 1999, at the age of forty-eight, Leite was convicted of corruption in Lisbon for selling RCMP information to the Cali drug cartel and was sentenced to three years in prison. But to the dismay of Canadian authorities, the sentence was soon overturned and replaced with four years of probation and a $1,500 fine when a Lisbon appeal court judge ruled that the Mounties had failed to adequately prove their case. He was again a free man.

Westlake is still convinced that Leite, if not the shooter himself, was involved in Leithman's murder before fleeing Canada shortly thereafter. As for Leite's fate, Kenny Fisher, a West End Gang drug importer who between 2002 and 2010 spent eight years in prison, first in Mexico and later at the Laval Leclerc Penitentiary, today insists, "I know for a fact that Leite is now dead," adding, "He was eliminated by RCMP agents in Portugal in order to shut him up." Fisher was referring to the relationship between Ross, Leithman and Savoie. However, there is no proof of that.

### The Dragnet Closes

Meanwhile, Canadian and American authorities had, since 1986, been slowly gathering evidence and interviewing accomplices in order to build a case against Alan Ross on charges of international drug trafficking and murder. Eventually they nailed him.

At 1 p.m. on Monday, October 7, 1991, U.S. federal marshals showed up at Ross' Casa Del Sol oceanfront condo in Fort Lauderdale with a sealed indictment charging him with leading a criminal enterprise that had been smuggling cocaine and marijuana from Colombia and Mexico into the United States and Canada between 1975 and 1989. The indictment, which listed 14 Canadian, American and Colombian co-conspirators, named Ross as the kingpin in the operation. One of the arresting officers, Christopher Dale, later testified in court that a very desperate Ross had offered him a $200,000 bribe to release him while he was being transported in handcuffs by car to the downtown Broward County U.S. Marshal's Office.

Among the co-conspirators named in the indictment were George Lawrence Neill and Joseph Bernard Cadieux, former West End Gang members who were Ross' West Coast drug distributors during the 1980s. In January 1990, forty-two-year-old Neill and thirty-year-old Cadieux were nabbed by the Alberta RCMP in a sting operation, and in June 1991 were convicted by the Alberta Court of Queen's Bench of conspiring to smuggle cocaine and marijuana into Canada, and sentenced to 18 years in prison. They later testified against Ross during the latter's trial in Florida. In October 2000, Neill, while on parole, was again arrested by the RCMP in Vancouver on charges of being the head of a Canadian-Russian network trafficking in some 240 kilos of hashish and 100,000 ecstasy tablets in Canada. Two of his accomplices, Gary Maybee of Austin, Quebec, and Thomas Dunn of Verdun, were also arrested by the Montreal police.

Another indicted co-conspirator was Bertram "Bert" Gordon, Ross' principal pilot for drug shipments, which he delivered on his plane from Colombia to Canada in 1987 and 1988, stopping along the way in the Bahamas, Florida and Nashville, Tennessee. Although he was an American, he obtained a false Canadian passport under the name of George Light. Gordon was arrested on cocaine-smuggling charges in Amsterdam on February 13, 1989, and deported to the United States in 1991, where he copped a plea by testifying against Ross in Florida in May 1992.

The prosecution now had a strong case, backed up by surveillance reports, wiretapped phone conversations, and more than a dozen informants ready to testify against Ross. His trial began on April 6, 1992, in the Gainesville, Florida, Federal Court where he faced multiple charges of drug trafficking and running a criminal organization.

Among those testifying in the heavily guarded courthouse was sixty-seven-year-old James "Jimmy" Allardyce, a Ross associate who was arrested at his Lachute, Quebec, home by the RCMP on March 20, 1992 on charges of importing hundreds of kilos of cocaine from South Florida to Montreal from 1981 through 1988. A week later he accepted extradition to the United States to be tried and sentenced there, as well as to testify against his former boss. On June 5, 2007, Allardyce, then eighty-one and out of jail, died of cancer at his home in Lachute.

Another who supplied damning testimony at the trial was Gaétan Lafond, a major cocaine supplier for the West End Gang. He was shot to death at the age of forty-five as he sat sipping coffee at an outdoor cafe in the city of Medellin, Colombia, on October 8, 1997.

Yet another witness for the prosecution was David Sabio, a cocaine importer who testified that he had arranged a meeting between William Blackledge and Ross in 1986 to enable Angel Sanchez to supply huge quantities of cocaine the following year. Blackledge, a Scotsman originally from Coalburn, Lanarkshire, and an international drug importer, has been on Interpol's most wanted list for the past 20 years and is still on the lam. While he was living in Fort Lauderdale, he allegedly had direct links to the Cali cartel during the 1980s and early 1990s as their conduit for major cocaine shipments to North America, especially to Montreal's Hells Angels and the West End Gang. Sanchez was one of Ross' main cocaine and marijuana suppliers. His and Blackledge's names came up often during the trial.

Apart from the bad guys who testified against Ross, there were also members of the Montreal police, particularly sergeant detectives Kevin McGarr and Michel Amiot, and RCMP narcotics detectives taking the stand, plus agents from the Florida State Police, the FBI and the DEA. The evidence against Ross was overwhelming.[1]

On May 15, 1992, after the jury had heard from more than 100 witnesses, 15 of whom were gangster informants, Ross was found guilty under the U.S. 1970 federal RICO (Racketeer Influenced and Corrupt Organizations) Act of conspiring to import and traffic more than 10,000 kilos of cocaine and more than 300 tons of marijuana (altogether totaling about $80 billion worth of drugs on the street) from South America and elsewhere to the United States and Canada between 1975 and 1989. Following the trial, one DEA agent described Ross as "the biggest non-Hispanic drug dealer ever arrested in the United States."

In July 1992, the forty-nine-year-old Ross was sentenced to three concurrent life sentences, fined $10 million, and ordered to pay $1,492 a month for the cost of his confinement and supervision. A year later he took his case to the U.S. Court of Appeals, with arguments on various grounds, but lost on October 11, 1994.

Meanwhile, in a separate trial in Fort Lauderdale, Ross was tried for the May 10, 1985, murder of David Singer in Dania, Florida. Included in the evidence linking him to the crime were hotel records which showed that he and his wife, Laine Cohen, were registered at the Fort Lauderdale Marriott Harbor Beach Hotel from late April to early May 1985, at the time when Singer was whacked. Coincidentally,

---

1 One Montreal detective who testified told me that as Ross was being led out of the Gainesville court-room, "He looked at me and muttered, 'Your new TV and VCR is on its way.'" A court guard overheard the remark and, suspecting that a bribe was being discussed, reported it to the judge, who later called the cop into his chambers for an explanation. The detective laughed and told the judge that Ross was employing sick humor in reference to the November 25, 1984, apartment bombing.

Sidney Leithman and Jean Guy Trepanier (Allan Strong's alias) were also registered there at the same time. John Quitoni, who had already testified against Strong, also testified against Ross. On October 29, 1993, Ross was found guilty of conspiracy in Singer's murder and had 30 years tacked on to the time he was already serving.

Ross is now serving consecutive sentences for second-degree murder and drug trafficking in a U.S. federal prison in Canaan, Pennsylvania, with no possibility of parole until 2060, at which time he'd be one-hundred-and-seventeen years old![2]

Following the assassination of Dunie Ryan and the lifetime incarceration of Alan Ross, there was a vacuum to be filled in the leadership of the West End Gang. The two likely Montreal contenders were William MacAllister and Gerald Matticks, both of them ambitious and successful Irish mobsters.

2 I last heard from Ross in February 2009 when he wrote me from prison to say "I will enjoy reading your book, and I will be more than happy to drop you a line and tell you if you were on the money" regarding the West End Gang.

# CHAPTER 16

# The MacAllister Family

The three Irish MacAllister brothers, George, William (Billy) and Peter, grew up during the 1940s in Lachute, Quebec, and the Montreal North area of Ville St. Laurent, in what was described by a 2005 National Parole Board assessment report on Billy as "a dysfunctional family" in which their "father was an alcoholic and abusive." All three boys went on to become criminals, robbing banks and armored trucks, or importing and trafficking in illicit drugs.

George, the oldest, was first busted at the age of twenty-two in 1960 for passing $444 worth of bad cheques in Ottawa and Cornwall, Ontario, and spent a year in the Ontario Reformatory. He was next charged with holding up the Canadian Imperial Bank of Commerce Branch on Montreal's Victoria's Square in May 1963, but was acquitted on the basis of insufficient evidence. The following year he was arrested again, this time for being part of a gang that included his younger brother Billy and had robbed $73,500 from the same bank three months later. George pleaded guilty and confessed to having received $12,000 as his share of the loot. He served three years in prison. After his release, he was arrested again, this time in connection with a $115,000 fraud. He got another seven years.

At 2:10 p.m. on September 12, 1973, George, Billy and three other West End Gang members, Richard White, twenty-eight, William "Willie" Lyndon, twenty-seven, and Donald "the Duck" McMillan, ambushed a Brink's armored truck while it was making a delivery to a Bank of Montreal branch at 5355 Côte de Liesse Road. During a sidewalk shootout, a Brink's guard, Claude Vienneau, was killed and another guard, Robert Brunette was injured. The desperados escaped with $276,000 in a stolen getaway car, but were arrested separately within days and sent to trial.

George MacAllister, who admitted to having received $40,000 from McMillan for his share in the robbery, insisted that his brother Billy was not present during the heist. In fact, at Billy's trial on November 22, 1974, he was a defense witness for his sibling. Knowing that his testimony could not be used against him, George boasted, "I'm a professional gunman; I make my living with a gun and I'm one of the best." He added, "I'm tired of all this talk about the MacAllisters. I'm the only MacAllister [criminal]." It was a noble brotherly gesture, but the jury didn't buy it. As for the shooting of the Brink's guard, it was never determined which of the bandits had fired the fatal bullet. During his testimony, George even oddly suggested that the victim was at fault. "We thought he would use his head as anyone else and not go out with his shotgun and open up on us," he stated. Eventually, all five were found guilty as accomplices in the holdup and death of Vienneau and received lengthy prison sentences. George, now a free man at the age of seventy-two, lives in Hawksdury, Ontario.

Peter J. MacAllister, the youngest and shrewdest of the three boys, managed to avoid arrest until November 16, 1994, even though he'd previously been hauled in for questioning by police with respect to his brothers' activities.

On October 13, 1994, a Port of Montreal Canada Customs official who was spot-checking recently offloaded containers happened across one with ceramic tiles originating from Uden, Holland. Upon closer inspection he discovered that among the 509 cartons of tiles, 34 of them were crammed with 202 kilos of hashish, with an approximate street value of $3 million. The RCMP was alerted and they maintained a 24-hour watch on the container until its contents were picked up by a truck three days later and delivered to the warehouse of Céramique Daniel Thériault, a ceramics tile supplier owned by a forty-four-year-old man of the same name in Montreal's southwest Ville Lasalle district.

The Mounties then surreptitiously tailed Thériault as he distributed some of the boxes of "tiles" to the home of his girlfriend Danièle Berniquez in Saint Placide, near Lake of Two Mountains west of Montreal, to sixty-six-year-old James McArthur in a Ville Lasalle shopping mall parking lot, and indirectly to forty-eight-year-old Peter MacAllister in Piedmont, north of the city. The cops then pounced, arresting all four on charges of conspiracy to import and distribute drugs. Following several trials and appeals, they were found guilty in December 1998, and were later sentenced to between four and seven years in prison.

During the search of MacAllister's home, the Mounties turned up $12,000 in cash, a hashish-processing tool, a weighing and packaging machine, and a bulletproof vest. Peter was clearly a major importer and distributer, and the cops were certain he'd gotten away with more deliveries prior to that. But, unlike his brothers, he had only this one conviction against him, and following his release from prison he wisely quit the drug game. Now, at the age of sixty-four, Peter spends most of his time with his children and grandchildren in Montreal and Bermuda.

In 2002, Peter MacAllister published a semi-autobiographical novel entitled *Dexter*, replete with thinly disguised references to many West End Gang members. It's actually quite a good read, and in some ways a morality tale. In a July 10, 2005, *Montreal Mirror* newspaper interview following the book's publication, MacAllister said of his time in prison, "I met young people [who] would come up to me and say, 'You've been successful. How do you get away with it? We can't seem to get away with it.' I thought, 'My God, they don't know what they're doing; they don't know the world they're in.' That's what inspired me to write the book ... There's a mythology I want to break for young people attracted to the drug world. Today's drug game is a pure cutthroat capitalistic pursuit. Twenty years ago it was an adventure. Today it's a very harrowing world to live in."

And then there is Billy MacAllister, a man who has spent more than half of his sixty-eight years in and out of jail and halfway houses for crimes that in quantity and quality far exceeded those of his siblings. His revolving-door prison history is unmatched by any other West End Gang member.

His rap sheet begins at the age of twenty-one, with a car theft and attempted bank robbery conviction in 1963, for which he served less than a year. Then, as previously mentioned, he was arrested while accompanying Dunie Ryan and two others in August 1966 to rob the Essex County Bank and Trust Company in Lynn, Massachusetts. Three years later, after serving only a fifth of his 15-year sentence, he was deported back to Canada. He was next arrested with two other men in 1970 for attempting to enter the United States by car in possession of guns, ammunition and balaclavas—all the accoutrements of a planned bank robbery. For that he served 30 months in the United States and was again sent back to Canada in 1973.

No sooner was Billy home than he pulled off the September 1973 Brink's truck robbery with his brother George and three others, during which a guard was killed. On December 6, 1974, he was given two concurrent life sentences, but was paroled on February 2, 1981. His parole was revoked several times over the next few years when he breached its conditions. In November 1986, while again on parole, MacAllister was busted along with seven others in London, Ontario, for attempting to import 100 kilos of cocaine from Venezuela, and on July 15, 1987, an Ontario court sentenced him to 15 years. He managed to escape from a London provincial holding pen that September but was soon after tracked down by the RCMP in Montreal. When arrested, he was in possession of cocaine and an Ingram machine pistol and silencer, as well as a loaded .357 Magnum handgun and several hand grenades.

He was sent to the federal maximum-security Millhaven Penitentiary in Bath, Ontario, to serve another 30 months on top of his 15-year sentence as a result of his escape and possession of weapons. But, much to the consternation of the RCMP and the prosecuting attorneys, the career criminal was once again let out on parole in July 1992.

By this time MacAllister was fifty years old, and had spent 22 of those years in various U.S. and Canadian prisons. Yet he would have more crime and prison time ahead of him.[1]

Once out of prison in 1992, MacAllister wasted little time in getting back into the game. But this time he was aiming for what he intended to be his most lucrative score ever, one that could involve the importation of up to 5,000 kilos of pure Colombian cocaine into Montreal via Florida. "In those days," says Guy Quintal, now a retired member of the RCMP drug squad, "cocaine was going for $35,000 a kilo," once it was cut and on the street. So the proposed shipment could eventually be worth as much $1.75 billion.

MacAllister's partners in the scheme were Paul Larue, Salvatore Cazzetta, Nelson Fernandez, Ashley Castaneda and Michael Dibben, all experienced drug importers or distributors.

Paul Larue began his criminal career dealing in small quantities of marijuana, hashish and cocaine during the 1970s while working as a bartender and waiter in several St. Denis Street bistros, and then escalated to selling coke by the kilo in the 1980s. His early convictions between 1974 and 1980 included drunk driving, possession of drugs with intent to sell, robbery and breaking probation conditions, for which he received only fines, weekends in jail or further probation. He later became a Billy MacAllister associate and one of his major cocaine contacts.

Salvatore Cazzetta was an original member of the Montreal-based SS motorcycle gang in the early 1970s. During the 1970s and early 1980s

---

1 I first met Billy in the late 1970s while I was coordinator of the Dawson College program at the Leclerc Penitentiary. He was perhaps the most personable and glib prisoner I'd ever met, and an obvious leader who was highly respected by the other inmates. My colleague Greta Nemiroff was then co-director of Dawson's alternative New School, and she invited MacAllister, who was on parole, to come and talk to her students, hoping perhaps that he'd warn them about the evils and repercussions of crime. But as Greta recalls, "He had them eating out of his hand within minutes," while he charmed them with the derring-do of his personal misadventures. In fact, a 2007 National Parole Board psychological assessment report describes him as "a very articulate person [with] a highly manipulative capacity" to fool others.

he'd been a petty criminal along with his younger brother Giovanni but received only minor sentences for robbery and possession of stolen goods. In 1986, he became a founding member of the Rock Machine motorcycle gang, which eventually led to the 1994–2002 drug turf war between them and the Hells Angels. He was incarcerated, for a few months each time, in 1985, 1986 and 1988 for possession of a handgun and narcotics. In March 1992, he fell in with MacAllister.

Nelson Fernandez, another Rock Machine member, was Cazzetta's right-hand man. In early 1992 he was arrested but later acquitted on charges of threatening to kill two Montreal police officers. He too joined MacAllister later that year.

Ashley Castaneda, a Montreal resident of Colombian origin, and Michael Dibben were also MacAllister associates. MacAllister and his five cohorts had been busy since the summer of 1992 working out the logistics of what, if successful, could amount to the largest Colombian cocaine shipment ever into Canada.

However, they weren't the only ones in a planning mode. Unbeknownst to them, an integrated police task force known as Project Choc was also quietly doing its own investigating and planning. A major sting operation was carefully being crafted, one that would definitely come as a shock to the conspirators. The members of the task force included Montreal police narcotics detectives Kevin McGarr and John Westlake, plus Guy Quintal and Mike Lang of the RCMP drug squad. They later coordinated their investigation with members of the Drug Enforcement Administration in Jacksonville and Gainesville, Florida, particularly with agents Ed Dickey and John Burns. The latter went undercover for nine months, posing as a major drug supplier in order to infiltrate the gang. Throughout this time the cops were busy tapping into telephone conversations between the principals in Montreal and Florida, as well as, via Burns, surreptitiously recording their clandestine meetings. The bait was in place, the mice were eager to nibble and the trap was about to be sprung.

### Burned by Burns

As would later be revealed in court, the face-to-face transactions began in July 1992 when Paul Larue and Burns, posing as a drug-delivery middleman, met at a hotel in upstate New York. Larue gave Burns $220,000 in seed money to transport Colombian cocaine by road from Florida to Montreal. They met again three months later at a bar inside Montreal's Dorval International Airport terminal, this time with MacAllister. Burns and Ed Dickey, another DEA undercover agent, showed them 67 kilos of coke that they said had been hidden in a car that had been driven up from Florida. They were promised that a good deal more could be on its way, as much as 5,000 kilos, in lots of about 1,000 kilos each over the next three months. But Burns insisted that he first needed to show his people some cash up front. MacAllister, convinced that Burns was the real deal, then set about arranging the financing. Within two months he had raised $875,000 U.S., mostly from the Rock Machine and other Montreal biker gangs, for the first installment in the proposed mega-kilo and megabucks transaction.

In January 1993, Larue contacted Burns in Florida and told him they had the money for the first delivery, but they first wanted to check out the quality of the cocaine. "No problem," said Burns. On March 10, 1993, Larue sent twenty-seven-year-old Ashley Castaneda, a man with a nose for coke, to Jacksonville, where he was taken aboard a yacht being used by the DEA, in order to sample the product. He reported back to the others in Montreal that it was top-grade blow. The deal was on.

On Friday, March 19, Salvatore Cazzetta, thirty-eight years old, and Nelson Fernandez arrived in Florida with a $660,000 payment, which they delivered to Burns in a Jacksonville motel room. The agreed-upon plan was for Burns to drive up to Burlington, Vermont, and deliver the first 1,000 kilos by truck to Paul Larue and Ashley Castaneda at a Denny's restaurant on Shelburne Road in South Burlington in two days' time. It would then be up to them to get it across the U.S.–Canada border and into Montreal.

And that's when the trap snapped!

Early Sunday morning on March 21, Kevin McGarr of the Montreal police and RCMP officers arrested a very surprised Billy MacAllister at his Mont Rolland chalet in the Laurentian Mountains north of the city. He was named in a Florida indictment, charged with conspiring

Kevin McGarr, 2008

to import 5,000 kilos of cocaine into Canada. Extradition proceedings were immediately begun.

Simultaneously, John Burns and other DEA agents, accompanied by John Westlake of the Montreal police and Guy Quintal of the RCMP, arrested thirty-nine-year-old Paul Larue and Ashley Castaneda at Denny's restaurant on the same charge while the supposed drug transaction was under way.

"People were coming out of church from across the street and into the restaurant," recalls Westlake, noting that it was a very public bust, with Larue "totally taken by surprise that Burns was a double agent." Indeed, Larue could not believe what was happening as he and Castaneda were handcuffed and read their rights by Burns. The DEA officers also stripped him of his $50,000 mink coat and a $35,000 jewel-encrusted Rolex watch, informing him that these had been purchased with the proceeds of crime and they were now the property of the U.S. Government.

"Larue was in total shock," recalls Quintal. "His English was not very good, so John and I told him in French that he was under arrest, and what for. He was in tears about his fur coat and watch, saying that they were presents from his wife. So I told him that they no longer belonged to him."

The two culprits were immediately flown down to Jacksonville by the DEA officers, where they were formally booked and committed to trial.

During the same sting operation, thirty-eight-year-old Michael Dibben had contacted Burns from Montreal to place an order for 200 kilos of the supposedly available tons of coke. Dibben sent two associates, Francesco Rubbo, thirty-seven, and Sebastiano Di Maria, forty-six, to deliver $282,000 of up-front money and bring back the shipment. No sooner had Rubbo and Di Maria arrived in Jacksonville and handed over the cash than the DEA agents promptly handcuffed them and transported them to the local jail.

Fernandez and Dibben were shortly after arrested in Montreal and sent to face trial in Florida. Almost all the conspirators were now behind bars. And most, like MacAllister, who was being held at the Parthenais Detention Centre, faced extradition to a Florida court where they knew sentences were much harsher than under the Canadian judicial system.

The Choc sting, which had been more than nine months in the making, dealt a major blow to the West End Gang. It was an operation that could not have been pulled off in Canada, since it involved entrapment and the sale of drugs by law enforcement officers to criminals. "To get them ourselves we would have needed to flash some dope," says Quintal, "and that would have been illegal," in Canada. But not so in the United States. The RCMP and Montreal police acknowledge that without the DEA and the entrapment rules that apply in the United States, MacAllister and his cronies would never have been busted.

## The Fallout

In 1994, Westlake, McGarr and Quintal were given the International Award of Honor by the American Narcotics Enforcement Officers Association, crediting them with "outstanding performance in Project Choc, a drug investigation into the West End Gang, an organized crime group based in Montreal, Canada." Those arrested were all facing serious jail time before the U.S. court in trials that would take place over six years in a Jacksonville courthouse.

In May of 1993, Larue pleaded guilty to charges of conspiring to import 5,000 kilos of cocaine into Montreal via Florida. It was later revealed that in order to reduce his sentence, he'd become a police informant and testified against the others. His handler was RCMP drug squad officer Daniel Chartrand. Despite his cooperation, Larue was given seventeen-and-a-half years in prison, and all his expensive toys were taken away. Under the Canadian government's Bill C-61 (concerning money obtained through criminal activity), his $400,000 condo in the Tropique Nord complex in Cité du Havre across from the

Port of Montreal, his $1 million chalet on Lake St. François in Saint-Anicet near Valleyfield, Quebec, and his $3 million estate in Moulton Hill in the Eastern Townships were confiscated as properties that had been acquired through the proceeds of crime. This was on top of the mink coat and Rolex watch the DEA had seized at the time of his arrest in Vermont.

Salvatore Cazzetta remained on the lam for a year until he was arrested on May 6, 1994, at a pit bull farm near Niagara Falls, Ontario, where he owned two fighting dogs and was still head of the Rock Machine motorcycle gang. He was transported to Montreal, where he resisted being extradited to the United States. But he lost, despite several appeals that went all the way to the Supreme Court of Canada. On March 20, 1998, he was removed from his cell in Quebec's Donnacona Prison and sent in irons to face trial in Florida, where in June 1999 he pleaded guilty to drug trafficking and was sentenced to twelve-and-a-half years in prison.

Nelson Fernandez successfully fought his extradition and remained incarcerated on drug charges in Canada. While in prison at Rivières des Prairies in December 2000, he defected from the Rock Machine to the Hells Angels Nomads chapter. But a few months later, at the age of forty-three, he died of cancer while still in jail.

Ashley Castaneda was extradited to Jacksonville in July 1994, to stand trial in the drug caper. He was found guilty and served a seven-year sentence.

Michael Dibben, who was arrested in Montreal by Kevin McGarr on April 27, 1993, was extradited to Florida to face charges in connection with the crime. He too was declared guilty and sentenced to eight years in prison.

Minor players such as Francesco Rubbo and Sebastiano Di Maria received light sentences. On June 11, 1993, Billy MacAllister, the kingpin in the planned

A young Billy MacAllister

major score, was ordered to be extradited to the United States to face charges in the drug-import plot. He unsuccessfully fought his extradition through the Canadian justice system. In July 1994 he was taken from his cell in the Donnacona Penitentiary by Montreal detectives Kevin McGarr and Eddie Gravely and turned over to two U.S. marshals, who accompanied him on a DEA private jet to Jacksonville.

His lengthy trial began on July 14, 1994, with over a dozen witnesses from Montreal and Florida, mostly peace officers, testifying against him. On April 19, 1995, he was found guilty and sentenced to 19 years and 7 months by a Jacksonville federal court for his role in the conspiracy. While in a U.S. federal prison for seven years MacAllister continued to fight the verdict in the U.S. Court of Appeals, but lost on November 16, 1998. In January 2002 he was brought back to Canada to serve out the rest of his sentence.

On November 9, 2006, while incarcerated in Laval's minimum-security Montée St-François Institution, MacAllister was granted his first "Unescorted Temporary Absence" from prison, which was renewed several times more, each for a period of a month or two. On April 10, 2007, he gained day parole to live in a halfway house for six months, and on March 20, 2008, he eventually got full parole after having served a total of 14 years for his drug-related crimes. That year he married Martine St-Pierre, a French Canadian woman who loyally stood by his side during future parole board hearings.

But on March 27, 2009, his parole was revoked and he was sent back to prison for having violated various conditions, such as being in contact with known criminal elements during the summer and fall of 2008.

In its summation of that hearing, the National Parole Board stated: "At age sixty-six you are serving, since 1974, a life sentence for attempted murder, armed robbery, theft, attempted prison breach and conspiracy to import narcotics. Your criminal career spans over four decades and your offences are large in scale, requiring a high level of organization. [With] accomplices, you participated in bank robberies ... holding up armored vans and carrying out drug transactions. A guard was killed, some victims were threatened with firearms and police officers were injured. Numerous firearms, including loaded guns, were involved, and you had various ties to the criminal underworld." The report noted that from the time of his March 2008 parole, MacAllister had "elected to associate with individuals, at least five or six times, that were interested in similar criminal activities as the ones for which you were convicted in the past." It concluded that due to "the extreme gravity of your crimes [and] your very poor history . . . you present an undue risk on release, and there is no less restrictive measure than a revocation of your full parole."[2]

MacAllister's next hearing was on April 14, 2010, at the Montée St-François Institution. He was denied full parole, but was given a six-month pre-release day parole. On October 20 it was extended for another six months, to be spent in a halfway house and with many conditions attached, such as not hanging out with any past or present bad guys. His notice from the parole board states: "It is forbidden for you to associate, communicate in any way, for any reasons with anyone who has a criminal record or is involved in the drug subculture and organized crime." Given Billy's background, that definitely limits his circle of friends.

On December 22, 2010, MacAllister was finally granted full parole, again with the above stringent conditions. At his latest hearing, the parole board took into consideration that MacAllister was moving with his wife Martine to a town east of Quebec City, and thus well distanced from the Montreal criminal milieu. "However," warns the board's report, "William MacAllister will be on parole and accountable for his behavior for the remainder of his life."

## Westlake's Last Bust

During an extension of Project Choc, Montreal police narcotics investigator John Westlake chalked up the final bust of his career with the arrest of Glen Cameron, a major West End Gang importer of hashish and cocaine into Canada. A tip from the DEA alerted the

---

2 I attended Billy's 2009 hearing, after which I asked him about the West End Gang. His response was: "There is no such thing as a West End Gang . . . Anyway, I just want to get away from all that stuff; it's all behind me now." He did, however, acknowledge that since his parole conditions always included not associating with anyone with a criminal record, it was pretty difficult to have any sort of social or family life outside of prison with the people whom he knew. As he admitted to the parole board members, "I'm back here [in prison] for being stupid."

local cops to Cameron's activities, and the Montreal drug squad, together with the RCMP, began surveillance on him. Cameron, who owned several homes in the Montreal area, as well as a hobby farm in Green Valley, Ontario, just west of the Quebec border, proved to be as elusive as Westlake was persistent. The surveillance even involved a wild car chase which had the bad guy pursuing the good guys.

John Westlake, 1988

Westlake recalls one August night in 1996 when he and fellow Montreal drug-squad investigator Michel Leclerc were in an unmarked Ford Probe coupe, cruising past one of Cameron's houses in the West Island suburb of Beaconsfield to see if he was there and who might be visiting him. "It was twelve o'clock and Cameron was standing in the driveway. We drove by slowly, rounded the block and came to a stop sign. The next thing we know, there's this big fucking SUV barreling down behind us . . . So I gunned it, and he pulled up beside us and I looked and it was Cameron [behind the wheel]. I hit the gas and the chase [east on the Trans-Canada Highway] was along Route 40 . . . He didn't know who the fuck we were. He thought somebody was out to whack him." (The Hells Angels had previously made two attempts on Cameron's life). "Anyway," continues Westlake, "we're hitting, 100, 120 miles an hour, and the fucking Probe is shaking like a bastard, and he's coming up the rear with that big SUV tank . . . Then we come up to a big truck and I was able to squeeze past it, and Cameron in his big fucking SUV couldn't . . . So we exit off the ramp on Jean Talon [Boulevard], make a right, make a left, and then fuck off. That was the end of that." It was a chase scene straight out of *The French Connection*.[3]

---

3 I can well imagine the scene. One afternoon in 1988 while I was researching a CBC *fifth estate* piece on heroin being smuggled into Montreal from Iran, I was in the back of an unmarked police car with John Westlake at the wheel and his drug-squad partner, Gaston Pitre, in the passenger seat. We were on the crowded Ville Marie expressway on our way to meet with an Iranian informant, and we were running late. John was weaving in and out of traffic, cursing, blowing the horn, and flashing his badge out the window at drivers impeding his progress. It was one of the wildest car rides I've experienced. But we made it on time for the rendezvous.

Glen Cameron's 1997 arrest by John Westlake and the RCMP

The investigation, involving surveillance and telephone wiretaps, continued for another year while the authorities gathered incriminating evidence. At dawn on June 20, 1997, thirty-seven-year-old Glen Cameron was arrested at his luxurious Green Valley farm by Westlake, accompanied by the DEA and the RCMP, and charged with importing 45 kilos of liquid hashish, hidden in plastic tubes, from Jamaica to Montreal.

As Westlake recalls the take-down: "It's 5 a.m. and our SWAT team went through the fields to his house. He had a long driveway that was alarmed, and if he didn't know you, he'd fucking blow you away. Up in his house he had a fucking machine gun beside his bed . . . But we managed to bust him cold." Westlake adds that as Cameron was handcuffed and led shirtless out of the house, "he says to me, 'Hey, John, I heard this was the last fucking shot for you; I'm your last guy.' I said, 'Well, looks like I'm gonna pack it in; and you too, you fucker!', and then he wishes me a happy retirement."[4]

On May, 8, 1998, Cameron was found guilty and sentenced to 27 months in prison plus a $150,000 fine. On June 22, 2000, the Quebec Justice Ministry and Canadian government seized his various properties in Quebec and Ontario, as well as his collection of rare cars valued

---

4 The following year, fifty-eight-year-old Westlake retired after 33 years on the force, with most of that time spent on the drug beat. According to his superiors, during his career he probably made more successful busts of individual narcotics dealers than any other Canadian cop. Having witnessed John in action several times while he arrested and grilled suspects, I can believe it. At six-foot-two and 220 pounds, he takes no guff from those whom he arrests. His distinctive features are his neatly trimmed beard and a toothpick that's usually hanging from his mouth, a habit he picked up decades earlier when he quit smoking. But John's most intimidating feature is his accusatory scowl and intense gaze which pierces into the eyes (and perhaps the soul) of anyone unfortunate enough to be collared and questioned by him. Today, when he's not relaxing by fishing for bass and pike at his cottage north of Montreal, Westlake runs a successful private investigator business with fellow retired cop André Savard of the Brink's robbery fame.

at $1.6 million, since it was all purchased through the proceeds of crime. Westlake recalls that a large barn next to Cameron's farmhouse contained "all kinds of fancy cars; Ferraris, Mustangs, you name it. He even had [Jorge] Leite's fucking Mercedes in there."

In July 2000 Cameron successfully avoided extradition to the United States, where the DEA wanted him on a previous charge of importing 700 pounds of marijuana from Canada to Florida. He is now a free man.

"He was my last bust," says Westlake today, "but he only did short time." He ruefully adds that "Cameron is a major crook who never worked a day in his life; and he's active again now—big time."

# CHAPTER 17

# Gerald Matticks: King of the Port

To paraphrase Sir Walter Raleigh: "He who controls the seaport controls the wealth." In terms of the drug trade, this is precisely what the West End Gang, through the Matticks family, managed to pull off in the 1980s and '90s.

Apart from several cruise ship berths, the 180-year-old Port of Montreal consists of dozens of commercial wharfs, warehouses, acres of container storage areas, rail spurs and 350 grain elevators in its 13-mile stretch along the southern side of the island. It is the world's largest inland port, unloading over 90 percent of all goods destined for Quebec and eastern Ontario, and is the port of entry for cargo heading west through the St. Lawrence Seaway to major American Great Lakes cities such as Buffalo, Cleveland, Toledo, Duluth, Detroit, Milwaukee and Chicago.

The facility employs some 850 dockworkers, most of them longshoremen, truck and forklift drivers, crane operators and cargo checkers, all of whom are members of unions affiliated with Local 375 of the Canadian Union of Public Employees (CUPE), the country's largest labor organization.

Gerald Matticks, circa 2001

Gerald "Gerry" Matticks, once the powerful president of the port's Coopers and Checkers union, was in a position to know what foreign ships were scheduled to arrive and when. More important, he knew from his and his customers' drug contacts in Europe, Africa, Asia and South America exactly which container on which ship contained contraband narcotics, right down to the container's serial number and where it was stowed on the ship—hence his sobriquet "King of the Port."

With Dunie Ryan having been whacked in 1984, Alan Ross serving life for murder and drug trafficking in an American prison since 1992, and Billy MacAllister extradited to Florida in 1994, Matticks went on to become the ex officio head of the West End Gang. In his position on the waterfront he profited hugely from payoffs by Montreal drug importers.

Matticks was born on July 4, 1940, the youngest of 14 children raised in an eight-room apartment in the Irish slums of Goose Village, adjacent to Griffintown. He quit school at the age of twelve, barely able to read or write. He was married at the age of seventeen and fathered four children by the time he was twenty-one. But he was a hustler with a lot of street smarts. He and four of his brothers, Frederick, Richard, John and Robert, had been associated with the West End Gang since the 1960s, initially specializing in truck hijackings and thefts from Montreal warehouses. Much of their stolen swag was fenced through Dunie Ryan at the Cavalier Motel.

The oldest brother, Frederick "Fred" Matticks, although arrested a couple of times, had no major convictions. Billy Morgan today recalls, "Him and I were best of friends. We spent time in Weredale [a Montreal juvenile detention home] and later partied together." Elaborating on that connection, he adds, "I could walk through The Point and The [Goose] Village with no problem, because in those days [the Matticks clan] had to know you." According to Morgan, Fred died prematurely of a heart attack at the age of fifty in 1989.

Richard "Richie" Matticks' criminal record dates back to 1957 when, at the age of twenty-three, he served two years for breaking and entering. He was jailed again in 1959 for two years on charges of theft. Once out, he was arrested several times, mostly on charges of truck hijackings, theft, assault and possession of stolen goods between 1963 and 1969, for which he received fines and/or short jail time. But Richard apparently could not break the habit. In one month alone, between September 25 and October 27, 1973, he and his brother Gerry were busted on 15 charges of truck hijacking, theft and possession of stolen goods, but again received only light sentences. The merchandise they boosted from the semis ranged from liquor to frozen meat, stereo systems, TV sets, leather goods, fur coats, blue jeans, cigarettes, cosmetics and lingerie. All of it was stuff that could easily be sold on the street, often in taverns and bars to honest citizens who were only too happy to purchase something that "fell off the back of a truck" at a real cheap price.

Richie was last arrested at the age of sixty-three in his Lachine home on May 20, 1997, along with Frank Bonneville, Donald Waite and Giovanni Cazzetta, leader of the Rock Machine biker gang. They were charged with possession and intent to traffic eight kilograms of cocaine, valued at $312,000. The following month Richie pleaded guilty and received a three-year prison term plus a $50,000 fine. He was denied parole that September when the National Parole Board declared him to be "a dominant figure in organized crime in Montreal over a period of many years." He served his full time and was released in June 2000.

In the fall of 1979, the CECO Commission, which had been looking into Quebec organized crime, singled out Richie, Gerry and

Fred Matticks as being Montreal's most prolific truck-hijackers between 1972 and 1979, and they were subpoenaed to testify under oath before the tribunal. They, of course, denied everything. Following the inquiry, on November 12, 1979, the brothers, along with Dunie Ryan, André "Sappy" Martin, Fred Griffith and several other West End Gang members, were charged with 158 counts of theft and possession of stolen goods, as well as perjuring themselves before the commission. All were released on $25,000 bail. But in December 1981, following a three-month trial, they were acquitted, despite the fact that Maurice "les Fesses" (the Buttocks) Villeneuve, a West End Gang armed robber and hijacker, had turned police informant in May 1978 and testified against them. In the course of the trial Richie admitted to knowing Villeneuve, describing him as a "little bit of a nut." Asked to explain, Richie said, "Any guy that starts to butt out cigarettes on a girl's chest is nuts."

Robert Matticks, who had the least number of charges against him, died of cancer in the fall of 1981. The informant Villeneuve died in prison in July 1988.

Meanwhile, the cops continued their pursuit of the Matticks family.

At 4 a.m. on November 15, 1988, Richard, Gerald and twenty-eight-year-old Normand Beauregard were caught red-handed by the Montreal police anti-gang squad in a Point St. Charles warehouse on Bridge Street, where they were in the process of unloading a hijacked tractor-trailer containing imported suitcases and travel bags worth approximately $150,000. While they were out on bail, their case dragged on in fits and starts for almost four years, partly as a result of the May 13, 1991, murder of their defense lawyer Sidney Leithman. On June 8, 1992, the three pleaded guilty and got a mere 90 days jail time to be served over 45 weekends in Bordeaux prison, as well as two years' probation and a $10,000 fine each for their part in the hijacking.

John Matticks was arrested at the age of thirty-nine along with his kid brother Gerry for the attempted murder of Allan Seller, whom they suspected was ratting to the cops about their activities. The prosecution alleged that on October 14, 1971, the brothers picked up Seller and took him for "a ride" in the back seat of his own car, and that while

Gerald was driving, John, in the passenger seat, turned around and shot Seller twice before dumping what they assumed was his corpse in a parking lot on Notre Dame Street East. But the injured Seller managed to crawl away to a nearby police station, and he later testified against them. Nevertheless, on January 17, 1972, the brothers were acquitted on the basis of a mistrial resulting from a procedural error on the part of the Crown. In 1975, John also beat the rap on charges of breaking and entering and possession of stolen goods. He later died of a brain aneurysm.

Gerald, although the youngest, was obviously the "baddest" of the bad boys in the family. His rap sheet begins at the age of twenty-six in 1966, with convictions for theft, break and enters, drunk driving, and possession of weapons and stolen goods. Then came his 1971 arrest on murder charges with his brother John, and his 1973 to 1988 truck-hijacking arrests with his brother Richard.

But it was on the waterfront where Gerry would make a name for himself. By the mid-1980s he was in charge of the Coopers and Checkers Union. (The term originates from the 18th and 19th century when wet cargo such as molasses, beer, whale oil and vinegar, and dry cargo such as flour, cereals, cement and fruit, was normally shipped aboard schooners, brigantines or barkentines in large sealed oak barrels. After the sailing ship was offloaded, the checkers examined the casks for leakage or damage, and if there was any, it became the cooper's job to seal and reinforce the barrel with wooden staves and metal hoops before it was transported off the wharf). In the 1990s the union performed a similar task, although now they were checking 20-foot-long steel maritime containers instead of oak barrels. This allowed Matticks and his hand-picked crew to smuggle tons of narcotics past customs and out of the port to be delivered to whomever had consigned the contraband goods.

During that same decade when Matticks was considered the "door to the Port of Montreal," Paul Matthew Arthur served the same function in the Port of Halifax, until his arrest by the RCMP in July 2000. Police wiretaps showed that he had connections to gangs in Montreal, including the Hells Angels, and to Colombian drug cartels. Using inside information, Arthur and his cohorts on the docks would set aside transport containers containing drugs, remove the drugs, and then ship them by van or truck to Montreal and other cities. Arthur pleaded guilty to drug trafficking and was sentenced to 14 years in jail. In August 2005, having served a sixth of his sentence, he was let out on supervised day parole. He eventually was living in a halfway house, working in construction, and keeping his nose clean. On July 30, 2007, he finally gained full parole, but with strict conditions attached.

However, the majority of illicit drugs entering Canada from overseas came through the Port of Montreal. Testifying before a November 2001 Canadian House of Commons Special Committee on Non-Medical Use of Drugs, Pierre Primeau, an RCMP intelligence officer with the organized crime task force in Montreal, noted that the port handles "over a million containers a year." He said, "There are two types of jobs in the port that are very important. The longshoremen are the individuals who unload the containers from the ships, put them on rail cars or trucks and send them out. But one of the most important positions is the checker—in French they call them *vérificateurs*. They have what is called a stow plan, a document which says exactly what will be coming off a boat, and this way they'll know exactly which container must go to which place, and they will have these containers placed in a stack to move them with transport of any kind."

Primeau added, "We have noticed in various investigations that some containers, which were supposed to be placed in a certain place, were moved a few minutes later, and then five minutes later moved to another spot, and then moved to yet another spot, five or six times. This is because [the checkers] know there are cameras there and they know that sometimes police could be around with cameras or conducting surveillance on them. So this way it's like the shell and nut kind of game and they're trying to avoid being detected. And we know for a fact that they are doing this every time there is a specific container with illegal drugs." He also stated that Matticks charged a "user fee," going on to explain, "Anybody could use the Port of Montreal to import illegal merchandise; but there's one condition: If you want to go through with a container with drugs in it, you have to pay [Matticks] 25 percent to 35 percent of the value of the container. And it's not [always] in money; it's in product." He also acknowledged that probably "less than 10 percent" of the drugs that enter through the Montreal port are ever detected and seized by authorities.

Furthermore, the officer told the committee, "What was really frightening to see is that when we went through the list of [port] employees, we found that 15 percent [of longshoremen] have criminal records, and 36.3 percent of the checkers have criminal records." He told the committee that one criminal name which kept coming up was "the Matticks in Montreal."

Finally, Primeau said, "To become a [Coopers and Checkers] union member you need to be sponsored by someone who will vouch for you. Most of the employees . . . are either family members or very close friends [of Gerald Matticks]."

Donald Matticks

One such nepotistic employee was Gerald's son Donald "Donnie" Matticks, who began working at the port in 1988 at the age of twenty-four under the tutelage of his father. As a container checker, he worked alongside his dad and his uncle Richard identifying and clearing shipments containing drugs destined for members of the West End Gang, the Montreal Irish mafia, or the Hells Angels and Rock Machine motorcycle gangs. It had become an extremely lucrative family-run business.

But the family eventually ran into problems, beginning with Operation Thor, a Sûreté du Québec (formerly known as the Quebec Provincial Police) anti-gangster squad project. In May 1994, Gerald and Richard Matticks, Donald Driver, Steve Brown, Felice "Felix" Italiano, Roger Goulet, Pierre Friedman and William Hodges were arrested separately at their homes after 26 tons of hashish, valued at $360 million, was seized in the container ship *Thor*. The SQ figured they'd finally nailed the bad guys and had closed the leaky port. But it was not to be.

The tale of the *Thor* began in January 1993 at a Point St. Charles restaurant when Pierre Friedman happened to strike up a conversation with Roger Goulet, one of Gerry's West End Gang associates. Goulet, interested that Friedman was an executive with the Canadian Pacific Steamship Company's international freight division and had access to worldwide maritime firms and their schedules, took his number. He called him sometime later and they met with Matticks at a West Island restaurant where Gerry offered him $50,000 to use his connections to expedite shipments of hashish into the Port of Montreal. As Friedman, who was living beyond his means and needed cash, later acknowledged in court, "I saw a bit of a chance for an adventure to play the lottery, but I didn't win. That's why I'm here."

On March 17, using Friedman's information, 10 tons of hashish were successfully smuggled through the port. Then a much bigger shipment was set up: 26 tons of hash from Mozambique and Uganda, hidden in three containers, supposedly containing tea, spices and women's blouses, aboard the *Thor* that was to arrive via Durban, South Africa. The *Thor* tied up at a Montreal wharf at midnight on May 3, 1994, and its cargo of 300 containers was immediately offloaded. However, the SQ, who'd been tipped off about the shipment, placed 24/7 surveillance on the three suspect containers, waiting to see who would pick them up. But nobody did, since the bad guys suspected that the cops were watching. Nevertheless, it was, to the delight of the SQ, the biggest drug seizure in Canadian history, and they knew who was involved.

Friedman was arrested eight days later. To avoid a three-year prison sentence, Friedman agreed to become an informant and was put into the witness-protection program where he'd eventually be shipped out of Canada with his family. But the quid pro quo was for him to wear a police wire in order to get incriminating evidence during his next meeting with the Matticks brothers. He subsequently became the Crown's star witness, testifying against Gerald, Richard and the others who had been arrested shortly thereafter. Their trial began on September 26, 1994.

With Friedman's testimony and his recorded conversation with the Matticks brothers while they discussed the abortive *Thor* shipment, the SQ had put together a strong case. But then, through overzealousness and stupidity, they blew it.

On June 15, 1995, Quebec Court Judge Micheline Corbeil-Laramée ordered a stay of proceedings when it came out that Sûreté du Québec (SQ) detectives had planted incriminating evidence in the form of four fictitious maritime lading documents at the offices of Warner Philips Ltd. in order to bolster their case against the accused. She angrily denounced the cops for what she called "reprehensible conduct," and effectively dropped all charges against the seven defendants. They were again free men.

Apart from the Matticks brothers, those who were set free included:

- **Donald "Don" Driver,** fifty-four, a long-time Matticks associate. He was later arrested during a drug bust on July 17, 2002, and released on $100,000 cash bail, plus an 11 p.m. curfew and other conditions. He pleaded guilty on October 4, 2004, and was sentenced to eight years in prison on January 18, 2005, for his role in importing marijuana and cocaine from Mexico to Montreal. He became eligible for restricted parole in June 2006.
- **Steve Brown,** twenty-five, who claimed to be the adoptive son of Gerald Matticks and the son of Matticks' mistress. He had a notorious fiery temper, and in 1989 and 1991 had spent several months in provincial jail on charges of aggravated assault. He later became the manager of Mickey's Restaurant, a South Shore country-and-western bar that was owned by Matticks. In 1997, Brown was handed a nine-year sentence for his role in trafficking 150 kilos of cocaine. He was denied day parole on August 18, 1999, when the National Parole Board declared him to "have a tendency for violence," going on to explain, "[because of] your association with the Matticks clan and your role as a leader in drug trafficking for which you are presently incarcerated." He appealed the decision and was granted day parole on January 11, 2000, with many conditions attached. But he was re-arrested on February 25, 2005, during a cocaine sting operation involving the Hells Angels. His parole was therefore revoked, and on February 19, 2007, while still in prison, he was handed another

five-year term for his role in the cocaine bust. He was finally granted restricted day parole on April 27, 2010.

- **Felix Italiano,** forty-nine, a Lachine, Quebec, car-dealership manager, who soon after returned to his native Italy. He and several others were later arrested there on October 23, 2007, on charges of money laundering and stock market fraud.
- **Roger Goulet,** sixty-three, the Matticks associate who had made the initial contact with Pierre Freidman of Canadian Pacific in January 1993. He was later arrested on drug charges on July 18, 2002.
- **William Hodges,** sixty-nine, a friend of Gerald Matticks and president of Warner Philips International, a Montreal maritime-salvage company. He was alleged to have assisted in the planned shipment of drugs aboard the *Thor*.

The bungled *Thor* bust became known as "The Matticks Affair" and led to the suspension of four SQ detectives who were charged with perjury and evidence-tampering. Although they were acquitted on June 9, 1996, it was clear that the SQ hierarchy, while supposedly conducting an internal inquiry, was in fact doing its best to cover up the embarrassing fiasco. This led to the Quebec government Poitras Commission, established on October 23, 1996, and mandated to inquire into the operations and investigative practices of the Sûreté du Quebéc. It was not a pretty picture.

The commission's 1,734-page final report, issued on December 30, 1998, at a cost of $20 million to Quebec taxpayers, was a scathing indictment of the province's police force and its internal investigation department. The report concluded that apart from the Matticks Affair, the force "routinely broke laws during its criminal investigations." The commission noted that there were "serious problems" within the SQ, and recommended that the government establish a "civilian body" that would oversee the force.

Undoubtedly Gerry Matticks must have gloated over the public scorn heaped upon the SQ. But he would not gloat for long, for the cops were still hot on his trail, and soon they would need no fabricated evidence to put him away.

Operation Springtime 2001, a combined investigation by the RCMP, the SQ and various municipal police forces in Quebec and Ontario, had begun its investigative work in 1998. The operation, aimed primarily at the Hells Angels and other biker gangs, resulted in the March 28, 2001, arrest of some 45 persons, including a few non-biker members such as Gerald Matticks. The charges ranged from murder to drug-smuggling and trafficking.

Gerry's trusted partner and accountant, Luis Elias Lekkas, was arrested on similar charges. He immediately turned police informant, becoming a key Crown witness in July 2001. That summer Lekkas twice attempted suicide at the age of thirty in his Bordeaux prison cell while awaiting trial, apparently in fear of retribution by prison associates of the Matticks clan and the Hells Angels. In exchange for his information about the connection between Matticks and Hells Angels members Maurice "Mom" Boucher and Normand Robitaille, and how the drugs were being shipped through the port, Lekkas was given a relatively light seven-year sentence. He later went underground via the government's witness-protection program.

Matticks originally denied his guilt, insisting that he was being set up by the SQ in retaliation for the embarrassing Matticks Affair debacle. His lawyers even played the Robin Hood card, introducing several character witnesses, including a parish priest, who lauded Gerry's largesse when he would play Santa Claus every Christmas and pass out turkeys and cash to the poor and elderly in Point St. Charles.

However, once confronted with Lekkas' credible and damaging testimony, plus police-taped audio and video surveillance recordings, Matticks changed his plea to guilty on the condition that he would not be extradited to the United States, where some of the drugs had been delivered. On August 6, 2002, he was sentenced to 12 years in prison, convicted of gangsterism and drug importation, mostly on behalf of the Nomads chapter of Hells Angels.

Coincidental with Operation Springtime was another combined-force investigation known as Project Boeuf, beginning in June 2001. This operation, so named because Gerald Matticks had a beef cattle ranch in La Prairie, and a meat wholesale business in St. Hubert, just

John McLean

south of Montreal, was aimed specifically at the West End Gang.

It culminated in the arrest of 14 persons on December 4, 2002, on charges of importing 33 tons of hashish and 260 kilos of cocaine, worth a total of $2.1 billion, through the Port of Montreal between January 1998 and February 2001. Among those arrested were Gerald's son Donald, thirty-nine; Donald Driver, sixty-one; John McLean, fifty-two; Serge Charron, fifty-three; Frederick Bougie, thirty-two; Normand Beauregard, thirty-nine; Michael Thomas, forty-three; Danny Fraser, forty; Darren Wilding, thirty-six; and James Morrison, sixty. In exchange for a reduced eight-year sentence, McLean became an informant against the others who were caught in the operation. His first application for day parole was turned down in 2004 on the basis that no Montreal halfway house would be safe with him there, since the Mattickses and their associates still had it in for him. By this time, of course, Gerald Matticks was already behind bars, serving his 12-year sentence as a result of Operation Springtime.

In October of 2004, Donald Matticks pleaded guilty to 14 charges of importing drugs through the port, and on January 18, 2005, he received an eight-year prison term. Since it was his first criminal conviction, he was granted pre-release day parole on May 5, 2006, to live in a halfway house, and then full parole on August 24, 2007. But he was sent back to prison in July 2008 after being stopped for impaired driving and using cocaine. He again gained day parole on September 29, 2010, and at year's end, at the age of forty-six, he was back in a halfway house.

At that last National Parole Board hearing, Matticks was ordered to "refrain from using any drug and alcohol [and] from frequenting certain places such as drinking establishments." Moreover, the NPB panel warned: "You are to avoid any contact with your accomplices as well as any person with a criminal record, including your father and any other person associated with the Port of Montreal . . . because in the past you committed your crimes with such persons while in contact with them or under their influence."

As for his father Gerald, the King of the Port was twice denied early parole as "an undue risk to society." But on August 6, 2010, once he had served the statutory two-thirds of his sentence, he was released at the age of seventy. However, he came out a far poorer man than when he went in. During his trial in 2001, police investigators estimated that Matticks had personally pocketed $13 million in 2000 as a result of his drug-import dealings with the Hells Angels. Upon his arrest, his assets, which included two South Shore farms, 300 head of cattle, a meat processing business and stock in several other companies, were seized by the government. And to add insult to injury, in June 2004 the Quebec Department of Revenue sent him a $2.1 million bill in prison for the unpaid 7.5 percent provincial sales taxes on his drug-related earnings.

Moreover, his strict National Parole Board conditions prohibit him from ever entering the Port of Montreal and from "any type of communication with any person having a criminal file as well as those related to the drug subculture or to any criminal activities or with criminal organizations." In effect, Gerald Matticks has to sever all ties with much of his family and most of his former friends in order not to be sent back to prison to complete his full 12-year sentence in 2014.

# CHAPTER 18

# The Bloody Biker War

S hortly after noon on Wednesday, August 9, 1995, eleven-year-old
Daniel Desrochers was happily playing on the lawn in front of
the Saint-Nom-de-Jésus elementary school with his ten-year-old
friend Yan Villeneuve on Adam Street in Montreal's East End when
Marc Dubé, a twenty-six-year-old drug dealer and member of the Rock
Machine motorcycle club, climbed into his Jeep Renegade across the
street. Seconds later, there was a thunderous explosion.

A shard of hot metal struck Desrochers in the head, and several small
pieces hit Villeneuve in the arms and legs. Villeneuve looked on in horror
as his friend fell to the ground and Dubé's mangled body was hurtled
skyward from the open Jeep. Desrochers and Dubé soon after died in
hospital, victims of a remote-controlled bomb that had been placed
under the vehicle, possibly by Gaetan Comeau of the Hells Angels.

The two youngsters happened to be in the wrong place at the wrong time during a war that had begun the year before between the Hells Angels and other Montreal motorcycle gangs, particularly the Rock Machine, over control of the city's drug turf. It was to last eight years, from 1994 to 2002, and would claim some 160 victims, almost all outlaw bikers with criminal records. In the war's opening year, more than a dozen bikers on either side were shot through the head or ripped apart with machine-gun fire before their bodies were (usually) dumped into a stolen car or van, which was then set on fire to destroy the evidence.

The public and the cops had at first accepted it as simply bad guys killing other bad guys and, although the murders were investigated, no one was overly concerned. "I remember seeing a headline in a newspaper one day [that read]: 'Hells Angels 4; Rock Machine 2', like it was a fucking hockey game," says André "Butch" Bouchard, today a retired Montreal police homicide detective. "So the people looked at that and they laughed; they didn't give a shit, because [the bikers] were killing each other."

However, when young Daniel was inadvertently killed in the crossfire, the public's attitude switched to one of outrage. And that led to the formation of the Wolverines ("les Carajous" in French), an anti-biker unit consisting of 60 officers from the RCMP, SQ, the Montreal police anti-gang squad and other municipal police forces. This special unit declared all-out war against Quebec's outlaw biker gangs, specifically the Hells Angels and the Rock Machine. Bouchard was a senior member of the Wolverine Squad.

## The Hells Angels in Quebec

The Hells Angels, the world's largest criminal biker group, had its genesis in Oakland, California, in 1948, and initially was a collection of freewheeling, open-road Harley Davidson riders, who were largely disenchanted vets from the Second World War. It was incorporated as a club in 1966, by which time it had changed its image to that of an outlaw organization, adopting its winged death's-head crest. By then, it had become heavily involved in crime and intimidation. Members referred to themselves as "the one-percenters," in response to the

American Motorcycle Association's insistence that 99 percent of its 300,000 members are law-abiding citizens who just enjoy riding their bikes and occasionally getting together to party at jamborees or motorcycle-racing events. By 2010, the Angels had approximately 3,000 full-patch members, plus a network of associates in puppet gangs, within 248 chapters in some 30 countries around the world. In Canada today there are about 460 full-patch members in 34 chapters, mostly in Quebec, Ontario and British Columbia. But most of the Quebec members are currently behind bars, after having been convicted on charges of murder, drug trafficking and gangsterism during the early 2000s.

The first Canadian chapter was formed in Montreal on December 5, 1977, cloaking under its death's-head wings several local gangs such as the Popeyes, at the time the city's most violent bikers, and other smaller clubs in the city and across the province. Its first president was Yves "Le Boss" Buteau, who was later shot to death in November 1983 during a pre-opening salvo of the biker war. Their headquarters were in a heavily fortified bunker, replete with bulletproof window coverings, motion detectors and surveillance cameras, in the town of Sorel on the St. Lawrence River, a 45-minute drive northeast of Montreal. On October 18, 2008, long after most of the Hells Angels had been sent to jail, the abandoned bunker was destroyed by fire when someone drove a stolen fuel tanker truck through its wall and set it ablaze. The residents of Sorel were only too happy to see the destruction of this blight on their community.

Soon after their arrival in 1977, the Hells Angels set out to seize control of Montreal's retail drug trade by intimidating bar owners and local street dealers. Two of their main sources for product in bulk were Dunie Ryan and Gerald Matticks of the West End Gang. However, they didn't hit their stride as Canada's most powerful and feared biker gang until Maurice Boucher took over the helm 10 years later.

Maurice "Mom" Boucher was born on June 21, 1953, in the town of Causapscal, on the Lower St. Lawrence near the New Brunswick border, and was later raised in Montreal's tough East End district, where he had several run-ins with the law during his teenage years. His initiation into

Maurice "Mom" Boucher, circa 2005

a motorcycle club was in the early 1970s with a small white-supremacist group known as the SS, of which Salvatore Cazzetta was a founding member. After being released from a 40-month sentence for armed sexual assault, Boucher first joined the Hells Angels in May 1987, and quickly rose to become its charismatic yet authoritarian president.

In 1992, he created the Rockers, a puppet gang of loan-sharking thugs and drug dealers, and in June 1994 he formed the Hells Angels' Nomads chapter, an elite cadre of assassins who were primarily responsible for instigating the biker war. Their principal targets were members of the Rock Machine, the city's second largest biker gang. The two sides were soon involved in a no-holds-barred struggle over control of the lucrative retail drug trade on the streets and in the bars of Montreal.

Prior to the war, the Hells Angels had some internal business to take care of. One of its chapters was based in Laval, just north of the city. It was founded by Yves "Apache" Trudeau, the freelance hitman who later did "jobs" for Dunie Ryan and Alan Ross of the West End Gang. Trudeau, who had founded the Popeyes in the 1960s, was among the first to join the Hells Angels in 1977. But he branched off in September 1979 to form its Laval chapter, a group known for its violent and often irrational behavior and excessive drug use. In the spring of 1982 the Canadian Hells Angels passed a bylaw prohibiting its members from consuming cocaine or any other drug heavier than marijuana or hashish. The reasons were twofold: it ate into the profits that could be made by selling cocaine, and a coke-head biker was not at his best when it came time to whack a member of a rival gang. Trudeau and the rest of the Laval members shrugged off the fiat and continued to snort. As Gilles "Le Nez" Lachance, a former member of the Laval branch, would later testify in court, most of them, and especially their chapter president, Laurent "L'Anglais" Viau, were often stoned out of their minds on cocaine.

The Hells Angels hierarchies in the Quebec and Nova Scotia chapters were more than a little annoyed by the Laval chapter's continual flaunting of the rules. They were also angered by the fact that Trudeau had expanded his gun-for-hire business to work for the West End Gang, namely his killing of Hughie McGurnaghan in October 1981, and the apartment bombing of four others in November 1984. The chapter presidents conferred and decided that drastic action had to be taken.

On March 24, 1985, eight top-ranking Laval members, Laurent Viau, thirty-three; Jean-Guy "Brutus" Geoffrion, forty-eight; Jean-Pierre "Matt Le Crosseur" Mathieu, thirty-five; Guy-Louis "Chop" Adam, thirty-one; Michael "Willie" Mayrand, twenty-nine; Claude "Coco" Roy, thirty-one; Gilles Lachance and Yves Trudeau, both forty-one, were summoned to a meeting of the Hells Angels' Sherbrooke chapter at their Lennoxville, Quebec, bunker in the Eastern Townships. Fortunately for Trudeau, he couldn't make it, as he was then in a Montreal detox center where he was trying to kick his cocaine habit.

Apart from Lachance and Roy, the five others successfully kicked their coke habit for good that day. Shortly after they arrived, they were each shot through the head by members of the Sorel and Sherbrooke chapters. Their bodies were stuffed into weighted-down sleeping bags and dumped off a pier into the St. Lawrence River where they weren't fished out until three months later.

It became known as the "Lennoxville Massacre," and led to the arrest of Luc Michaud, Robert "Snake" Tremblay, Réjean Lessard and Jacques "La Pelle" Pelletier on charges of first-degree murder of the five Laval bikers. The four were eventually found guilty in 1987 and were sentenced to life in prison. Michaud, who was considered the driving force behind the killings, was released on full parole in June 2005. Tremblay, a member of the Sherbrooke chapter, went on the lam in France and England for a few years, but was arrested by Scotland Yard and extradited back to Canada in July 1987 and is still behind bars.

Lessard and Pelletier were both granted day parole in October 2008 after serving lengthy sentences.

Trudeau, realizing that he'd been targeted to be whacked by his Hells Angels brethren that day, became a police informant against them in July 1985. Lachance, a surviving witness to the purge, also turned informant. In November 1986, he testified against the assassins, in exchange for which he was given a new identity (including plastic surgery for his bulbous nose) in the government's witness-protection program.

## The Bandidos in Ontario

The purge of a group of bikers lured into a deadly trap by fellow gang members would later be duplicated and even exceeded in Ontario by the Bandidos, a biker club formed in 1966 in Houston, Texas. Its initial membership consisted of Vietnam War veterans and, as an outlaw motorcycle gang, it is second in size to the Hells Angels. It has chapters worldwide, including several in Canada.

On April 7, 2006, eight Bandidos from the Toronto-area chapter, known as the "No Surrender Crew," arrived for a weekend conference (known in biker parlance as a "church") and to party at a farm near Shedden, Ontario, southwest of London. Winnipeg Bandidos member Wayne Kellestine owned the 50-acre farm. Over the course of that night and early morning, six Winnipeg-based Bandidos executed all eight, apparently under orders from the Bandidos overall leader, Jeff Pike, known as "El Presidente," in Houston. Their crime had been to run afoul of the Houston head office over dues payments and a refusal to surrender their Bandidos patches. The Winnipeg branch was ordered to take care of the problem by "pulling their patches" by whatever means necessary. It resulted in one of Ontario's largest mass slayings and the most dramatic internal purging of outlaw bikers. Following a seven-month trial in the Ontario Superior Court, on October 29, 2009, all six Winnipeg men were found guilty of first-degree murder and sentenced to life in prison.

The Crown's key witness in the case was a police informant identified only as M.H., a forty-year-old drug dealer and former senior member of the Winnipeg Bandidos who was present during the slaughter.

He is now living under another identity in the witness protection program. During the trial M.H. admitted that he had once been a member of a Hells Angels puppet club, which he likened to "a farm team," and said that he'd sometimes provided security for the infamous Mom Boucher in Montreal. In one telling statement, he told the jury, "The leading cause of death amongst Hells Angels is other Hells Angels."

True. But in a broader sense, the death of an outlaw biker was usually at the hands of a competing outlaw biker, as was evident during the eight-year clash between the Hells Angels and the Rock Machine in Quebec.

## The Rock Machine in Quebec

The Rock Machine was founded by Salvatore Cazzetta and his younger brother Giovanni in 1986 when their SS biker gang was absorbed into the Hells Angels. Salvatore wanted nothing to do with an organization that flaunted its colors and so openly attracted heat from the cops. He also wanted no part of a gang that would brazenly eat its own, as it had the year before in the "Lennoxville Massacre." He therefore shunned overtures from his former friend Maurice Boucher to ride with the Angels.

Salvatore Cazzetta

Cazzetta, born in 1954, grew up in the tough southwestern Montreal area of Saint Henri, a neighborhood then controlled by the notorious Dubois brothers, who specialized in extortion and drug dealing. In his early twenties he served several short jail stints for burglary or possession of stolen goods and rode with the SS bikers.

In 1986, at age thirty-two and sporting a bushy dark beard and pony tail that would become his distinctive trademark, Cazzetta wanted a piece of the lucrative street-level drug trade that was being increasingly monopolized by the Hells Angels. By the early 1990s the Rock Machine had over a dozen members and was still growing. It had also formed a chapter in Quebec City and was soon muscling its way into drug-distribution territory that Mom Boucher and his gang considered their own. It was only a matter of time before war would erupt.

During the opening skirmishes, it was clear that the Rock Machine was outnumbered and outgunned. Cazzetta sought to even the odds by creating the "Alliance" (akin to the mafia style "Syndicate"). Under the Alliance umbrella, small biker gangs such as the Dark Circle, the Palmers Clan and the Pelletier Clan joined the fray. The Alliance shunned jacket colors, and instead wore identifying rings engraved with the acronym *ALVALM* (À la vie, à la mort; roughly translated to "As We Live, So Shall We Die"). They went head-to-head against the powerful Hells Angels, particularly its Nomads hit-squad division and puppet gangs such as the Rockers and the Evil Ones. The battle lines had been drawn and the carnage began.

Cazzetta personally missed most of the war, since he was arrested on May 6, 1994, during Project Choc, and was extradited to serve time in a U.S. prison. In 2002 he was shipped back to Canada to serve out the rest of his sentence at Archambault Penitentiary until being paroled on statutory release on July 9, 2004, after convincing the National Parole Board that he'd given up the criminal biker life.

Nevertheless, the battle of the bikers flourished without him. In fact, while he was incarcerated in the States, one of its casualties was his brother-in-law, thirty-seven-year-old Richard Parent, a cocaine trafficker who was gunned down on the street by the Hells Angels on August 5, 1999. The police at the time chalked up Parent's death as number 116 in Montreal's ongoing biker turf war. There were many more victims to come.

By the turn of the century the Montreal Hells Angels had racked up a much higher body count than had the Alliance, and Boucher is alleged to have placed an outstanding cash bounty of $100,000 for any full-patch Rock Machine member who was whacked. So, in order to even the odds, on December 1, 2001, the Rock Machine, in sort of a reverse corporate takeover, was absorbed into the Bandidos, an international biker gang with 45 full-patch members in Quebec. This would make the battle for supremacy of Montreal's drug trade even more deadly.

Following the 1995 death of eleven-year-old Daniel Desrochers, and several other innocent victims later, the authorities came down hard on the biker gangs. They were assisted in their arrests and prosecutorial convictions by the federal government's Bill C-95, passed in 1997, which amended the Criminal Code of Canada to acknowledge and include crimes that were committed "for the benefit of, at the direction of, or in association with" a recognized criminal organization. In effect, "gangsterism" became an indictable offense, with convictions carrying a mandatory five to fourteen-year prison sentence. The law now made it illegal to belong to a known criminal group, such as the mafia, the Hells Angels or any other biker gang. It was similar to the RICO Act that had been adopted in the United States in 1970 and had been used to put away members of the Italian mafia as well as full-patch American members of the Hells Angels and the Bandidos.

While the Wolverine Squad was busy amassing evidence against the bikers, the Hells Angels made three more outrageous hits. The first was the attempted murder of Michel Auger, a senior investigative crime reporter for *Le Journal de Montréal*, a Montreal daily tabloid, which was chronicling the biker war on a day-to-day basis. On September 13, 2000, Auger was getting out of his car in the *Journal's* parking lot when he was shot five times in the back by a gunman who immediately fled the scene. Auger survived, but the attempt on his life brought even more heat down on the Hells Angels.

Even more blatant was the murder of two off-duty Quebec penitentiary prison guards. On June 26, 1997, Diane Lavigne was shot and killed in her car by Stéphane "Godasse" Gagné while she was driving home from work. Three months later, on September 8, 1997, Pierre Rondeau was driving a prison van when he was ambushed and killed by Hells Angels member Paul "Fon Fon" Fontaine on a Laval side road. Robert Corriveau, a guard in the passenger seat, was also a target, but escaped unhurt.

As would later be disclosed in court, the killings had been ordered by Mom Boucher in an attempt to rattle the justice system and to demonstrate his power to any biker would-be informant. But on November 27, 1998, Boucher was acquitted for lack of evidence and he left the Montreal courthouse smiling and waving a two-fingered V sign to his compatriots. That night he attended a boxing match in the Montreal Molson Center, surrounded by a coterie of patch-wearing Hells Angels. He appeared to be untouchable and remained a free man for almost two years.

But the cops had built a strong case, primarily by encouraging witnesses to testify against Boucher. Stéphane Gagné, a Hells Angels member and major drug dealer, was the first to flip, turning police informant in December 1997 against Boucher and Fontaine in return for a 15-year sentence instead of the mandatory 25-year term he was facing for the murder of Diane Lavigne. The next to flip was André "Toots" Tousignant, a Nomads biker who was Boucher's bodyguard and who admitted to taking part in the prison guard murders with Gagné. Unfortunately, before he could testify in court, Tousignant was slain at age thirty-four by fellow Hells Angels. His bullet-riddled body was found in the Eastern Townships on February 27, 1998.

In 1997, Fontaine, a full-patch member of the Hells Angels Nomads chapter went on the lam in Mexico and elsewhere for seven years under the alias of Jean Goyer. He was arrested near Quebec City in 2004 and put on trial in Montreal in October 2008 for the murder of Pierre Rondeau. He was found guilty on February 1, 2009, and, at the age of forty-two, was given a life sentence with no chance of parole for 25 years.

On October 10, 2000, following the Crown's successful appeal of the 1988 verdict, Maurice Boucher was re-tried, this time with strong evidence consisting of wiretaps, video surveillance tapes and Gagné's credible testimony. On May 5, 2002, after 11 days of deliberation, the jury found forty-eight-year-old Boucher guilty of ordering the execution of the two prison guards. He was given an automatic life sentence with no possibility of parole for at least 25 years.

Boucher is currently diagnosed with throat cancer and is incarcerated in Canada's only super-maximum penitentiary in Sainte-Anne-des-Plaines, Quebec. Among his SHU fellow inmates are Canada's notorious child murderer, Clifford Olson, and the one-time Canadian Hells Angels national president Walter Stadnick.

As former homicide cop André Bouchard sees it, "Mom will either kill himself in prison or he'll die of cancer, or he'll be killed the first chance they get to kill him ... We've heard that [the Hells Angels] in the United States got together and they said to take the fucker out. They say that this is the guy that caused all the trouble." They blamed him for bringing down the heat on the Hells Angels in Canada. In fact, on October 23, Boucher survived several wounds during an altercation among four inmates in the prison.

With Mom out of the picture, there were still the rest of the bikers to be picked up and put away. The Wolverine Squad would accomplish that in three stages.

## Operation Springtime 2001

The first was Operation Springtime 2001, a combined investigation by the RCMP, the SQ and various municipal police forces which began in 1998 and culminated on March 28, 2001, with the arrest of some 42 members of the Hells Angels Nomads chapter and the Rockers biker gangs, plus dozens of their associates on charges of drug-dealing and murder during their battle over drug-distribution turf. Among those arrested was Mom's twenty-six-year-old son, Francis "Le Fils" Boucher, a member of the Rockers. On November 18, 2002, he pleaded guilty to drug trafficking, gangsterism, and conspiracy to commit murder, and received a 10-year sentence. He was granted statutory release on July 18, 2009, after having served two-thirds of his sentence.

## Operation Amigo

Next came Operation Amigo, another combined police force investigation which, on June 5, 2002, resulted in the arrest of some 60 members and associates of the Bandidos in Quebec and Ontario on charges of conspiracy to commit murder (mostly against Hells Angels members), drug trafficking and gangsterism. By September 2004, most had either pleaded guilty to reduced charges, or were found guilty and sentenced to various prison terms by the Quebec Court.

## Operation SharQc

Finally there was Operation SharQc (Stratégie Hells Angels Région Québec). It was a three-year joint investigation by the RCMP, the

SQ and various municipal police forces which on April 15, 2009, involved more than 1,200 officers arresting or issuing warrants for some 156 members and associates of the Hells Angels in Quebec, France and the Dominican Republic in the Caribbean on charges of gangsterism, drug trafficking and conspiracy to murder rival gang members of the Alliance (primarily the Rock Machine) between 1994 and 2008. Much of the evidence supplied to the investigators came from Sylvain Boulanger, a full-patch member and former sergeant-at-arms of the Hells Angels' Sherbrooke chapter from 1993 until 2005, who became a police informant in 2006.

SharQc was essentially an extension of Operation Springtime 2001. As of January 2011, 16 of those arrested in Operation SharQc were out on bail awaiting trial, 23 of the accused were still at large, and the other 117 were behind bars. The most recent capture, on November 1, 2010, was accused murderer and drug-trafficker Marvin "Casper" Ouimet, forty-one, who had managed to hide out for 18 months. Because of the large number of defendants involved, their trials have been split up into individual groups of 15 each, and could run as long as into 2014.

None of those investigations and subsequent convictions could have succeeded without police informants who made a deal with the Crown in order to reduce their sentence, make money, or disappear forever in a witness-protection program. Apart from stoolies like Gagné, Tousignant and Boulanger, two other major biker informants were Eric "Rat Killer" Nadeau and Dany Kane.

Eric Nadeau was a 1980s member of the Montreal Hells Angels who defected to the Bandidos in 1991 following an attempt on his life by his own gang. In reality, he was a paid police informant hired to infiltrate the Bandidos. By early 2002 he'd become the Bandidos' Canadian National Secretary, all the while supplying police with details about the gang and its drug-turf war with the Hells Angels. With his inside information, the Wolverine Squad executed Operation Amigo. Nadeau later complained that he had been abandoned by the police and filed a civil suit against them for the money he says he was promised for his efforts.

Dany Kane was an early Hells Angels member, drug trafficker and contract killer for the Rockers. Beginning in October 1994, he also secretly worked for the RCMP and later the SQ (under the source code name "C-2994") for six years, being promised $1,750,000 for his inside information. Kane surreptitiously recorded hundreds of hours of audiotapes, which supplied most of the evidence that eventually convicted many of the Quebec Hells Angels in Operation Springtime 2001. During those years Kane led four lives: a husband and father of four young kids; the bi-sexual lover of a Hells Angels associate; a driver and bodyguard for one of Mom Boucher's top lieutenants; and a mole for the cops.

On August 7, 2000, at the age of thirty-one, Kane was found suffocated to death by carbon monoxide poisoning while sitting in his car with the engine running in the garage of his home in the village of Saint-Luc, on the Richelieu River southeast of Montreal. This was shortly before he was due to testify in court and to collect the bulk of his promised source money and disappear into the witness-protection program. His death was officially declared a suicide, but has since led to all kinds of conspiracy theories, with many believing that he was killed by either the Hells Angels or the cops, who made it look like suicide. There's even a rumor that he's not dead at all, but faked his death and is now living the good life somewhere on the proceeds of his ratfink money.

Butch Bouchard doesn't buy any of that. "A lot of people say that we killed him, and a lot of people say that he was killed by the Hells Angels and a lot of people say he's not dead. But I can tell you that he's dead, because my friend [in the Montreal major crimes division] was his controller and was the one who identified him in his car." Bouchard adds, "Dany was the best source we had . . . He'd call [the Wolverine Squad] before he had a meeting with Mom, and we'd put cameras in . . . that's how we got them. Dany even gave us Matticks on Beaubien Street where we got Matticks coming in there with fucking hockey bags full of money." Bouchard suggests that Kane finally killed himself out of shame that he'd ratted on his biker brothers and because he knew, "as Project 2001 was coming to completion, [the Hells Angels] would eventually get him . . . and he was worried about the way he would be killed—tortured, things like that."

By 2002, the bloody Quebec biker war was essentially over. Following several mega-trials most of the bad guys who'd been fortunate enough not to have been whacked were behind bars. Still others were rounded up during Operation SharQc, with their trials still to be held. What's left of the Montreal Hells Angels today is the Big House Crew, a name adopted by the gang for their incarcerated members who remain in good standing. By mail, by phone or by word of mouth behind prison walls they continue to keep up to date on North America's Hells Angels chapter activities.

# CHAPTER 19

# The RCMP's Largest Drug Seizure

What would amount to the RCMP's largest-ever drug seizure, and one directly connected to the West End Gang, ironically had its roots in a drug and alcohol rehabilitation center where people were attempting to kick the habit.

The plot began in the Heritage Home Foundation in Huntington, Quebec, 46 miles southwest of Montreal, near the New York State border. The foundation's director was Catherine Cosgrove Toman, a psychotherapist who'd previously worked at Addington House, another Montreal rehab center. She also happened to be the wife of Peter Toman, a West End Gang associate and convicted fraudster from the Town of Mount Royal.

Over an eight-month period between August 1, 1996 and March 31, 1997, Toman had been grossly inflating the value of the accounts receivable for two failing companies he owned—Trekka Sportswear Inc. and Vêtements Avenues des Amériques Inc., both on Chabanel Street in Montreal's garment district—in order to secure bridge financing from the National Bank of Canada and the Bank of Nova Scotia. When his companies went belly-up and declared bankruptcy in March 1997, the banks were left holding the bag to the tune of almost $2.5 million, and they accused Toman of fraud. He was arrested, tried and found guilty. On April 13, 2005, he was sentenced to two years to be served in the community and was ordered to make full restitution to the two banks. A motion by the Crown to have him serve prison time was rejected by the Quebec Court of Appeal on December 5, 2005.

## 22.5 Tons of Hash

In a desperate bid to come up with the money to reimburse the banks, or else face jail time, Toman, at the age of fifty-nine, turned to the world of drugs. And in a very big way. In fact, he intended to make a lot more money than he owed the banks. He devised a plan to smuggle tons of hashish from Pakistan by ship into Canada, and approached James Frederick Cameron, a former heroin addict who worked at the Heritage Home Foundation, in order to set the plan in motion.

Cameron had previously been busted on drug charges, but was now doing his best to stay clean. He saw this overture from Toman as an opportunity to earn some quasi-legal money as an RCMP informant and to later disappear under a different identity. This led to Project Chabanel, an 18-month RCMP sting operation. Cameron, who was paid several hundred thousand dollars for his undercover work, is now living under another identity, either in his home province of Nova Scotia or in Ontario.

In November 2004, Cameron contacted the RCMP and told them about the scheme. As fifty-one-year-old Staff-Sergeant André Potvin, head of the Mounties 136-member drug section in Montreal, recalls today, "We received information [from a source whom he will only officially identify as "James"] that Peter Toman was seeking to introduce a very large shipment of hashish into Canada, and he wanted to find a method of transportation. So we set up Project Chabanel

RCMP Montreal drug squad head, André Potvin

[named after the street where Toman had once operated his bankrupt companies] and began to investigate."

Toman's point man on the other end of the deal was fifty-seven-year-old Sidney "Sid" Lallouz, who was connected to the Montreal Jewish mafia and had close ties to the West End Gang and the Italian mafia. In 1983 he'd been sentenced to two-and-a-half years for conspiring to import 700 kilos of hashish into Montreal from Pakistan and was released in 1985. A few years later he was sued by various Montreal banks for $5 million for his role in suspicious real estate transactions in Old Montreal, as well as for tax evasion. He immediately fled to Spain to avoid prosecution, but snuck back into Montreal in 1994, using his Hebrew given name of Sidney Chimeon. He became co-owner of a health spa and small shopping mall, both of which went bankrupt, leaving investors holding the bag for almost $1 million. He was also suspected to have been involved with renegade cop Jean Belval in the 1994–1996 Marché Central shopping center financial scam in Montreal North, which had fleeced the Roman Catholic Sisters of the Good Shepherd nuns out of some $85 million. He was never charged in that case. By 2004, Lallouz was in Pakistan, where he was setting up the proposed shipment for Toman.

Potvin and his drug squad then set up what is undoubtedly the most elaborate (and expensive) sting operation in the history of the RCMP. But the rewards, in terms of contraband seized, would be enormous, amounting to 22.5 tons of high-grade hashish originating from Afghanistan and Pakistan.

"We set up a sting through our undercover man [Cameron] who by this time had gained [Toman's] trust," explains Potvin. "You can compare it to going fishing, and [Toman] really caught onto the hook." Toman was looking for a boat with a trusted captain that could pick up the drug shipment and deliver it to Canada. The RCMP provided it by chartering a 150-foot cargo vessel out of Halifax and a "captain" who, in reality, was an RCMP agent. The fake captain met with Toman, who paid him $195,000 cash up front and the promise of another $5 million once the hashish was delivered and sold. The plan was to rendezvous with another cargo vessel off the coast of Angola where the drugs would be transferred to the Canadian vessel, which would then bring it back to Canada.

Potvin adds, "We now had a covert boat, but we needed to have a second boat just in case something went wrong. You're going out in the middle of the Atlantic Ocean, and obviously there's [RCMP] officer safety involved in case of possible attacks, or burns from the drug lords or whatever ... Because once [the drugs] are taken aboard by the recipient, you're kind of opening yourself up to the people that gave it to you. If those guys want to do a burn on you, they can call any of their buddies and say, 'Listen, we just gave 22.5 tons of hash to a Canadian boat. Do you guys want to rip it off?' Which could have happened." So the Mounties enlisted the help of the Department of National Defense, which agreed to put the Canadian Navy frigate HMCS *Fredericton* at their disposal.

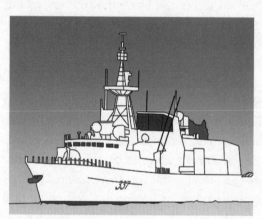

HMCS *Fredericton*

In early April 2006 the covert ship, with 15 armed RCMP officers aboard posing as crew members, sailed out of Halifax. On the same day, the *Fredericton* with its complement of about 200 sailors and a squad of RCMP officers pulled out of St. John's, Newfoundland, staying about 20 miles behind so as not to be picked up on radar as the pickup ship approached the southern coast of West Africa.

On May 10, 2006, the RCMP pickup vessel and the delivery ship, which had sailed from East Africa and had rounded the Horn with its cargo of hashish, met approximately 200 miles off the coast of Angola. The coordinates for the rendezvous point had been established earlier between Lallouz and the "captain" of the covert ship and the vessel, with a Filipino crew, that was delivering the drugs. Using GPS and brief UHF radio communications, the two boats eventually pulled alongside one another in a calm sea, and 959 bales of hashish, each weighing about 50 pounds, were transferred from one ship to the other. Neither vessel could be identified, since both had their hull names and port of origin covered over.

The delivery vessel immediately headed south while the RCMP's covert ship sailed west to meet up with the *Fredericton* a day later where its bales of hash were offloaded and stored in the frigate's holds. Both then steamed back to Halifax. The 43-day mission at sea had been accomplished. All that was now left was to arrest those who had set it up.

The operation and transfer at sea "went like clockwork," says Potvin. His only regret is that, although he had headed the operation, he was not aboard either Canadian ship when the drug transfer took place. "I should have been," he explains, "but my son was in the RCMP training camp at the time and he was scheduled to graduate on April fourth. I wasn't going to miss out on that [ceremony], so there was a superintendant from the RCMP on the *Fredericton* to act as the commanding officer for me."

Once the *Fredericton* had delivered its cargo to Halifax, it was offloaded and shipped by a heavily guarded convoy of trucks to the RCMP's Montreal storage vaults on St. Antoine Street. Potvin now had to close the trap. "So basically what we did is we [via the undercover agent posing as the ship's captain] told Toman that we would bring the dope right into Montreal [and] he didn't have to worry about any trucking; we guaranteed him door-to-door service." The next arrangement was to deliver a sample ton of the hash to Toman where he could pick it up and test it for quality before having to pay any more money.

On Friday morning, June 2, 2006, the boat's "captain" arrived in a rental truck with the sample ton, consisting of 20 bales of hash-ish, at a hotel parking lot on St. Jean Boulevard in Pointe Claire on

Montreal's West Island, where Peter Toman and his twenty-year-old son Andrew were waiting for them in their own rental truck. The truck-to-truck transfer was closely observed by Potvin and other RCMP officers seated in unmarked cars parked some distance away. "We didn't want to make the arrest then," explains Potvin, "because he was going to deliver it to some obvious buyer, and we wanted to see who." The Mounties followed Toman's truck to a home on the outskirts of St. Jean sur Richelieu, about 30 miles southeast of Montreal, where the bales were being unloaded into a garage. And that's when the cops pounced.

"We arrested Peter and his son Andrew, as well as another individual who subsequently wasn't charged because we could not make a case against him that he knew what was being stashed in his garage," recalls Potvin. He adds, "[the Tomans] were taken completely by surprise—especially Peter when he actually met the undercover operator [the supposed boat captain]—because until then he had no idea that the whole thing was linked to the actual transport" of the drugs. "He probably thought it was somebody that tipped off the police here, and that we just acted on a tip." The two were being handcuffed and read their rights and, says Potvin, "It was kind of interesting. Here we had Peter utilizing his son to do this, but [Andrew] was worried about his dad and saying, 'Don't harm him; he's an old man; he's not violent.' And Peter's just saying, 'Keep your mouth shut; keep your mouth shut,' which he eventually did, because when we ended up interviewing them [back at RCMP headquarters] they didn't have much to say."

Later the same day Potvin and his men arrested Sidney Lallouz, who had flown back to Montreal, expecting to become a rich man with his share from the sale of the hashish.

It's estimated that the 22.5-ton shipment would have netted Toman and Lallouz more than $19 million by selling it wholesale at $8,500 per kilo off the boat. Potvin says that Toman's likely buyers were the Hells Angels and other organized gangs in Montreal and, "as we later found out from our U.S. counterparts, a good chunk of it was scheduled to go to New York City and Boston." Once the hash was broken down and sold on the street at $10 to $15 a gram, the RCMP estimated

22.5 tons of hashish aboard the HMCS *Fredericton*

the value of the seizure at approximately $225 million.

On the other side of the balance sheet, Potvin says that Project Chabanel cost the Canadian taxpayers "close to 7 or 8 million dollars … the bulk of it for wages of the hundreds of police officers involved … and also a big chunk went to the military for the use of the frigate to cross the Atlantic twice." He chuckles as he recalls, "One day [the *Fredericton*] gassed up, and I think it was like $250,000 worth of fuel. And my boss was telling me, 'I hope they don't send us the bill.' But sure enough [the Department of National Defense] did." Nevertheless, shrugs Potvin, "It all comes out of the same pocket at the end of the day; it's all the Federal government."

On August 15, 2006, Peter Toman pleaded guilty and received an 11-year sentence for his role as the mastermind behind the scheme. He was granted day parole in a halfway house on April 28, 2008, and gained full parole on March 28, 2010, after having served one-third of his sentence. His son Andrew also pleaded guilty the same day and, since he had no previous criminal record, was sentenced to only two years in prison. He was paroled eight months later in June 2007. Sidney Lallouz was tried separately and on September 25, 2006, he was sentenced to six-and-a-half years for his role as the broker in the attempted shipment. After having served the statutory two-thirds of his sentence, he was paroled on January 24, 2011, but with many stringent conditions attached.

Several minor players were arrested in connection with the scheme, including the infamous Donald Matticks. But he was soon released for lack of evidence. Another was Shawn Daoust, Peter and Catherine Toman's thirty-year-old son-in-law from Candiac, Quebec. He had previously served prison time for marijuana production, and on August 15, 2006, he was handed a four-year sentence for his role in the smuggling plot. He was paroled two years later.

## Operation Cabernet

Following Project Chabanel, RCMP Staff-Sergeant Potvin and his squad made several other successful drug busts, some of which were tied to the West End Gang. They consisted mostly of seizures of cocaine smuggled by container ship into Montreal by various means, including a June 2007 shipment of 160 kilos of coke hidden in buckets of frozen mango puree from Mexico.

One bust that turned sour against Potvin and his drug squad was Operation Cabernet. (All of the RCMP's Montreal "projects" or "operations"—a name that is used interchangeably—begin with the letter "C", the letter designated by the federal force for the province of Quebec).

Operation Cabernet, which began in late 2005, was similar to Chabanel in that it involved a sting operation that would lure drug smugglers into an RCMP trap using a decoy ship's captain. The targets were West End Gang associates Christopher Tune, fifty-two years old; Steeve Morin, twenty-seven; Martin Belhumeur, thirty-five; and Daniel Rivard, forty-six, all of whom had previous drug-related convictions. The four had come up with a plan to smuggle up to a ton of cocaine by boat from Colombia via Venezuela and Martinique to Montreal in the summer of 2006. But, like Peter Toman, they first had to find the right boat and a willing captain. And that's when Pierre "Panache" Tremblay entered the picture.

Tremblay had a colorful background. He was in a halfway house on drug charges in November 1998 when he was arrested by the RCMP for his role with West End Gang member Raymond Desfossés and two others to import 210 kilos of cocaine into Canada aboard a private plane in 1989. In 1991, while out on day parole, he and Desfossés were forced to sink several tons of hashish on a boat off the south coast of Nova Scotia when the truck that was supposed to pick it up never showed up. Using a diver, Tremblay later tried to recover the drug shipment, only to find out that it had already been retrieved by the RCMP. He was re-arrested and found guilty of drug smuggling in November 1998, and given a 15-year sentence in 2000. In January 2005, while on conditional parole, he agreed to work as a tipster for the RCMP, and on September 2, 2005, he signed a contract with his Montreal RCMP drug squad investigator and handler, John Golden, which promised him $400,000 to work as an undercover agent. Tremblay is probably the first person to have signed such a deal with the RCMP while still on conditional parole. And that is where the drug squad's problems began, especially once it turned out that Tremblay was still an active drug dealer while working for the cops.

Wearing an RCMP-supplied hidden wire, Tremblay met with Christopher Tune at the Atwater Market on March 31, 2006, and a couple of times thereafter to discuss the plan by which Tune and Daniel Rivard intended to smuggle the Colombian cocaine into Canada. Another West End Gang associate, Donald Waite, attended one of the taped meetings in order to check out Tremblay's street cred as a "bad guy" rather than a police plant. Tremblay's role was to introduce Tune to a trustworthy boat captain who would pick up the drugs off the coast of the island of Martinique.

The deal was eventually set up. But unlike the complex Chabanel Operation, there was no need to go to sea. The Mounties figured they had enough evidence from the incriminating taped conversations as well as telephone wiretaps to go directly to court instead. Tune and his cohorts were arrested that December on charges of conspiring to import between 500 and 1,000 kilograms of cocaine into Canada and were held without bail to await trial. Martin Belhumeur died of heart failure in January 2009 at a Rivière des Prairies detention center, and the trial for the others began later that year.

However, on January 25, 2010, Quebec Court Judge Hélène Morin ordered a stay of proceedings after Tune's lawyer, Julio Peris, filed a motion pointing out that Tremblay had been violating his parole conditions by associating with known criminals while working as an RCMP informant to gather evidence against the accused. As a result of the judge's ruling, Tune was released from custody. Similar rulings were later made in the case of the other defendants, who will remain free unless the Crown comes up with additional evidence to appeal Judge Morin's decision.

Despite the setback in that particular operation, Project Chabanel remains the feather in the RCMP drug division's cap. "It was our biggest drug seizure ever," boasts Potvin. "When we were taking it off the *Fredericton* [docked in Halifax Harbor], we had about 100 or so RCMP officers making a human chain from the ship's hull onto our trucks, and it took almost two hours. That's how much dope there was!"

CHAPTER 20

# The Gelding of Montreal's Italian Mafia

*"There are many things my father taught me in this room: keep your friends close, but your enemies closer. If anything in this life is certain, if history has taught us anything, it is that you can kill anyone."*
—Michael Corleone, in a scene from the
1974 film *The Godfather: Part Two*

Perhaps the closest to the fictional Corleone family in Montreal are the Rizzutos, who arrived on the set when thirty-year-old Nicolo "Nick" Rizzuto Sr., with his wife and eight-year-old son Victor "Vito" Rizzuto, immigrated from Palmero, Sicily, in February 1954. They were relatively late mafioso émigrés, arriving decades after the Cotroni and Violi families had come from Italy's southern Calabria region to establish roots in Canada. As discussed earlier, there was no love lost between the Sicilians and Calabrians, and the two were soon fighting over control of Montreal's drug trade, well before the Irish mafia or the biker gangs entered the picture.

Nick Rizzuto Sr.

Unlike the Hells Angels and its Rock Machine rivals, the Italians managed to be a lot more circumspect in their internecine warfare, and thus drew less public attention. But they did draw blood. The Rizzutos were behind the January 1978 slaying of Paolo Violi, then the "godfather" of the Cotroni Family mob, as well as the murder of his brother Rocco in October 1980. The brothers headed the Montreal arm of New York's powerful Bonanno crime family, which supported the Cotroni mob. Two suspects in the killings were Vito Rizzuto and Paolo Renda, Nick Rizzuto's son-in-law, who'd immigrated to Montreal in 1958 and married Nick's daughter, Maria. Despite strong circumstantial evidence, neither man was ever convicted of the Violi murders. Vito later went on to replace his father as head of "the family," while Renda became their respected consigliere.

By the late 20th century, the Rizzutos were Montreal's dominant Italian crime family. But to wield such power was one thing; to hang on to it was another, as they would discover in the early 21st century.

Vito Rizzuto

Among the first of the immediate family to take a fall was Vito Rizzuto. On January 20, 2004, he was arrested at his Montreal mansion (on the basis of FBI informants Salvatore Vitale and Frank Lino) for the May 5, 1981, execution of three Bonanno renegade capos—Alphonse Indelicato, Philip Giaccone and Dominick Trinchera—in Brooklyn, New York. After many unsuccessful appeals against extradition, Rizzuto was deported from his Quebec prison cell to New York in August 2006 to face racketeering and murder charges.

On May 4, 2007, he pleaded guilty in a New York federal court to his involvement in the 1981 triple slaying, and was sentenced to 10 years in prison, with no chance of parole until he'd served 85 percent of his sentence. He will likely serve five years in a Florence, Colorado, federal penitentiary, plus another three years of supervised release in Canada before being eligible for full parole. On October 23, 2007, Italian police, with the assistance of the RCMP and Interpol, dismantled a major cocaine-smuggling and money-laundering ring, which Italian authorities, based on wiretapped conversations, claimed was being run by Vito from his Colorado cell. In May 2010, he challenged the length of his U.S. sentence, but was turned down. He filed an appeal against that decision in the U.S. Court of Appeals, but it too was rejected on August 19, 2010. Vito Rizzuto won't be released from prison until 2012, when he'll be 64 years old.

## A Marked Family

But it was not always Italians killing fellow Italians. The West End Gang also took its lumps. At 2:30 in the morning of July 12, 2006, forty-one-year-old Richard "Rick" Griffin pulled up in front of his home on Terrebonne Street in the residential neighborhood of NDG. As he stepped out of his car, he was mowed down by a hail of bullets. He died in hospital a few hours later, while crime scene investigators were picking up more than 40 spent shell casings in front of the home. They also recovered an Uzi machine pistol and a revolver on the lawn of the Rosedale Queen Mary United Church across the street from Griffin's house. The shooters were never apprehended, although the cops are certain it was a Rizzuto hit.

Griffin, one of eight siblings in an Irish Catholic family, was known to police. He'd had several run-ins with the law during the late 1980s and early '90s, but received only a six-month concurrent sentence on December 2, 1991, for obstruction of a police officer and for possession of a Mauser 7.65-caliber automatic pistol and silencer. He was brought up on extortion charges later that year, but acquitted in 1993. Griffin was also a partner-in-crime with another former West End Gang member and loan shark, Robert "Robbie" Brewer.

Through wiretaps and hidden cameras and microphones in the Cosenza Social Club, a mafia hangout on Jarry Street East in Montreal's St. Léonard district, investigators later discovered that 18 months prior to his death, Griffin had become involved with the Rizzutos in an abortive attempt to smuggle 1,300 kilograms of cocaine from Venezuela to Montreal via Newark, New Jersey. The delivery never happened, but the up-front money, amounting to $2 million, was apparently invested in the Bahamas by Francesco "Frank" Faustini, a forty-one-year-old online gambling networker, and Griffin's business partner. The Rizzutos wanted their money returned, but Faustini kept stalling, telling them that Griffin was holding it up as it had been invested in securities that had lost most of their value. Further recorded conversations at the Cosenza Social Club indicate that by June 27, 2006, Nick Rizzuto (referred to by mobsters on the tapes as "the old man") was fed up with the delay. His men leaned again on Faustini and Griffin with none-too-subtle threats, but got no satisfaction. By this time Griffin had, with good reason, become paranoid and was often accompanied by an armed bodyguard. But he was alone during those fateful wee hours of July 12.

Two days after the murder, police intercepted and recorded a cell phone conversation in Italy between Rizzuto henchmen Rocco Sollecito, fifty-eight, and his thirty-year-old son Giuseppe. Referring to the killing, Rocco says, "It would be a shame if they arrested someone because of that piece of shit. And they did it in front of his house, eh?" Giuseppe later says to his father: "You can't say that we did not do [Nick Rizzuto] a favor," agreeing that Griffin was indeed "a piece of shit!"

By coincidence, Griffin was killed on the day that his older brother John turned forty-nine, a birthday he happened to be spending in prison. John Griffin, a former professional boxer with ties to the West End Gang and the Hilton brothers, was first arrested at the age of twenty-nine on December 24, 1986, on two charges of assault, but was freed on both counts. He was next busted in 1995 for possession of hashish, and again in 2000 for possession of a restricted firearm, and got off both times with light sentences. On February 5, 2003, he was arrested and charged with first-degree murder in the shooting death three days earlier of thirty-eight-year-old Denis Poirier, a West End

Gang cocaine dealer, over an unpaid $80,000 drug debt, near the corner of Atwater Avenue and Workman Street in the city's southwestern St. Henri district. He was also accused, along with fifty-two-year-old Earl Harris, a West End Gang enforcer, of kidnapping and beating two men, Joseph Besso and Matthew Demaine, on January 22, 2003, in order to make them reveal where Poirier was hiding out.

In February 2003, Griffin was convicted and sentenced to life in prison for Poirier's murder by the Quebec Court, a ruling that was upheld by the Quebec Superior Court on February 11, 2005. But on May 2, 2008, the Quebec Court of Appeal ordered a new trial on the basis of supposed Superior Court trial judge errors. The Crown immediately appealed to the Supreme Court of Canada for a reversal of that decision, and on June 18, 2009, the High Court restored Griffin's first-degree murder conviction. He is still in jail. His accomplice, Harris, who'd acted as lookout when Griffin whacked Poirier, was charged with manslaughter for his role in the killing, and sentenced to nine years in prison. He was released in January 2010 after serving two-thirds of his sentence.

A third brother, Michael "Mike" Griffin, a Montreal businessman and boxing referee, has no criminal record, yet says he is constantly being harassed by police due to his family name. He is the owner and operator of Honey Martin's bar on Sherbrooke Street West in NDG. In October 2009, the police tried to close it down by having its liquor license revoked on the basis of previous noise complaints from neighbors and claims that it was a hangout for known gangsters, was serving alcohol to minors, and was a source of street-level drugs. But none of those allegations has ever been proven, and the Irish bar remains one of the most popular in NDG.

A close friend of the Griffin parents, John and Ann, who originally hailed from Verdun, today recalls that they were "an ultra-Catholic family" and that Ann "always worried about her oldest boys who were rebellious as teenagers." She adds that their mother "was especially concerned by the fact that young John and Richard looked up to The Fonz [the cool badass character played by Henry Winkler in the 1970s TV sitcom *Happy Days*] as a role model."

Other Montreal non-Italians also incurred the wrath of the Rizzuto Family during the early years of the 21$^{st}$ century, usually for competitive drug dealing, failure to repay usurious loans, or for running investment schemes in which the family lost money. Those hapless targets received a severe beating, or in some cases were murdered. The chief strong-arm enforcers for the Rizzutos at the time were Francesco "Chit" Del Balso and Lorenzo "Skunk" Giordano, two men who were about to be swept up in Canada's biggest ever mafia takedown.

## The Fall of the Rizzutos

At dawn on Wednesday, November 22, 2006, the ax came down on Montreal's Italian mobs, particularly the Rizzuto Family and its associates, during Project Colisée (Coliseum) when a combined police force, coordinated by the RCMP, arrested 70 persons and issued warrants for 20 others. The joint force, which had patiently been accumulating evidence for more than four years, was comprised of some 700 officers from the RCMP, the SQ, the Montreal and Laval police departments, the Canada Border Services Agency, and Revenue Canada. In a blitzkrieg of simultaneous raids, the officers, armed with arrest and search warrants, descended on the homes and businesses of almost everyone associated with the city's mafia, charging them with crimes committed between 2003 and 2006.

The seven major players targeted that morning were:

- **Nick Rizzuto Sr.**, eighty-two, the family patriarch. He was charged with extortion, bookmaking and drug smuggling. On September 18, 2008, he plea-bargained his way down to two counts of possessing profits from organized crime. On October 16, 2008, after having spent two years in detention since his arrest, he was released on three years' probation, with the condition that he not associate with known criminals. It essentially amounted to house arrest. He was later assasinated on November 20, 2010.
- **Francesco Arcadi**, fifty-three, a high-ranking lieutenant. He was considered the heir apparent to Nick's son Vito, who was then serving time in a Colorado penitentiary. On October 16, 2008,

Arcadi was found guilty of drug smuggling, racketeering, extortion and gangsterism, and was sentenced to 15 years in prison. He is still behind bars.

- **Paolo Renda,** sixty-seven, Vito Rizzuto's brother-in-law. He pleaded guilty to charges of gangsterism, drug trafficking, extortion, and weapons offenses, and received a six-year sentence on October 16, 2008. During an unsuccessful bid for early release, he was described at his National Parole Board hearing as "one of the leading members of the mafia in Montreal" and the right-hand man to Nick Rizzuto. On February 12, 2010, after reaching his statutory release date, Renda gained day parole, but with strict conditions, including observing curfews, not frequenting Italian cafés or communicating with known criminals until his full sentence ended on October 16, 2012. But he was later kidnapped on May 20, 2010.

- **Rocco Sollecito,** fifty-eight, a Rizzuto lieutenant with previous run-ins with Revenue Quebec and Revenue Canada, and a suspect in the murder of Richard Griffin. On October 16, 2008, he received an eight-year sentence after being found guilty of racketeering and gangsterism. He was also wanted by Italian police in connection with a $600 million money-laundering scheme headed by Beniamino Zappia, who was busted by the Carabinieri in Sicily in October 2007. On November 22, 2006, Sollecito pleaded guilty to conspiracy for drug smuggling, racketeering and extortion. He was found guilty on October 16, 2008, and sentenced to 15 years. He is still inside.

- **Lorenzo Giordano,** forty-three, a Rizzuto lieutenant. His arrests date back to an attempted April 2004 murder at the Globe Restaurant on St. Laurent Boulevard, and a November 2005 assault on John Xanthoudakis, CEO of Norshield Financial Group. But nothing was proven against him in either charge. Giordano had escaped the November 22, 2006, Project Colisée roundup, but was tracked down in Toronto and brought back to Montreal to face trial on May 9, 2007. He pleaded guilty on Sept. 18, 2008, to conspiracy and extortion charges, and was given a suspended sentence in the Court of Quebec on top of the time he'd already served. The Crown appealed, and on February 9, 2009, he was sentenced to 15 years in prison for gangsterism, extortion, and conspiracy to import drugs. Counting the time he had already served, Giordano faced 10 more years behind bars.

- **Francesco Del Balso,** thirty-six, a Rizzuto mob enforcer and hitman. In 1992 he was charged with arson, but was eventually cleared. In 2001 he pleaded guilty to assault with a weapon, and was sentenced to two years' probation. He was also suspected of murdering Magdi Garas Samaan over a money-laundering scheme that went bad in 2005, as well as participating with Giordano in the November 2005 assault on John Xanthoudakis. He's also still a suspect in the murder of Richard Griffin. Del Balso, arrested at his Laval home during Project Colisée, pleaded guilty on September 18, 2008, to conspiracy to smuggle drugs, racketeering and extortion. On October 16, 2008, he was given a 15-year prison term. He is still inside.

- **Giuseppe "Ponytail" De Vito,** forty-four, a mafia associate and cocaine importer who managed to skip town just before Project Colisée. He was finally arrested in Montreal's St. Léonard district on October 4, 2010, where he had changed his name and appearance. During his four years on the lam, his wife, forty-one-year-old Adele Sorella, the mother of their daughters, eight-year-old Sabrina and nine-year-old Amanda, was arrested on charges of murdering the two girls in their Laval home on March 31, 2009. As of February 2011, she was out on bail and her trial is still in progress. As for De Vito, he is locked up with his trial scheduled to begin in June 2011.

Apart from those seven, there were dozens of others, including a few members of the West End Gang, who were convicted on lesser charges and sent to jail as a result of Project Colisée, which continued into 2009. Most were not Mafiosi members, but were persons abetting them to smuggle drugs into the country through the Port of Montreal, across the Quebec–New York State land border, or through Montreal's Pierre Elliott Trudeau International Airport. Following the November 22,

2006 raids, an RCMP spokesman described it as "a very serious blow to Italian organized crime" and "one of the most significant" assaults against organized crime in Canada, comparing it to the Operation Springtime 2001 roundup of Quebec's outlaw biker gangs.

The authorities had succeeded in breaking the back of the Montreal mafia, reducing it to a scattered flock of lame ducks. And some of those ducks in the Rizzuto mob were about to be picked off one at a time by their underworld enemies.

The first to go was thirty-seven-year-old Sam Fasulo, a convicted heroin and crack cocaine dealer with close ties to Nick Rizzuto's right-hand man, Francesco Arcadi. On Friday afternoon, January 16, 2009, Fasulo was driving his Jeep Cherokee SUV in Montreal North when a vehicle pulled up beside him in traffic and its driver or passenger fired several shots at him before speeding away. Fasulo died of his wounds in hospital two days later. His murder remains unsolved.

Next to go was fifty-nine-year-old Frederico Del Peschio, who in 1988 was in a Venezuela jail with Nick Rizzuto Sr. when they and two others were arrested on charges of attempting to smuggle 1.5 kilos of cocaine through the Caracas airport. He later went on to become a close associate of Nick's son Vito and was co-owner and operator of the La Cantina restaurant on St. Laurent Boulevard. On Friday morning, August 21, 2009, Del Peschio had just gotten out of his silver Mercedes-Benz in the parking lot behind his restaurant when he was shot down by one or two gunmen. He died hours later in hospital. His murder remains unsolved.

But Fasulo and Del Peschio were mere bottom feeders in the Rizzuto organization. There were bigger targets to come.

Nick Rizzuto Jr., grandson and namesake of the family patriarch, and the son of Vito Rizzuto, was never charged for any crime more serious than impaired driving, although police suspect that he'd

Nick Rizzuto Jr.

been handling the financial end of his father's criminal affairs following Vito's 2004 incarceration in a U.S. prison. In 2007 he got into real estate development in partnership with Tony Magi, a man whom police had been investigating in connection with two alleged extortion attempts. Magi's firm was FTM Construction, with its offices on Upper Lachine Road in NDG.

At 10 minutes past noon on Monday, December 28, 2009, Rizzuto was about to get into his Mercedes sports car parked by the corner of Upper Lachine Road and Wilson Avenue, near the offices of FTM Construction, when a gunman approached and pumped four bullets into his chest. He died on the spot at the age of forty-two. The shooter immediately ran off and was never identified or captured.

Nick's casket lay for two days at the Complexe Funéraire Loreto, a St. Léonard funeral home owned by his mother, Giovanna, and his aunt Maria Rizzuto Renda, during which time a steady stream of family friends dropped by to pay their respects. His elaborate Roman Catholic funeral took place on Saturday, January 2, 2010, at the 90-year-old Romanesque-style Madonna della Difesa (Our Lady of Defense) church on Dante Street in Montreal's Little Italy. It was attended by an estimated 400 mourners inside the church, as well as hordes of journalists and assorted rubberneckers outside.[1]

One mafia mob boss who was unable to show up was Nick's own father Vito. His request for an escorted passionate leave was denied by U.S. prison authorities in Colorado. But Nick's eighty-six-year-old grandfather, Nicolo Rizzuto, although still on probation and technically prohibited from being in the company of anyone with a criminal record, was permitted to attend. It would be the last time he'd ever enter that church on his feet.

Five months after Nick's death, while the police and the press were still speculating about who might have killed him and why, the Rizzutos were dealt another blow.

---

1 I was at the church that day, curious to observe a funeral for a major mafia figure. I was slightly bemused by the fact that some of the men pouring out of stretch limousines, black Cadillacs and SUVs looked like they'd arrived from Central Casting, sporting fedoras and full-length charcoal cashmere coats, as extras in yet another "Godfather" film. It was also obvious from the blinking pinpoints of red light behind the tinted windows of two nondescript vans across the street that the cops were videotaping everything. As one RCMP agent later told me, "We're just as interested to see who doesn't show up as who does."

On Thursday afternoon, May 20, 2010, seventy-year-old Paolo Renda, Nicolo Rizzuto's closest associate and Vito Rizzuto's brother-in-law, left home in his Nissan Infiniti luxury car to run some errands. When he failed to return several hours later, his wife Maria grew worried and drove off to look for him, retracing his regular route. She soon spotted his car parked by the side of the road on Gouin Boulevard, not far from their home in Montreal's Cartierville area. The car, with its windows open and

Paolo Renda

keys in the ignition, was empty. Renda apparently had been waylaid and kidnapped. By January 2011, there was still no sign of him or his body, nor any ransom note delivered. Police and his family fear it's perhaps another Jimmy Hoffa case never to be solved.

As outrageous as the abduction of the mafia's Number Two man in Montreal was, more was yet to come. Around six in the evening on Wednesday, November 10, 2010, the family patriarch, Nicolo Rizzuto, was standing in the kitchen with his wife and daughter in their Antoine Berthelet Avenue home when a single bullet smashed through the window, killing him instantly at the age of eighty-six. The unknown sniper, whom police assume was a professional hitman, had fired a high-powered rifle from a secluded wooded area behind the house. The luxurious mansion on a street police refer to as "Mafia Row," is next door to that of Paolo Renda and two doors away from an equally impressive home owned by the incarcerated Vito Rizzuto.

Five days later, a second lavish funeral was held at the Madonna della Difesa church in Little Italy, only 10 months after Nicolo had last been there to bury his grandson.[2]

---

2 Nicolo was barely in his grave when the Montreal and national press launched a series of articles alleging that the Rizzuto Family was involved in intimidation, payoffs, collusion and bid-rigging on certain Quebec public works construction projects. The allegations came on the heels of an incediary October 4, 2010, Maclean's magazine cover article which declared Quebec to be "The Most Corrupt Province in Canada" with respect to political patronage, fraud, contract kickbacks, bribery, corporate tax-evasion, and other scandals.

Yet another Rizzuto-connected mobster was killed on January 31, 2011. Forty-four-year-old drug-trafficker Antonio Di Salvo was found shot through the head in the garage of his Rivière des Prairies home in Montreal's east end. He was closely connected to Rizzuto enforcers Francesco Del Balso and Francesco Arcadi, both of whom were busted during Project Colisée and are still in jail. Di Salvo's murder remains unsolved.

The brazen attacks on senior members of the Rizzuto mob have left the police bewildered. Guesses as to who is behind the purge range from an internal palace revolt to a power struggle originating from other mafia families in Ontario or New York, or perhaps upstart street gang members who, as one Montreal anti-gang detective says, "have absolutely no respect for their elders." Today the only major Rizzuto left is Vito, the family's so-called godfather. He's eligible for parole from his Colorado prison in 2012. He'll be returning home to a battered shell of a criminal empire that was once the most powerful in the city.

# CHAPTER 21

# Tobacco:
# The Mob's Latest Addiction

S ince the early 1900s, the importation, distribution or manufacture of illegal drugs has been the main source of wealth for
Montreal's criminal gangs. First it was heroin, brought in by
the Italian mafia from Marseilles in the 1930s and '40s. In the 1960s
and '70s, marijuana, hashish, amphetamines ("Speed" and "Poppers")
and hallucinogens such as LSD became the drugs of choice, and by
1980 cocaine was the biggest moneymaker of all. By the 1990s the list
of gangland revenue-producing drugs was expanded to include crack
cocaine, the psychoactive drug known as "Ecstasy," and even Rohypnol,
the so-called "date-rape" drug.

Anyone convicted for the distribution of those illicit drugs could
expect to serve some serious prison time. Yet not so for another drug:
nicotine, an addictive yet legal substance which has led to the deaths

of far more people than all of those other narcotics combined. A 2009 report by Health Canada estimated that each year more than 37,000 Canadians die of illnesses such as heart attacks, strokes or emphysema due to cigarette smoking. However, the Canadian and provincial government are themselves addicted to nicotine through the billions of dollars they receive each year from the taxes they impose on the sale of tobacco products to the nation's estimated 5 million smokers.

Beginning in 1980, the federal and provincial governments began to gradually increase the tax on tobacco, as well as forcing manufacturers to place health warnings on the packages, in the hope of discouraging young people from taking up the habit, and encouraging those already hooked to quit. By the mid-1990s, the retail price of a pack of cigarettes in most provinces had tripled in cost, with anywhere from 50 to 70 percent consisting of federal and provincial taxes.

While these punitive taxes worked to some extent in reducing the number of smokers, they also created a whole new drug source for organized crime—cigarette smuggling. This was especially true in Quebec and Ontario, two provinces with First Nations reserves whose borders straddle the United States across the St. Lawrence River in upstate New York. And, just like in the U.S. Prohibition rum-running days of the 1920s and early 1930s, the river became a conduit for contraband goods. But this time the trade ran from south to north—and tobacco rather than liquor was being smuggled.

It initially involved the sale of cheap American brands shipped through the reservations into Canada, usually from North Carolina which, being a tobacco-growing state, supplied the cheapest cigarettes. But many Canadians preferred their traditional smokes to American brands. Big Tobacco came to their rescue. In a contraband operation that the RCMP has referred to as "the biggest corporate fraud in Canadian history" several Canadian cigarette manufacturers, including Imperial Tobacco Ltd. and RJR-Macdonald Inc., began exporting their product to subsidiaries in the United States, thereby avoiding Canadian excise levies. The cigarettes were then smuggled back into Canada, usually through aboriginal reserves, and sold to Canadian customers for half of what they'd pay for legal ones at their local store.

The ruse was eventually exposed, and on April 13, 2010, after 10 years of litigation, the companies were forced to pay $550 million in excise taxes and penalties to the federal and provincial governments. That was only half of the $1.15 billion the companies were originally sued for. Moreover, not a single corporate bigwig involved in the scheme spent a day in jail, much to the disgust of Garfield Mahood, executive director of Canada's Non-Smokers' Rights Association. He described the settlement as "a sweetheart deal."

Apart from the white-collar crooks, there were others who recognized that the demand for cheap cigarettes was a way to make money by dealing in an addictive drug whose consumption is perfectly legal. Pretty soon, the manufacture, importation and sale of contraband tobacco involved members of the West End Gang, biker gangs and the aboriginal people, particularly those on the Kahnawake, Akwesasne and Kanesatake Mohawk reserves. Those territories, which straddle the American and Canadian border are, by virtue of long-established treaty rights, off limits to provincial or federal police officers. The Mohawks are allowed to manufacture and sell tax-free cigarettes within the reserve, but they are prohibited from selling them to non-Indians. Nevertheless, on the immediate outskirts of those reserves are dozens of roadside "smoke shacks" offering cheap cigarettes to anyone who stops by.

And then there are those ubiquitous cellophane baggies containing 200 untaxed cigarettes, labeled "Native" or "Mohawk Blend" that are sold for $10 to $20 in Montreal and other cities by people who, in effect, are illegally dealing in a legal drug. According to a May 17, 2010, report by the Canadian Convenience Stores Association, contraband cigarettes make up 35 to 50 percent of tobacco sales in Ontario, Quebec and the Atlantic provinces.

The bulk of the profits were being made by the smuggling of contraband raw tobacco from the United States to Canada and by the manufacture of cigarettes on the Mohawk reserves. And that's when outside gangs entered the picture to ratchet up sales. In 2008, the RCMP seized almost 1.1 million cartons of contraband cigarettes, up 73 percent from the previous year. And in January 2010 alone, they seized approximately $1 million worth of contraband tobacco and arrested 22 persons accused of smuggling. These illegal smokes are estimated to cost the federal and provincial governments some $1.5 billion in lost taxes each year, with an estimated $200 million in Quebec alone. In addition, police say that Quebec and Ontario organized gangs use the reserves as a conduit to smuggle American weapons into Canada, and Canadian-grown marijuana and even illegal aliens into the United States.

This led to Project Machine, a combined investigation by the SQ, Montreal and other police departments and the Mohawk Police Service, in tandem with Canada Customs and U.S. Border Patrol agents, that began in March 2007. On June 3, 2009, 600 cops simultaneously arrested 46 persons in the Montreal area and on the Kahnawake Mohawk reserve, immediately across the river. Included in the roundup were former Rock Machine leader Salvatore Cazzetta, fifty-four, and his right-hand man Daniel "Putin" Leclerc, forty. The charges against them included trafficking in contraband cigarettes and other drugs such as crack cocaine, as well as committing crimes for the benefit of a criminal organization.

Cazzetta, who'd previously been busted in April 2009 during Operation SharQc, was charged while still in jail. During his court hearing, it was established that he was vice-president of Mustang Distribution Ltd., a Kahnawake manufacturer of black market cigarettes that were flooding the Canadian market. Two years were added to his original sentence and he is still behind bars.

He is but one outsider nailed in the illegal tobacco trade. The RCMP says that because dealing in contraband cigarettes merits a far easier sentence than being caught dealing in cocaine or other illicit drugs, it's a huge incentive for organized gangs to enter this lucrative market. But since the crime is initiated on Mohawk sovereign territory, the authorities can usually do little but wait until the goods are shipped across the St. Lawrence River into Quebec or Ontario. It then becomes a cat-and-mouse game that is played out daily, or rather usually nightly, while the RCMP agents wait to pounce on speedboats, laden with cases of contraband cigarettes, that roar north across the St. Lawrence to deliver the cargo to someone with a truck or SUV waiting on the opposite shore.

In the first half of 2010 the RCMP's Valleyfield, Quebec, detachment, which oversees the area where most of the smuggling takes place, arrested 99 people, seized dozens of boats and vehicles, and confiscated more than 39 million contraband

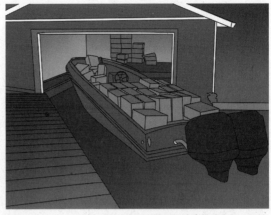

Contraband cigarettes seized by the RCMP in Valleyfield, QC, June 2010

cigarettes. Had those cigarettes been legally manufactured and stamped, they would have sold in Quebec for approximately $14 million, at least half of which would have gone to the federal and provincial government in taxes.

That represents a mere dent in the $1.5 billion annual loss of federal and provincial tax revenue as a result of the criminal smuggling of a legal drug. With money like that at stake, it's little wonder that many Montreal gangsters have recently become addicted to tobacco as their drug of choice.

CHAPTER 22

# Montreal's Modern Street Gangs

*"Nature abhors a vacuum."*
—Aristotle, 4th century BC Greek philosopher

Aristotle coined this phrase in describing why a thrust spear flies forward rather than immediately falling to the ground. He explained that air rushing into the vacuum created behind the end of the hurtling shaft helps to propel it until gravity eventually takes over. That abhorrence of emptiness also applies to the world of crime. If there is a demand for a product such as illicit drugs, and it's not being satisfied, someone will quickly step into the breach to fulfill that demand. That is exactly what various Montreal street gangs did following major busts against the Matticks family and biker gangs during Operation Springtime in 2001 and against the Italian mafia during Project Colisée in 2006. Most of the city's principal suppliers of hashish and cocaine had been locked up, but their traditional customers still needed their fix, and the vacuum left in the wake of the jailed suppliers needed to be filled.

The early street gangs sprang up in the 1980s, a bunch of punks in their teens and early twenties. They often were made up of ethnic groups, such as Haitian or Jamaican posses, who sometimes were employed by the biker gangs or Italians to peddle dope at the street level and to collect debts or commit arson and extortion. Originally, the biggest among them were the Haitian-Canadian Bo-Gars, operating in Montreal North and Laval. There were also the Bloods, also known as the Reds, who operated mostly on St. Lawrence Boulevard and other parts of the city core. As well as drug-dealing, these gangs were also involved in prostitution, extortion and loan sharking.

By 2010, the punks had grown up and become even more dangerous. According to Montreal police inspector Charles Mailloux, "The phenomenon has been evolving since the 1980s. Young people of fourteen and fifteen years old are now forty. So they're more structured and associated with organized crime."

## The Crack Down Posse

Today's largest street gang is the Crack Down Posse, or CDP, a collection of thugs originally operating in the Montreal North area of St. Michel. They began as the Crips or Blues, terrorizing their working-class neighborhood through protection rackets and robbery from local businesses, usually corner convenience stores, known as *dépanneurs*. The CDP was eventually led by Gregory Wooley, a Haitian-Canadian and a member of the Hells Angels' Rockers affiliate and a Mom Boucher bodyguard. In 1998 he brought the Rockers and the CDP together to form the Alliance or "Syndicate" during the height of the biker war against the Rock Machine. He was busted during Operation Springtime 2001 and charged with drug trafficking and for the December 20, 1996 murder of Rock Machine biker Pierre Beauchamp. In 2005, Wooley was committed to Kingston Penitentiary to serve a 13-year sentence. On February 12, 2009, at the age of thirty-nine, he was re-arrested in the pen in connection with Project Axe, a combined Montreal police and SQ operation against street gangs, culminating in some 50 arrests in February 2009, and another dozen in June 2010. Wooley is still behind bars and is facing further trials on multiple charges of gangsterism and other crimes.

## Ducarme Joseph and Tony Magi

Another major street gang figure is Ducarme "Kenny" Joseph, the Haitian-born founder of the Gangs de 67 in Montreal's St. Michel district, and later an influential member of the Bloods, a mob that sprang up in the 1980s and aggressively sought to wrest control of the city's drug trade from the traditional mafia and biker gangs, particularly in the bars and restaurants on St. Laurent Boulevard. His criminal record dates back to 1987, including charges of armed robbery, possession of weapons, pimping and sexual assault. The latter charge stemmed from January 1989 when, at the age of twenty, he lured a twelve-year-old girl into prostitution and raped her, for which he pleaded guilty and was sentenced to eight months in jail plus two years probation. In July 2009, he was hired by construction magnate Tony Magi, a fifty-year-old real estate developer in partnership with Nick Rizzuto Jr., as Magi's strong-arm enforcer to collect outstanding debts.

Magi, although never convicted of a serious offense, is thought by police to have close ties to the Italian mafia. At 6:30 a.m. on August 11, 2008, he was shot and critically injured by one or two unidentified men while driving his Range Rover SUV on Cavendish Boulevard in NDG. Police are certain that the attempted hit was connected to the mafia. A year later Magi was being investigated by authorities in connection with two alleged extortion attempts. On September 21, 2010, the cops raided his FTM Construction offices on Upper Lachine Road in NDG and arrested him and two of his bodyguards, Lucieno Canci, sixty-four, and Michael Fanelli, thirty-one, for possession of illegal weapons. Magi's heavily armored car was also seized during the raid. As of January 2011, he was out on $25,000 bail, under strict curfew conditions, while awaiting trial. On February 18, 2011, Magi's fifty-year-old wife, Rita Biasini, was the target of a gunman who fired several shots at her SUV as she was driving on Beaconsfield Avenue in NDG. Biasini escaped unhurt and drove to the nearest police station.

As for Magi's pal, Ducarme Joseph, he was next arrested on September 19, 2009, along with his bodyguard Peter Christopoulos, on charges of assaulting a doorman at the upscale Buona Notte

Ducarme Joseph

restaurant on St. Laurent Boulevard, and was released on $50,000 bail. But apart from collecting debts for Magi, he was obviously collecting some serious enemies.

On March 18, 2010, Joseph narrowly avoided being whacked at the age of forty-two when two gunmen entered his upscale FlawNego clothing boutique on St. Jacques Street West in Old Montreal and sprayed more than 50 rounds of automatic gunfire. Joseph managed to scurry out the back door, but Christopoulos, twenty-seven, and the store manager, Jean Gaston, sixty, were killed. Two other men were injured. The shooters ran down the street and escaped in a black Dodge Caravan. Ninety minutes later, Joseph was spotted by police detectives in Montreal's St. Michel district, meeting with a well-known enforcer known as "the Gunman," presumably planning a revenge attack on his would-be assassins.

At 2 p.m. the next day, Joseph was arrested while leaving Magi's FTM Construction headquarters. He was booked and later sentenced to 10 months in jail for breaching his September 2009 bail conditions, as well as being in possession of a gun silencer. At his bail hearing two days later, Joseph was described by police as one of Montreal's "most dangerous street gang leaders." His previous $50,000 bail was revoked and he was sent to a Rimouski, Quebec, detention center to await his previous assault trial. Two months later, he renounced his right to a Quebec Parole Board hearing, choosing to serve the remainder of his time in jail, no doubt aware that he was a lot safer in jail than on the outside.

## Gangland: A New Take

The attempted hit on Joseph remains unsolved, although police suspect it is linked to the December 2009 assassination of Nick Rizzuto Jr., and was carried out by members of another street gang. The Italian mafia and the biker gangs are known to outsource their dirty work to street gang members. On July 16, 2010, the cops arrested Carey Isaac Régis, forty-one, and Terrell Lloyd, twenty-seven, two members of the Bo-Gars, charging them with first-degree murder in the FlawNego boutique killings. A third Bo-Gars member, Kyle Gabriel, twenty-six, was also being sought. Their trials were still pending in January 2011.

A new twist to the violence began in September 2009 with a wave of Molotov cocktails being thrown in the middle of the night through the windows of various cafés and bars in Little Italy and adjacent neighborhoods, and sometimes as far west as Westmount and NDG. The rash of fire-bombings continued sporadically. Most of the targets were Italian-owned businesses, including, on January 6, 2011, the Loreto funeral home owned by the Rizzuto Family. The damage was usually minimal, as firefighters quickly arrived to put out the flames. But a message was being sent. Police believe the arsonists are street gang members either acting on their own or else hired by what's left of the established mobs, such as the bikers or the mafia, in the never-ending struggle over Montreal's drug turf.

"It's a whole new style of bad guys now since the Haitians came in," says former armed-robbery and homicide detective André Savard. "They have no rules and no organization. It's all guns and knives and violence on the street, and there's no respect for anyone else."

"You got these street gangs that are popping up left, right and centre," agrees André Potvin. "They don't give a rat's ass about how to do things. They want to do it, they do it their own way and they don't care that they need to talk to so-and-so or so-and-so, and then it becomes violent. They've got no morals, basically."

There are an estimated ten street gangs of various sizes now operating in the city. And, whatever their ethnic origin, they present a whole new challenge to Montreal police, given their unpredictability and lack of cohesiveness. Gone are the days when the cops could concentrate their sights on a single criminal structure such as the mafia, the Hells Angels, the Rock Machine or the West End Gang, and use surveillance, wiretaps and paid informants to whittle them down a piece at a time. Today's street gangs are a moving target with few rules and constantly shifting allegiances. Functioning more like guerilla fighters or anarchists, they're changing the reality of the Irish mafia—and organized crime—in Montreal.

# EPILOGUE

*gang [n.] (1): a group of persons working together. (2): a group of persons working to unlawful or antisocial ends.*

—Merriam-Webster Dictionary

The West End Gang, during the height of its activities in the 1970s through the early 2000s, consisted of perhaps 150 associates, most of them in their twenties to forties. Today the Irish mob is a mere shadow of itself, with its surviving members either in prison or else on the outside and trying to stay clean. Many of them are members of Alcoholics Anonymous, kicking a vice that goes back to their roots, often through their fathers, in the Irish ghettos of Griffintown, Point St. Charles and Verdun.

There still exists the debate as to whether any such organized and cohesive "gang" ever existed in the usual sense of the word. As previously noted, the term was coined by the French press back in the mid-1950s, and has stuck ever since. Nevertheless, there are good guys and bad guys both who still wince at the appellation.

I was having breakfast one recent morning with Kevin McGarr, a retired Montreal drug and anti-gang detective who'd arrested many of the Irish hoods and their associates back in the 1970s, '80s and '90s. We were at a table in the Green Spot restaurant in St. Henri, a west end neighborhood where he was raised and where I now live, and where many of the mobsters once committed their crimes. When I brought up the term "West End Gang," McGarr looked up from his plate of bacon and eggs and said, "D'Arcy, you're Irish and I'm Irish and we're meeting here and talking about drug deals done by some Irish guys. So couldn't that technically make us members of a West End Gang?"

It was a broad brush stroke, but I understood his point. Yet there's no getting around the fact that there once existed a bevy of gangsters with Irish roots who cooperated with one another for "unlawful or antisocial ends"—something that neither McGarr nor I were doing at the breakfast table.

Former Montreal police detective André Savard insists, "[there was] definitely a West End Gang" that was active in the 1970s and '80s on downtown Crescent Street and in the lower NDG area. "The Matticks were very close to the McGuires [and] the Matticks were also close to Dunie Ryan. That I know for a fact . . . That's where they used to all hang around at one time or another, either at Peg's [Motel] or Smitty's [bar], and certainly Crescent Street, because this was the place, especially for the English people."

But, as John Westlake, a retired Montreal police drug squad sergeant-detective, points out, "There was no West End Gang" in the sense of a leader "who sits you down and says, 'You do this and you do that.' It's just a bunch of guys in the west part of the city who sometimes cooperate with each other."

Former bank robber John Phillips, who hung out with most of the Irish boys, agrees. "West End Gang is not a correct term. There is no gang per se . . . But because [the press] put that term together, the police are always looking for a gang, like a company president or mob boss with his staff under him." He adds, "Like when I'd meet with Dunie, we'd maybe talk about a score I was planning with Rory [Shayne]. But Dunie and I aren't a gang. I don't work for him and he don't work for me. Just like [Billy] MacAllister doesn't work for [Mickey] Johnston and Johnston doesn't work for MacAllister, and neither works for [Gerald] Matticks, and Matticks don't work for Johnston." Nevertheless, Phillips does acknowledge a kind of organization, explaining, "[Although] there was no boss, there were associations, like as much as we'd drink together in the olden days and talk about stuff."

And, as convicted drug traffickers Billy MacAllister and Kenny Fisher have both vehemently insisted during my conversations with them, "That is total bullshit. There is no such thing as a West End Gang."

André Potvin, head of the RCMP's Montreal drug squad, says, "Basically, there is no such group. It's just a bunch of Irish descendant people that have got together since they were kids and started to do a few thefts and kinda graduated and did business ventures together. So what makes it unique with them is that even though you're going to dismantle one cell, you won't dismantle the organization, because it doesn't exist. You won't be able to tie in other known people from the West End Gang automatically, because you're only going after one [drug] deal or one cell." Potvin adds that although the West End Gang is not as big as it once was, "our intelligence suggests that they are still busy."

Perhaps the final word should go to retired homicide detective André Bouchard, who in his 34-year career dealt with all of Montreal's unsavory gangs. "In my early uniform days in the 1970s we never saw the West End Gang because they weren't the type of guys who were gonna cause trouble in the streets or sell drugs on the corner or beat up somebody . . . These were the intelligent guys that did hijackings, bank jobs and safe cracking . . . They had the best safecrackers. These guys were really good." Bouchard adds, "Eventually the French Canadians would go and hire these guys [as in the Brink's robbery] through Dunie [Ryan] because nobody else intelligent could do that . . . French Canadians would try it, but only with a lot of shooting and killings."

Bouchard says that by the 1980s he was working in the narcotics division, where they noticed the proliferation of cocaine in all the downtown bars and discotheques. "People were literally sniffing it right there on the bar and on the tables, even on broads' bellies. I mean, they weren't even hiding it in the toilets . . . So we said, 'Wait a minute, how the fuck is all this shit coming in?' And that's when the name Matticks started popping up. We'd bust a dealer downtown and he'd give up a name. It was always Gerry Matticks and the West End Gang . . . That's when we realized how big these guys were."

Finally, warns Bouchard, even if the glory days of the Irish mafia appear to be behind them, "It's not over yet . . . The West End Gang still exists today."

## BIBLIOGRAPHY

**Books**

Akenson, Donald. *An Irish History of Civilization*, Vol. 2. Montreal: McGill-Queen's University Press, 2005.

Asbury, Herbert. *The Gangs of New York: An Informal History of the Underworld*. New York: Alfred A. Knopf, 1928.

Auger, Michel. *The Biker Who Shot Me* (Translated by Jean-Paul Murray). Toronto: McClelland & Stewart Ltd., 2002.

Beare, Margaret E. *Criminal Conspiracies: Organized Crime in Canada*. Toronto: Thomson Canada Ltd., 1996.

Brandt, Charles. *I Hear You Paint Houses: Frank "The Irishman" Sheeran and the Inside Story of the Mafia, the Teamsters, and the Last Ride of Jimmy Hoffa*. Hanover, NH: Steerforth Press, 2004.

Burns, Patricia. *The Shamrock and the Shield: An Oral History of the Irish in Montreal*. Montreal: Vehicule Press, 1998.

Butts, Ed. *The Desperate Ones: Forgotten Canadian Outlaws*. Toronto: Dundurn Group, 2006.

Caine, Alex. *The Fat Mexican: The Bloody Rise of the Bandidos Motorcycle Club*. Toronto: Random House Canada, 2009.

Carr, Howie. *The Brothers Bulger: How They Terrorized and Corrupted Boston for a Quarter Century*. New York: Warner Books, 2006.

Capeci, Jerry. *The Complete Idiot's Guide to the Mafia*. New York: Alpha Books, 2004.

Charbonneau, Jean-Pierre. *La Filière canadienne.* Montreal: Éditions Trait d'Union, 2002.

Charbonneau, Jean-Pierre. *The Canadian Connection: An Expose on the Mafia in Canada and its International Ramifications.* Ottawa: Optimum Publishing Company Limited, 1976.

Cherry, Paul. *The Biker Trials: Bringing Down the Hells Angels.* Toronto: ECW Press, 2005.

De Champlain, Pierre. *Le Crime Organisé à Montréal (1940/1980).* Hull, QC: Les Éditions Asticou, 1986.

De Champlain, Pierre. *Mafia: bandes de motards et traffic de drogue.* Hull, QC: Les Éditions Asticou, 1990.

De Champlain, Pierre. *Mobsters, Gangsters and Men of Honour: Cracking the Mafia Code.* Toronto: HarperCollins Canada, 2005.

Desroches, Frederick J. *Force & Fear: Robbery in Canada.* Toronto: Canadian Scholars' Press Inc., 2002.

Desroches, Frederick J. *The Crime That Pays: Drug Trafficking and Organized Crime in Canada.* Toronto: Canadian Scholars' Press Inc., 2005.

Driedger, Sharon Doyle. *An Irish heart: How a Small Irish Immigrant Community Shaped Canada.* Toronto: HarperCollins Publishers Ltd., 2010.

Durney, James. *The Mob: The History of Irish Gangsters in America.* Tampa, FL: Self-published, 1997.

Edwards, Peter. *The Bandito Massacre: A True Story of Bikers, Brotherhood and Betrayal.* Toronto: HarperCollins Publishers Ltd., 2010.

Edwards, Peter; Auger, Michel. *The Encyclopedia of Canadian Organized Crime.* Toronto: McClelland & Stewart Ltd., 2004.

English, T.J. *Havana Nocturne: How the Mob Owned Cuba ... and Then Lost It to the Revolution.* New York: HarperCollins Publishers Ltd., 2007.

English, T.J. *Paddy Whacked: The Untold Story of the Irish American Gangster.* New York: HarperCollins Publishers, 2005.

English, T.J. *The Westies: Inside New York's Irish Mob.* New York: St. Martin's Griffen, 2006.

Germain, Georges-Hébert. *Souvenirs de Monica.* Montreal: Libre Expression, 1997.

Gravenor, Kristian; John David Gravenor. *Montreal: The Unknown City.* Vancouver: Arsenal Pulp Press, 2002.

Humphreys, Adrian. *The Enforcer: Johnny Pops Papalia, A Life and Death in the Mafia.* Toronto: HarperCollins Canada, 1999.

Hustak, Alan. *The Ghost of Griffintown: The True Story of Mary Gallagher.* Montreal: Price-Patterson Ltd., 2005.

Knuckle, Robert. *A Master of Deception: Working Undercover for the RCMP.* Renfrew, ON: General Store Publishing House, 2007.

Lamonthe, Lee; Humphreys, Adrian. *The Sixth Family: The Collapse of the New York Mafia and the Rise of Vito Rizzuto.* Mississauga, ON: John Wiley & Sons, 2008.

Langton, Jerry. *Fallen Angel: The Unlikely Rise of Walter Stadnick and the Canadian Hells Angels.* Mississauga, ON: John Wiley & Sons Canada Ltd., 2006.

Lavigne, Yves. *Hells Angels at War.* Toronto: HarperCollins Publishers Ltd., 1999.

Lavigne, Yves. *Hells Angels: Into the Abyss.* Toronto: HarperCollins Publishers Ltd., 1996.

Lavigne, Yves. *Hells Angels: Taking Care of Business.* Toronto: Ballantine Books, 1987.

Leacock, Stephen. *Montreal, Seaport and City.* Toronto: McClelland & Stewart, 1942.

Leblanc, Marc; Ouimet, Marc; Szabo, Denis. *Traité de Criminology Empirique*. Montreal: Les Presses de l'Université de Montréal, 2004.

Lehr, Dick; O'Neill, Gerard. *Black Mass: The True Story of an Unholy Alliance between the FBI and the Irish Mob*. New York: HarperCollins Publishers Inc., 2000.

MacArthur, Peter A. *West End Gang* (a novel). Toronto: Writer's Showcase Press, June 2002.

MacAllister, Peter J. *Dexter*. Ottawa: Legas Publishing, 2002.

MacDonald, Michael Patrick. *All Souls: A Family Story from Southie*. New York: Ballantine Books, 2000.

MacKay, Donald. *Flight from Famine: The Coming of the Irish to Canada*. Toronto: Dundurn Press, 2009.

Malarek, Victor. *Merchants of Misery: Inside Canada's Illegal Drug Scene*. Toronto: Macmillan of Canada, 1989.

Marrelli, Nancy. *Stepping Out: The Golden Age of Montreal Night Clubs*. Montreal: Vehicule Press, 2004.

Martineau, Pierre. *I Was a Killer for the Hells Angels: The Story of Serge Quesnel*. (English translation by Jean-Paul Murray). Toronto: McClelland & Stewart, 2003.

McSherry, Peter. *The Big Red Fox: The Incredible Story of Norman "Red" Ryan, Canada's Most Notorious Criminal*. Toronto: Dundurn Press, 1999.

Morton, Suzanne. *At Odds: Gambling and Canadians, 1919–1969*. Toronto: University of Toronto Press, 2003.

Nicaso, Antonio; Lamothe, Lee. *Bloodlines: The Rise and Fall of the Mafia's Royal Family*. Toronto: HarperCollins Canada Ltd., 2001.

O'Gallagher, Marianna. *Grosse Île: Gateway to Canada; 1832–1937*. Sainte-Foy, QC: Carraig Books, 1984.

Palmer, Al. *Montreal Confidential: The Lowdown on the Big Town.* Montreal: Vehicule Press (reprint), 2009.

Paradis, Peter. *Nasty Business: One Biker Gang's Bloody War Against the Hells Angels.* Toronto: HarperCollins Canada Ltd., 2002.

Pileggi, Nicholas. *Wiseguy: Life in a Mafia Family.* New York: Simon & Schuster, 1986.

Pollock, Donald. *Call Me a Good Thief.* London: Howard Baker Press Ltd., 1976.

Redmond, Lar. *Emerald Square.* London: Corgi Books, 1987.

Reid, Stephen. *Jackrabbit Parole.* Toronto: McClelland & Stewart Ltd., 1986.

Sanger, Daniel. *Hell's Witness.* Toronto: Penguin Group Canada, 2005.

Savard, André. *The System.* An unpublished manuscript about the March 30, 1976, Montreal Brink's Robbery, 1992.

Schneider, Stephen. *Iced: The Story of Organized Crime in Canada.* Toronto: John Wiley & Sons Canada Ltd., 2009.

Schorow, Stephanie. *The Crime of the Century: How the Brink's Robbers Stole Millions & the Hearts of Boston.* Beverly, MA: Commonwealth Editions, 2008.

Shea, John. *Rat Bastards: The Life and Times of South Boston's Most Honorable Irish Mobster.* New York: HarperCollins, 2006.

Sher, Julian; Marsden, William. *The Road to Hell: How the Biker Gangs Are Conquering Canada.* Toronto: Vintage Canada, 2004.

Silverman, Robert A.; Teevan, James J. *Crime in Canadian Society.* (Third Edition). Toronto: Butterworths, 1986.

Simard, Réal. *The Nephew.* Toronto: Doubleday Canada Ltd., 1989.

Stanké, Alain. *Le Tueur: Confessions d'un ex-tueur à gages.* Montreal: Les Éditions au Carré, Inc., 2004.

Weeks, Kevin; Karas, Phyllis: *Brutal: The Untold Story of My Life inside Whitey Bulger's Irish Mob*. New York. HarperCollins, 2006.

Weintraub, William. *City Unique: Montreal Days and Nights in the 1940s and '50s*. Toronto: McClelland & Stewart, 1997.

**Crime Commission Inquiries and Other Reports**

Alain, Mark. "The Rise and Fall of Motorcycle Gangs in Quebec." Nathanson Centre. University of Toronto. 1995.

"Annual Report on Organized Crime in Canada," 2002. Criminal Intelligence Service Canada. Ottawa.

Barlow, John M. "'Forgive My Nostalgia': The Construction of Griffintown, Montreal, as a *lieu de mémoire*." Canadian Historical Association, 2005.

*Canadian Journal of Criminology* (1994–2000; volumes 36–42). Canadian Criminal Justice Association. Ottawa, September 1977.

Desrochers, Fred. "Drug Trafficking and Organized Crime in Canada: A Study of High Level Drug Networks." Nathanson Centre. University of Toronto, 1999.

"Étude sur les Vols de Banque dans la Communauté Urbaine de Montréal." Rapport du Comité Conjoint Formé par l'association des Banquiers Canadiens et le Service de Police de la CUM. September, 1977.

"McLellan Senate Committee Report on Organized Crime and Illicit Traffic in Drugs." Canadian Government Senate, 1964.

"Québec Police Commission Report of the Commission of Inquiry on Organized Crime and Recommendations." Editeur Officiel du Québec. Québec City, 1977.

"Report of the Public Inquiry Commission appointed to inquire into the Sûrete du Québec" (Summary and recommendations). Les Publications du Québec. Sainte-Foy, QC, 1998.

"Report on Organized Crime" (Dealing with the Port of Montreal). Criminal Intelligence Service Canada, 1999.

"Statistics Handbook: Canadian Criminal Justice." Solicitor General of Canada. Ottawa, 1977.

**Newspaper Articles and Other Media Sources: 1940–2010**
*The author drew upon the following sources for background, research and cross-referencing of details.*

*Allô Police* (Montreal) (A popular French-language crime tabloid that lasted from 1953 until its demise on July 13, 2004)

*Boston Globe*

CBC News

*Chicago Tribune*

*Corriere Canadese* (Toronto)

CTV News

Cyberpresse.ca

*Daily News* (Bowling Green, KY)

*Daily Record* (Glasgow, Scotland)

*Edmonton Herald* (Edmonton, AB)

*Ellensburg Daily Record* (Ellensburg, WA)

*Gainesville Sun* (Gainesville, FL)

*Gazette* (Montreal) (The city's longest-running English-language daily newspaper)

GLOBAL TV News

*Globe and Mail* (Toronto)

*Hamilton Spectator* (Hamilton, ON)

*Herald* (Montreal) (A 146-year-old daily tabloid that folded in 1957)

*L'Action Catholique* (Montreal)

*L'Actualité* (Montreal)

*Lakeland Ledger* (Lakeland, FL)

*La Presse* (Montreal)

*La Voix Populaire* (Montreal)

*Le Devoir* (Montreal)

*Le Droit* (Ottawa)

*Le Journal de Montréal* (Montreal)

*Le Journal de Québec* (Quebec City)

*Le Soleil* (Quebec City)

*London Free Press* (London, ON)

*Maclean's Magazine* (Toronto)

*McGill Tribune* (Montreal)

*Miami Herald*

*Miami News*

*Montreal Daily News* (Montreal) (A daily tabloid newspaper that existed from 1988 to 1989)

*Montréal Magazine*

*Montreal Mirror*

*Montreal Star* (An English-language broadsheet afternoon paper that was launched in 1869 and folded in 1976)

*Ottawa Citizen* (Ottawa)

*Palm Beach Post* (Palm Beach, FL)

*Perspectives-Dimanche, La Presse Magazine* (Montreal)

*Photo Police* (Montreal) (The sister tabloid to *Allô Police*)

*Quebec Chronicle-Telegraph* (Quebec City)

Radio-Canada.ca

*Reader's Digest,* Canadian edition (Westmount, QC)

*Reading Eagle* (Reading, PE)

*Register-Guard* (Eugene, OR)

Ruefrontenac.com (An online newspaper put out by striking reporters
of *Le Journal de Montréal* during their 2009–2010 lockout)

*San Francisco Chronicle*

*Sarasota Herald-Tribune*

*Saskatoon Phoenix.*(Saskatoon, SK)

*Saturday Night* (Toronto)

*Schenectady Gazette* (Schenectady, NY)

*St. Petersburg Times* (St. Petersburg, FL)

*Suburban Weekly* (Montreal)

*Sunday Sun* (Vancouver)

*The Bulletin* (Bend, OR)

*The Record* (Kitchener, ON)

*The Standard* (St. Catharines, ON)

*This Magazine* (Toronto)

*Times Herald* (Seattle, WA)

*Toronto Star* (Toronto)

*Toronto Sun* (Toronto)

*Town of Mount Royal Weekly Post*

*Vancouver Courier* (Vancouver)

*Vancouver Sun* (Vancouver)

*Victoria Times-Colonist* (Victoria, BC)

*Wall Street Journal* (New York)

*Washington Post* (Washington, DC)

*Windsor Star* (Windsor, ON)

**Films (Documentary And Drama)**

*And Then You Die*. Directed by Frank Mankiewicz, 1986. Based on the 1984 assassination of Montreal West End Gang leader Dunie Ryan.

*Gangs of New York*. Directed by Martin Scorcese, 2002. Based on the 19th century bloody rivalry between the Irish and Anglo-Saxon gangs in Manhattan's Five Points district.

*Ghosts of Griffintown: Stories of an Irish Neighbourhood*. Produced and directed by Richard Burman, 2003. A video documentary.

*Goodfellas*. Directed by Martin Scorsese, 1990. Based on Irish-American hoodlum Henry Hill.

*Monica la Mitraille*. Directed by Pierre Houle, 2004. Based on the exploits of Monica "Machine Gun Molly" Proietti, Montreal's infamous 1960s bank robber.

*The Brink's Job*. Directed by William Friedkin, 1978. Based on the $2.5 million heist from the Boston Brink's headquarters on January 17, 1950.

*The Departed*. Directed by Martin Scorsese, 2006. Based on Boston Irish mobster Whitey Bulger and FBI agent John Connolly.

*The Point*. Produced by William Weintraub and directed by Robert Duncan of the National Film Board of Canada, 1978. Based on the residents of Point St. Charles and their Irish heritage.

## Criminal Court Records and Other Official Document Sources: 1950–2010

*The author drew upon the following sources for background, research and cross-referencing of details.*

Correctional Services of Canada

Court of Quebec

Florida Court of Appeals

Florida Dade County District Court

National Parole Board (Quebec Region)

Ontario Court of Appeal

Ontario Superior Court

Quebec Coroner's Office

Quebec Court of Appeal

Quebec Superior Court

Supreme Court of Canada

# INDEX

Bill C-95 (criminal organization), 207
Bisaillon, Jean-Alain, 110
Blackledge, William, 165–66
Blass, Michel, 58, 146, 147, 150–51
Blass, Richard, 58–59, 62, 110, 147
Bloods, 242, 243
Bo-Gars, 242, 244–45
Bonanno family, 21, 30, 32, 224
Bonanno, Joseph, 22
Bonaventure Expressway, 12, 95
Bonfire Restaurant, 24, 30, 46
Bonneville, Frank, 187
bootlegging, 6
Bordeaux Prison, 31, 38, 48, 54, 70, 74, 188, 195
Bouchard, André, 83–84, 111, 159, 200, 208–9, 211, 249
Boucher, Francis, 209
Boucher, Maurice "Mom," 27, 195, 201–2, 205, 206, 207–9, 211
Bougie, Frederick, 196
Bougie, Leo, 55–56
Boulanger, Sylvain, 210
Bourré, Gilles, 113
Bowman, William, 47
boxing, 158–59
Brabant, Denis, 71
Brecher, Pincus, 35–36
Breen, William, 134
Brewer, Robert, 225
Brink's Canada Ltd., 87, 88
Brink's Incorporated, 87–88
Brinks robberies, 85–98, 100–6, 151, 170, 172, 249
Brockville heist, 82–83
Bronfman, Sam, 6
Brown, Steve, 191, 193
Brunette, Ronald, 88, 89–96, 115, 119
Bulchalter, Louis, 35
Bulger Task Force, 8

Bulger, James, 7
Bulger, Whitey, 161
Burke, Charles, 15–16
Burke, Dan, 162
Burke, Hetty, 15–16, 47
Burns, John, 174–77
Buteau, Yves, 201

Cadieux, Joseph Bernard, 164
Café Roma, 55
Calabrian/Sicilian mobs, 21–32, 223 (See also Italian Mafia)
Cali drug cartel, 151, 157, 159–60, 162–63, 166
Cameron, James Frederick, 214–15
Cammelleri, Giovanna, 31
Canadian Imperial Bank of Commerce, 71, 102–3, 124, 169
Canadian Industries Limited (CIL), 64
Canadian National Bank, 144
Canadian Union of Public Employees (CUPE), 186
Canci, Lucieno, 243
Carignan, Roch, 89, 90–96, 116, 119
Caron Report, 43, 44
Caron, François, 43
Cartierville Airport, 126
Caruana-Cuntrera families, 21, 30
Castaneda, Ashley, 173, 174, 176, 178
Cat's Den Lounge, 101
Catania, Giuseppe, 25
Cavalier Motel, 101, 136, 138, 141, 186
Cazzetta, Giovanni, 174, 187, 205
Cazzetta, Salvatore, 173–74, 175, 178, 205–6, 238
CBC, 19, 162
CECO (Commission d'Enquête sur le Crime Organisé), 23, 28, 81, 135, 187–88

police corruption, 23, 34, 39, 42, 43, 44, 103, 162–63, 194
political corruption, 7, 8, 23, 34, 35, 42, 43
Popeyes, 98–99, 148, 201, 202
Port of Montreal, 138, 171, 178, 185–86, 189–92, 196, 197, 230
Potvin, André, 114, 214–20, 222, 245, 249
Pretula, Daniel, 46
Pretula, Donna, 46
Pretula, Frank, 24, 30, 37, 38, 46–50, 51, 52, 55, 83
Pretula, Frankie, Jr., 46
Pretula-Greco mob, 16
Primeau, Pierre, 190–91
Primeau, Roger, 110
Primeau, Roland, 77–78
Prohibition, 6, 22
Proietti, Monique, 72–74, 145
Project Axe, 242
Project Boeuf, 195–96
Project Chabanel, 214–19
Project Choc, 174–77, 180, 206
Project Colisée, 228, 229–30, 234, 241
Project Machine, 238
Provençal gang, 88, 90
Provençal, Bernard, 117, 118, 121
Provençal, Françine, 112
Provençal, Grace, 112
Provençal, Jacques, 112
Provençal, Murielle, 112
Provençal, Roger, 88–89, 90–91, 98, 112, 113, 115, 116, 118, 119, 120, 120, 121
Provincial Bank of Canada, 125

Quebec Department of Revenue, 197
Quebec Organized Crime Inquiry, 142

Quebec Police Ethics Commission, 110
Quebec Provincial Police, 112, 128, 129, 149, 153 (See also Sûreté du Québec)
Quebec Superior Court, 130, 227
Quintal, Guy, 173, 176, 177
Quintal, Pierre, 80
Quitoni, John Robert, 151–52, 167

Racketeer Influenced and Corrupt Organizations Act. See RICO
Randolph, Bernie, 51
Randolph, Joseph, 51–52
Raphael Motel, 101
Raso, Francesco, 25
RCMP, 22, 23, 24, 26, 35, 43, 47, 48, 49, 79, 81, 114, 115–16, 150, 152, 153, 159, 160–61, 162, 163, 165, 171, 172, 173, 174, 177, 181, 182, 194, 200, 209, 213–22, 228
Red Hood Gang, 66–68
Reeves, Jules, 71
Reggio Bar, 28, 29
Régis, Carey Isaac, 245
Reid, Stephen, 67–68
Renda, Maria Rizzuto, 224, 232, 233
Renda, Paolo, 29, 31, 32, 224, 229, 233
Ricciardi, Raymond, 104
Richardson, Bryce, 56
RICO (Racketeer Influenced and Corrupt Organizations) Act, 8, 166, 207
Rivard, Daniel, 220, 221
Rivard, Lucien, 78
Rizzuto family, 21, 26, 137, 156, 223–34, 245
Rizzuto, Maria, 31
Rizzuto, Nick, Jr., 231–33, 243, 244

# ABOUT THE AUTHORS

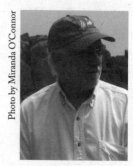

**D'Arcy O'Connor** is a veteran journalist, script writer, documentary producer, book author and round-the-world sailor. He has contributed to the *Wall Street Journal*, the *Montreal Gazette*, *People* magazine, *National Geographic*, and as far abroad as Sydney, Australia's *Daily Telegraph*, and the *Australian*. Among his books credits are *The Money Pit* (Putnam), *The Big Dig* (Ballantine), and *The Secret Treasure of Oak Island* (Lyons Press). Among his associate producer credits are a segment on Oak Island for ABC, the CBC/NFB's "Valour and the Horror," winner of three Gemini awards, and CBC/NFB's "The War at Sea," a docudrama on Canada's role in the North Atlantic in WWII. He teaches English and journalism at Montreal's Dawson College.

**Miranda O'Connor** has an MA in history and a keen knack for primary source research. She is bilingual in French and English and is currently studying law at McGill University. She can also be caught performing "Heartbreak Hotel" at karaoke bars across Montreal.